INTERNAL DIFFERENCE

INTERNAL DIFFERENCE

Twentieth-century writing in Wales

M. WYNN THOMAS

CARDIFF
UNIVERSITY OF WALES PRESS
1992

British Library Cataloguing in Publication Data

A catalogue record for this book is available from the British Library

ISBN 0-7083-1152-0

Published with the financial support of the Welsh Arts Council

Typeset in Wales by Megaron, Cardiff
Printed in England by Billings Book Plan, Worcester

I
Karen ac Elin

Heavenly Hurt, it gives us –
We can find no scar,
But internal difference,
Where the Meanings, are –

(Emily Dickinson)

Contents

Preface

'Internal Difference' would seem to be a reasonable, not to say politic, title for a book which consists of essays on a mixture of subjects. The studies collected here are ones written at different times, but always for the same reason – because the subjects interested me in ways I could scarcely begin to explain, even to myself. We live life forwards, but understand it backwards, said Kierkegaard. Only after completing the bulk of this book did I realize that preoccupations of which I had largely been unaware were revealed by the unexpected recurrence, from study to study, of certain themes and ideas. Whenever I had, in the past, thought of the Wales I mentally inhabited, Waldo Williams's wistful phrase had kept coming back to my mind: 'Ynof mae Cymru'n un. Y modd nis gwn.' ('In me Wales is single and united. I know not how.')[1] But as I read the essays that I had accumulated on the English-language literature of modern Wales, I realized that it was to the rich, but highly problematic diversity of the country that I had, for some reason, been primarily drawn.

In his highly readable book on Wales, Trevor Fishlock has nicely retold a familiar story:

> There is even a Rhondda society in Cardiff – and the Rhondda is only 16 miles from the Capital. Gwyn Morgan, who works for the European Commission, recounts with pleasure his encounter with a Welsh hotel porter in Stratford-upon-Avon.
>
> 'You're Welsh, aren't you,' the porter said when Gwyn spoke to him. 'Where do you come from?'
>
> 'Aberdare,' Gwyn said, naming his home town with proper pride.
>
> 'Don't generalise, man,' the porter chided, 'what part of Aberdare – Cwmbach, Robertstown, Trecynon, or Abernant?'[2]

Here difference 'presents' as being geographical, but is as we know infinitely more complex than that, since on the back of this one difference rides a whole host of others – historical, social, cultural, linguistic and so on. In the Welsh context, knowing your place can mean a great many things.

But one has to be Welsh in order to get the meaning – to appreciate the significance of the difference between Aberdare and Aberdaron, let alone between Cwmbach and Trecynon. The point has been well made recently by the anthropologist Anthony Cohen in his study of the 'symbolic boundaries' by means of which people demarcate identity:

> Rather than being drawn at the point where differentiation occurs, the community boundary incorporates and encloses difference, and, as Durkheim asserted for his organic model, is thereby strengthened. The boundary represents the mask presented by the community to the outside world; . . . . it is the community's public face. But the conceptualisation and symbolisation of the boundary from within is much more complex. To put this another way, the boundary as the community's public face is symbolically simple, but, as the object of internal discourse, it is symbolically complex.[3]

Some studies of Wales, and of its English-language literature, are primarily interested in the features that distinguish it, and differentiate it, from England. In Cohen's terms, they are (very properly) interested in the 'public face' of the culture. I, on the other hand, am mainly interested in what Cohen calls 'the internal discourse' of Wales, as that seems to me to be evidenced by its recent literature. In other words, I am interested in exploring, through the literature, what the Welsh make of themselves and of each other, and thereby what between them they 'privately' make of Wales.

In *The National Question Again*, the editor John Osmond referred to 'the fissile political geography of Wales' and noted 'that Welshness, as a political identity, is crossed by conflicting loyalties: by the local community on one hand, and by a wider sense of Britain on the other.'[4] Elsewhere in the same volume Denis Balsom outlined a very useful 'three-Wales model' in an attempt to explain 'the political sociology of Welsh identity.' He distinguished between the different – and some-times conflicting – identity perceptions of people in, respectively, Y Fro Gymraeg (the shrinking Welsh-speaking areas of Dyfed and Gwynedd); Welsh Wales (mainly corresponding to the old south Wales coalfield societies); and British Wales (a broad belt of border country, parts of the southern and north-eastern coastal districts, and much of Pembrokeshire). Valuable analyses of this kind have undoubtedly influenced my understanding of the modern literatures of Wales.[5]

To approach the literary evidence of Welsh identity in any such systematic, or schematic, fashion would, however, in my opinion, be a mistake, not least because it would be false to the elusive terms on which literature itself actually functions, and to the convoluted means by which it 'mediates' the life of the society which produces it. Although current intellectual fashions in literary studies would seek strongly and earnestly to persuade me otherwise, I am still attracted to the kind of approach implicitly recommended by Henry James, when he contrasted two styles of criticism :

> Just as [Sainte-Beuve] could never reconcile himself to saying his last word on book or author, so he never pretended to have devised a method which should be a key to truth. The truth for Mr Taine lies stored up, as one may say, in great lumps and blocks, to be released and detached by a few lively hammer-blows; while for Sainte-Beuve it was a diffused and imponderable essence, as vague as the carbon in the air which nourishes vegetation, and, like it, to be disengaged by patient chemistry. His only method was fairly to dissolve his attention in the sea of circumstances surrounding the object of his study, and we cannot but think his frank provisional empiricism more truly scientific than M. Taine's premature philosophy. [6]

Although scarcely a Sainte-Beuve, I certainly favour a 'frank provisional empiricism', and so am chary of separating generalizations from the specific contexts which give them authentic meaning. But of course these studies inevitably touch, at some point or other, on the issues in the very contesting of which Welsh identity could perhaps today be said precariously to reside: the issue of language, of a bicultural society and a divided sensibility; the rival symbolic geographies of Wales by means of which its various cultural groups orientate themselves; the different versions of history through which the present is defined and explained; the attempts to provide English-language culture with a legitimatizing Welsh point of origin; the threatened merger of Anglo-Welsh literature into British regional or provincial literature; the struggle to distinguish between authentic indigenous experience and the imputed experience that is the accompaniment to an imposed identity. The list could be extended almost indefinitely – no wonder the historian Dai Smith has wittily said that Wales is a singular noun but a plural experience.[7] However, the obvious danger in paying unremitting and single-minded attention to the cultural politics of literary works is that they end up seeming one-dimensional. Bearing this very real possibility in mind, I have conscientiously tried to guard against it throughout, but have specifically addressed myself to the problem in the case of R. S. Thomas. To me he seems to be a poet who has particularly suffered from being confined, by many of his readers, to a single political role. In the second of my two essays on his work I therefore deliberately set out to look at the neglected 'private' aspects of his poetry.

Of all the various matters upon which these essays all-too-lightly touch, however, the one that concerns me most is the co-existence of two literatures in modern Wales and the many consequences that flow from that single complex fact. Since every language inescapably creates a world unto itself there is, of course, a sense in which these literatures can have virtually nothing to say to each other. There is also obviously another sense in which both languages are, in the present social and political circumstances, directly competing for *Lebensraum* – although it might be thought that one has world enough and time already, while for the other both space and time are in imminent danger of running out – and the respective literatures can scarcely fail to reflect this struggle, sometimes in a form approaching *Kulturkampf*. I accordingly glance at this vexed problem of cultural confrontation (and, in the case of the Welsh language, of cultural survival) in my study of three novelists.

Nevertheless, my primary interest here is in beginning to explore ways in which these two cultures have to some extent developed in tandem, and share certain unnoticed common features that show them to have been the products (and producers) of the same history. The full literary results of this important historical association (which has involved much opposition, some co-operation, occasional mutual influence and many signs of a shared milieu) seem to me to have been generally overlooked and must still await proper investigation, but at least I try in some of these essays to show what can be done and what thereby can be achieved.

All this fuss over Welsh identity may strike some outsiders as (to paraphrase Henry James) very subtle talk about a very simple matter, whereas to me it is very simple talk about a very subtle matter. I am acutely aware of the inadequacies of these essays – inadequacies which are partly the weaknesses of my strengths, in the sense that they are the result of 'where I am coming from', in both the Welsh and the American senses of that phrase. In other words they are the result of my own limited socio-cultural background. But I believe that the study, and practice, of Welsh 'internal discourse' is important work, that has to be started somewhere. My debt is clearly great to those who have already started on the same project – distinguished critics like Glyn Jones, Raymond Garlick, Roland Mathias, Ned Thomas, Jeremy Hooker and Anthony Conran. This book is offered simply as a supplement to their excellent studies.

Parts of this study have appeared elsewhere, usually in a different form and sometimes even in a different language. I should therefore like to record my gratitude to the following for permission to reprint material: Mick Felton (Seren Books), Bedwyr Lewis Jones and R. Gerallt Jones (*Taliesin*), the Welsh Union of Writers, the Academi Gymreig (English Section), Belinda Humfrey (*The New Welsh Review*), Prys Morgan, University of Wales Press, Gwasg Gomer and *Llais Llyfrau/ Welsh Book News*. Friends and colleagues who have kindly spared the time to read sections of this book include Dr J. A. Davies, Professor Hywel Teifi Edwards, Dr John Harris, Emyr Humphreys, Professor Helen Vendler and the late Professor C. J. L. Price. I am also very grateful to Liz Powell and the University of Wales Press for the care taken in preparing this book and to Tony Daly for his work on the dust-jacket. Grateful acknowledgements are also due to Mrs Gweno Lewis and Allen and Unwin for permission to print material by Alun Lewis; and to R. S. Thomas, his son Gwydion, and the publishers for permission to quote extensively from the poetry. My greatest debt by far, however, is to my wife Karen and my daughter Elin, for their patience and understanding, and above all, of course, for the internal difference they daily make to my life.

1

All change:
the new Welsh drama before the Great War

The anonymous reviewer of *Barn y Brodyr*, a play by T. R. Evans, reported as follows in *The Welsh Outlook* for April, 1914:

> It is clear to the most casual observer of the intellectual activities of Wales today that we are on the verge of something in the nature of a dramatic intoxication. The men who, 20 years ago, would have been writing poor lyrics for publication in the sheltered columns of the *Goleuad* and *Llan a'r Dywysogaeth* are now spending laborious hours writing plays.[1]

He was saying nothing new. The emergence of a promising national 'dramatic movement' was the excited talk of intellectuals throughout Wales in the months before the outbreak of the First World War; and the best of the plays in English that appeared at that time could very reasonably be considered, in retrospect, as constituting the beginnings of an authentically Welsh literature in English. Caradoc Evans's collection, *My People*, did not, after all, appear until 1915, yet it has become customary to treat it as the undisputed founding text of Anglo-Welsh literature. Its reputation in this respect is, of course, based as much on the influence it had on subsequent developments as on the arresting qualities of the book itself. But that again prompts further thoughts. How different, one wonders, would the course of 'Anglo-Welsh Literature' have been, for a generation and more, had writers taken their cue not from the fiction of Caradoc Evans, but from the drama of J. O. Francis?

One of the most unfortunate aspects of the legacy Caradoc Evans left to later writers was the animosity his work had helped foster between the two cultures of Wales and their respective literatures. By contrast, one of the striking features of the drama movement in which Francis played such a distinguished part, was its bicultural and bilingual character. As the American scholar Olive Ely Hart remarked in her twenties study of *Drama in Modern Wales*, 'it is interesting to note that these first attempts to stimulate the writings and production of Welsh plays made no attempts to discriminate in the matter of the language in which the play should be written.'[2] Moreover several of the best plays were quickly translated from Welsh into English and vice versa. Such, indeed, was the sense of fellow-feeling and of common purpose uniting the Welsh-language and the English-language dramatists at the time that a full consideration of Francis's major contribution must involve not only a comparison of it with the work in English of a dramatist such as Naunton Davies but also an examination of the Welsh-language plays of D. T. Davies, W. J. Gruffydd and R. G. Berry. Fortunately, the history of the pre-war Welsh drama movement has already been splendidly mapped out in its entirety in the complementary work of two scholars. Professor Cecil Price has dealt very thoroughly with events in the English language, while the Welsh-language side of the story has been told by Professor Hywel Teifi Edwards, with his customary panache. Their combined work has provided the indispensable basis for the study that follows.[3]

The 'intoxication' of Wales by drama was no doubt due in no small part to the fact that virtually throughout the nineteenth century mainstream Welsh society had been characterized by total abstinence, as far as genuine theatrical productions were concerned. Non-conformity regarded all things theatrical with a puritanical disapproval which bordered on pathological horror.[4] It tolerated only the staging, under strict chapel control, of little improving dialogues and Temperance playlets. But towards the end of the century there was a slight, but significant, extension of this repertoire. Carefully selected scenes from the novels of Daniel Owen proved acceptable and popular. And Professor Price has convincingly argued that Joseph Parry's grand operas – 'pure' entertainment in both senses of the word – played an important part in reconciling Nonconformity at least to the amateur stage.[5] An appetite for drama, of a sort, had of course been created (and satisfied) by the Welsh pulpit for the best part of a century. Had not Dickens himself sat entranced through a long Welsh sermon at Bangor in 1852, professedly mesmerized by the performance of the preacher?:

> No other living actor could keep together such a vast concourse of people on such a broiling hot day as that Welsh preacher . . . Although I did not understand a single word he said except the word *Chalmers*, I could not tear myself from the spot until the sermon was over.[6]

Perhaps the time has come for us to consider the finest specimens of nineteenth-century Welsh pulpit oratory as maverick versions of Victorian melodrama.

The slight change in the climate of Nonconformist opinion about drama was eagerly exploited by enthusiasts like Beriah Gwynfe Evans, a concocter of improbable historical extravaganzas full of impeccably uplifting patriotic sentiment. Some of Evans's work is not without its serious side, but he did have his generous share of that unerring genius for the absurd that distinguished the great pageant-makers and national impresarios of the period. He deserves to be better known, if only as the producer of the first soap-opera for royals. His masterpiece, *Glyndŵr, Tywysog Cymru* (Glyndŵr, Prince of Wales), was performed at Caernarfon castle to celebrate the investiture of 1911. But since it was forbidden to use artificial lighting, there had to be an overnight break in the performance. The actors played until dark one afternoon and then returned to finish the play the following day. The Prince tactfully expressed his enthusiasm for this serialized history lesson, spelled out in Evans's Introductory Note to the published text of his drama:

> [The period covered by the play] distinguishes between the new and the old mutual relationship of England and Wales. Henry IV may be taken as representing the older policy of repression and of oppression which drove the whole nation into irreconcilable hostility, and left for centuries a rankling sense of injustice in the nation's heart. Henry V, in adopting the more statesmanlike policy of generous recognition . . . made it possible for those who had followed Glyndŵr into open rebellion to follow in turn the Victor of Agincourt, and to play no inconsiderable part in winning that notable and historic triumph. From that day to this Welshmen have figured prominently in the history of the British Nation.[7]

Since he prided himself that his play was based 'on the latest results of trained historical research', one wonders what Evans made of an earlier production of his play *Llewelyn ein Llyw Olaf* (Llywelyn our Last Prince), when the actors were allowed to give full, uninhibited, vent to their loyalist sentiments:

> Llewellyn [sic] was clothed in a Life Guard suit, with Wellington boots and tassels. Prince David wore a royal artillery uniform and the chieftains were magnificent in butchers' aprons. Pistols were brandished instead of bows and arrows, but there was some fine character acting and people came with great enthusiasm to all the performances.[8]

The future of Welsh drama did not, however, lie in this resourceful reinventing of the past. In fact, one of the distinguishing features of the serious drama, when it appeared, was its preoccupation with the present, considered as a period of unprecedented social change. Moreover the dramatists themselves were agreed that their plays were the complex product of that change as well as the best literary instruments for investigating it. Six or seven years after his own impressive debut as a dramatist, the most outstanding of the group of Welsh-language playwrights, D. T. Davies, wrote a sensitive piece on this subject for *The Welsh Outlook*. He noted that, for two hundred years, 'intellectual and moral effort in Wales has been concerned with the affairs of the individual soul, in pitiful isolation.' This approach, he argued, had been valid and should be valued, but it had also been emphatically lop-sided:

> I suggest, then, that the emergence of the drama can be accounted for briefly in this wise: a vital necessity has manifested itself in Wales that the individual's perception of his relationship with a higher and future life should be supplemented by an intelligent comprehension of his social adjustments on this earth. One could go further. It is demonstrable that our chief failings, both individual and national, are attributable to the neglect we have suffered in the latter training. An expansion of this thesis, with illustrations from educational, political and even religious spheres of activity, would make interesting reading.
>
> The future of the drama is indicated here. It will hold up the mirror not so much to individual man, contrasting his impotence and sinfulness with the omnipotence and holiness of an absolute being. The drama will rather present him with a more expansive reflection of his environment, wherein he will see how his daily traffic acts upon his fellow man, and eventually re-acts upon himself. This experience is a vital complement to the larger one. To appreciate your social adjustments is to realise all the more fully your own individual character; both are essential to the privilege of loving mankind, and in parenthesis there remains that story about Abou Ben Adhem.[9]

D. T. Davies's remarks quietly announce a profound, and profoundly important, shift in outlook, away from the religious individualism of classical Nonconformity and towards a new appreciation of social interrelatedness. His account of the change of attitude signalled by the emergence of the new drama is suggestively, if obscurely, related to the different phases in the history of Welsh Nonconformity: first its otherworldly, apolitical stance, then its wholesale conversion to political action that eventually turned the chapels into the Liberal party at prayer, and finally its eclipse by the new secular religion of socialism. As we shall see, the plays of D. T. Davies and several of his contemporaries can usefully be considered as responses to aspects of this last phase, with particular reference to the social turmoil that accompanied the development of a new, militant and politicized labour movement. But for the time being it is worth pausing to examine the best known of Davies's plays in the light of the comments quoted above.

Ble ma fa? (Where is he?) is a powerful one-act play that first attracted general notice when it (along with two other plays by the same author and *Ar y Groesffordd* [At the Crossroads] by R. G. Berry) won the Lord Howard de Walden prize for Welsh drama in 1913. The prizewinner the previous year had been J. O. Francis's *Change*, which will be examined in detail later. In outline Davies's play is extremely simple. A woman, whose collier husband has just been crushed to death in a roof fall underground, asks her friends and visitors the same urgent, plaintive, piercing question: where is he? At first, they think her sorrow must have made her distraught, and believe her to be searching for her dead Guto, supposing him to be still alive. But they soon realize that hers is in fact a very different and most uncomfortable question. Guto, although a good man, was not a chapel-member. Has he then gone to heaven or has he been sent to hell? The play shows the unnerving effect her anguished question has on two characters in particular: the sternly pious deacon whose callous self-righteousness caused Guto such pain when alive, and the more humane and considerate young minister.

The strength, and the originality, of *Ble ma fa?* is very largely owing to the use Davies makes of regional dialect. The play was of course written at a time when the achievements of Synge were on everybody's mind. Welsh dramatists writing in English never did succeed in following the Irishman's example, earnestly though some of them wished to do so. But in *Ble ma fa?* Wales did produce a play that managed to exploit dialect's power to suggest a density and intimacy of communal experience. It is also worth noting the play's ambiguous relationship to the homiletic and doctrinal literature which D. T. Davies quite rightly believed had delayed the appearance of a mature modern literature in Welsh. Reduced to an outline, the play seems to have taken over the didactic structure of conventional religious literature pretty well unaltered in order to preach a new message: the gospel of humanitarianism replaces the gospel of salvation by faith. But this is to overlook the textured and nuanced quality of a work whose meaning ultimately consists of the sum of those complex relationships between people which it shows us.

It could, of course, be argued that this new concept of dispersed, buried, or contextualized meaning is itself ideologically compromised. D. T. Davies would probably have been very ready to plead guilty to that charge. It is, after all, the point he had himself made in his *Welsh Outlook* article. The very form of a play, he had argued, was designed to show how human life needs to be understood not only in terms of a man's private relationship to God but also as an intricate nexus of social interactions. The medium of drama was therefore for him itself an important part of the message. This helps explain why D. T. Davies's work for the theatre is generally superior to that of his Welsh-language contemporaries – a fact astutely noticed by the young Saunders Lewis. 'The most important fact about Mr D. T. Davies', he observed in 1920, 'is that he is a dramatist, perhaps the only Welsh dramatist hitherto. I know nothing more of him than his three plays tell me, but I will hazard the statement that apart from his plays he has no means of expression. What he has to say needs the dramatic form to say it.'[10]

As it happens, Saunders Lewis was not particularly fond of *Ble ma fa?*. The play by D. T. Davies he particularly admired was *Ephraim Harris*, the three-act drama that shared the 1913 de Walden prize with *Ble ma fa?*. *Ephraim Harris* caused quite a stir when it appeared because it was seen by conservative Nonconformists as another of the plays besmirching the purity of the Welsh saints. It did, after all, centre on a deacon who in his youth had (supposedly) begotten an illegitimate child and whose (initially unwilling) concealment of that fact for half a lifetime served to intensify his bigoted intolerance of any hint of moral laxity in others. The element of despairing self-hatred in Ephraim's obsessive character is sensitively brought out by Davies. Indeed, for nine-tenths of its length the play has at least power enough to reveal the genuine possibilities for tragedy in the contemporary Nonconformist character.

Most of the first act is taken up with the attempts made by his mother to persuade the young Ephraim not to confess his guilt before the whole chapel. She pleads with him not to dishonour his dead father's memory by bringing the whole family into public disgrace – an argument in which Davies would clearly have us see the dilemma of a whole new generation of Nonconformists, prevented by ancestor worship and an

inherited passion for social respectability from reforming and liber-
alizing their faith so as to restore its moral credibility.[11] The patriarchal
aspects of triumphal Nonconformity are in fact subtly examined in
Ephraim Harris, including the belief in the strict and austere fatherhood
of an Old Testament God. Insanely possessed as he is by the very guilt
he has suppressed, Ephraim eventually drives away the only person to
whom he is genuinely attached, his only daughter, because he believes
that she is erring and disobedient. Rather like Hardy, Davies has the
ability to redeem theatrical situations which had become tainted by
melodrama, by grounding them again in real social and psychological
complexities. Unfortunately he draws back at the very last moment
from following through the dark logic of the situation he's created to its
tragic conclusion, and supplies his play instead with a frustratingly
happy ending. A reviewer mentioned this weakness at the time,
complaining that 'the spectator with any feeling for dramatic fitness is
literally shocked by the feebleness of the ending. ' He went on to make
an interesting suggestion:

> For this we are inclined to blame, not the author, but the unwillingness
> of an audience, whether Welsh or English, to witness the final ruin of a
> noble life; an unwillingness which makes the lot of the conscientious
> dramatist a particularly hard one.[12]

The character in *Ephraim Harris* nearest in point of view to D. T.
Davies himself is probably the outsider and free spirit Dinah, who feels
closest to God not in the claustrophobic chapel but on the hilltop
overlooking the village where the action is set. She explains at one point
what precisely it is she's able to see from that vantage point:

> Yes, Shakki, the top of the hill is a strange place: it would be a salvation
> for you to see yourself from up there exactly as you are down here, at the
> bottom of the valley ... Last Thursday afternoon I was sitting on top of
> that tump, with the village lying neatly under my feet. I'd seen it
> hundreds of times before, but I got a new view of it that time. There they
> all were, the homes of the men and women I'd been brought up with,
> and from every direction, along the street, through the fields and
> meadows, over hill and dale, I could see the old and the young, the
> strong and the weak, every one drawn to the same place, in the crook of
> the mountain, to the little old chapel in the middle of the graveyard and
> the white gravestones. And I realised that, in spite of all the lies and the
> narrowness, the hypocrisy and the pettiness, there was some strange
> force bringing people together and keeping them together.[13]

Here the emphasis, as one would expect from the author of the *Welsh Outlook* article, is on the extensive social landscape created and controlled by Nonconformity. At this point the stress is specifically on the beneficial aspects of the chapels' power, but all that some readers and listeners could see in *Ephraim Harris* when it was first performed was anti-Christian propaganda.

But then the nerves of hardline Nonconformists had been on edge for some time before ever *Ephraim Harris* was staged. Indeed the Nonconformist establishment had been on red alert to repel attack ever since it realized that it was losing its battle against the rising power of labour, and discovered in addition that there was a threat from within its own ranks corresponding to this massing threat from without. The arts were particularly suspect because they were clearly playing a leading part in the formation of a new, irreligious and anti-religious society. Touring metropolitan plays, the music-hall, and above all that new sensation, the cinema, were an evident danger, but at least their baleful influence was very largely confined to the Anglicized and industrialized areas. More insidious and much more threatening was the growth of an irreverend, subversive literature in Welsh. The poets had started the rot as early as 1902, when T. Gwynn Jones had dared enter the morally misty realms of myth in the controversial poem that won the eisteddfod chair that year, *Ymadawiad Arthur* (The Departure of Arthur). By 1914 the dramatists were proving equally unmanageable – a point underlined by the fact that two of this new school of Welsh playwrights had already written notoriously perfidious poetry. One was T. Gwynn Jones himself; the other was the scourge of established Nonconformity, the young Turk, W. J. Gruffydd.

For T. Gwynn Jones, the new Welsh-language drama was the second phase of literature's critical engagement with Nonconformity. But he also saw this second stage as in part a reaction against the characteristics of the first literary acts of rebellion, exemplified by his own early poetry. Looking back in 1920, he approvingly observed in the drama of 1914:

> . . . a tendency to depart from the romanticism of the preceding decade –
> I mean the romanticism which came as a protest against Eisteddfodic
> traditionalism, religious stagnation, and social materialism, which
> almost immediately became conventionalized itself, and which remains
> as another kind of insipidity in Eisteddfodic poetry. The tendency to
> rebel against the new tyranny continues.[14]

One of T. Gwynn Jones's most important contributions to this new literature of uncompromising realism was his translation into Welsh of Ibsen's play *Ghosts*. As Hywel Teifi Edwards has succinctly noted, Ibsen's work was an exhilarating and a liberating influence on the leading Welsh dramatists of the day. In particular they relished his skill at disinterring the buried life of a stultifyingly respectable society; and his exposure of the cant of so much high-sounding idealism.[15]

W. J. Gruffydd was undoubtedly the most vigorously and invigoratingly iconoclastic figure on the Welsh literary scene during the years immediately preceding and following the First World War. And so, when he turned his hand to drama, and produced *Beddau'r Proffwydi* (The Tombs of the Prophets), in March, 1913, it was only to be expected that the play would cause a stir. It was, in fact, a frontal attack on Nonconformity's part in maintaining an oppressive and exploitative social hierarchy. The piece shows the degradation of Emrys, a young idealist wrongfully convicted of poaching, who is duly excommunicated from the chapel through the majority vote of sanctimonious deacons anxious to safeguard their own position as prominent and prosperous local citizens. Embittered by their hypocritical conduct, Emrys abandons himself to a life of crime, eventually returning home to be revenged on his tormentors. At this point the play seems on the verge of turning into a crude, neo-Nonconformist version of an Elizabethan revenger's tragedy. But this scene of violent melodrama is capped by the kind of sentimental episode which we nowadays tend to associate with the Victorians. The play ends with Emrys a reformed character, saved by the love of a good woman, and rather piously embracing an ethic of forgiveness. But as the reaction of the Nonconformist establishment at the time confirms, what really distinguished *Beddau'r Proffwydi* was its power to disturb through the gibes, the raillery and the sarcasm of Emrys at his most uninhibited, when he borders in fact on the mentally unhinged.

Even some of those who were sympathetic to the new drama could still balk at *Beddau'r Proffwydi*. An anonymous commentator in *The Welsh Outlook* compared the play unfavourably with *Ble ma fa?* and admonished Gruffydd for his rashness. It should be remembered, said the writer, 'that the Welsh Drama is at present in its infancy, and there will be more likelihood of sturdy growth on its part if it appeals to the sympathy of all classes. This it will not do, if institutions which have played a great part in the life of the country are subjected to crude and unsympathetic attacks.' He therefore advised the playwrights to 'introduce a certain element of moderation into [their] protest.' Gruffydd's deacons, he argues, are distortions of the truth for the sake of satire. 'There is the less justification for this in that there is ample material for the dramatic element in a contrast between the past and the present – and still more the future – even of the 'Sêt Fawr' which shall be based on truer and more faithful portraits than some of those given us in *Beddau'r Proffwydi*.' This, he maintained, was where *Ble ma fa?* excelled.[16]

As can be seen, then, some contemporaries wilfully mistook the vehemence of Gruffydd's satire for virulence. But today we can relish the inspired intemperateness of parts of *Beddau'r Proffwydi*, particularly contrasted to the much more gentle and rather bland criticism found in the work of R. G. Berry. His unfortunately titled four-act play *Asgre Lân* (A Pure Bosom), for instance, deals with the case of a sincerely devout minister who brings disaster in his wake when he turns part-time insurance agent and persuades his flock to invest their money in a company which predictably goes bust. Enraged by bankruptcy they at first turn in their bitterness on the minister, who meekly accepts responsibility for the catastrophe; but all ends happily when the manse and its entire contents, put on the market to raise money to part-compensate the victims, is bought by the minister's faithful friends and restored to him, in an act of Christian charity that is also a triumphant reaffirmation of community spirit.

Attacks on the Nonconformist establishment were not confined to plays in the Welsh language. A pre-war work which quickly captured the public's imagination was J. O. Francis's one-act drama, *The Poacher* (1914). A play charmingly effective on its modest terms, it contained, in the simpleton Dici Bach Dwl with his innocent native cunning, a stock character who nevertheless acquired a new lease of life through being introduced, for the first time, into a distinctively Welsh context. Zealots and guardians of the faith were, however, most disapproving of a play where the main source of humour was a good-natured, chapel-going wife's efforts to de-convert her husband. Upon his religious conversion Twmas had renounced all his former sinful practices, obediently stifling his passion, and conspicuous talent, for poaching. His wife's pleasure, however, soon turned to exasperation, when she discovered her larder had become boring at best, and was frequently entirely bare. Her attempts, in collusion with Dici Bach Dwl, to entice Twmas back to the pleasures of illicit hunting and snaring, prove successful only when it emerges that Dafydd Hughes, a chapel stalwart, is on the point of using secret information confided to him by an unsuspecting Twm, to catch the gigantic, elusive rabbit that Twmas rightly regards as his alone, by virtue of his exceptional talents as a poacher.

Slight piece though it ultimately is, *The Poacher* possesses qualities that are, regrettably, seldom to be found in Welsh literature in either language of any period. Instead of obediently dealing with matters that moralists and social commentators regard as central and substantial, Francis has followed wherever the unpredictable and quixotic imagination of mankind seems to him in his chosen instance actually to lead, and he has ended up discovering that the deepest human passions have a habit of manifesting themselves in the most apparently inconsequential of ways. By employing this method, much greater writers than Francis, from Faulkner to Welty, have been able to show that hunting has its mythic aspects. To claim that *The Poacher* in any way plumbs comparable depths would be silly. But Francis's lightness of touch is more than an example of his professional dexterity; it is a reliable proof of the sensitivity and delicacy of his genuinely writerly imagination.

Unfortunately, some of Francis's contemporaries had eyes only for his 'mistreatment' of deacons, as he himself ruefully noted in his essay 'Deacon and Dramatist'.[17] The piece begins with a confident assertion: 'Today, without rashness and without reservation, we may believe that the drama has taken so strong a hold on Welsh-men that it must be counted one of their favourite literary forms.' Looking back, however, at the beginnings of this development in the years immediately preceding the war, he now penitently professes to 'think we somewhat overdid our indictment of the deacon. It began to get a little monotonous.'[18] He attributes this obsession in part to 'the old, and perhaps ignoble, desire to hit back. In our early days, we had known all the terrors in which the deacon moved enwrapped. Little boys who are some day going to write plays are not the little boys who sit meekly through long sermons.' But beyond this, he admits, lay a deeper reason for singling out the Sêt Fawr for special attention:

> A small and intimate nation was changing old lamps for new. In all that concerned industry and religion there was, in most acute expression, the age-long conflict between the power that waxes and the power that wanes. Apollo was once more challenging Hyperion, and near by stood the dramatists taking notes with feverish pens. Some of them, it must be said, had put their money on Apollo – and wrote accordingly.

There Francis reveals the real mainspring for much of the dramatic activity of the period, his own plays included. But when we turn to his finest work, we find that the emphasis has shifted from the 'changing [of] old lamps for new' in the field of religion, to the same process in the world of 'industry'.

J. O. Francis's play *Change* is today one of the nearly forgotten and sadly neglected key works of Anglo-Welsh literature. Yet in 1914 it was regarded as certainly a breakthrough and possibly a masterpiece. The winner of the de Walden prize in 1912, performed in London, produced in New York, played before a distinguished audience in Cardiff, and toured throughout south Wales, it was hailed as the outstanding English-language contribution to a Welsh drama movement that might shortly rival even the renowned Irish achievements at the Abbey. In his favourable review of the Cardiff performance the correspondent for *The Welsh Outlook* provided a serviceable summary of the play:

> The play is a powerful drama of Glamorgan life in which the author graphically depicts the 'change' that is taking place in the industrial districts of South Wales. We see this in the history of one small family. The father is the deacon of a local Methodist chapel and represents the 'old brigade'. He has worked hard and sacrificed much in order to secure for his sons advantages which were unknown in his younger days. But it was all in vain. The son who was destined for the ministry becomes an 'unbeliever', and is turned out of home; a second, an invalid, is killed in the course of some strike riots which had been caused by the young Socialist element, of which the third son is the recognised local leader. He, accused by his father of having on him the brand of Cain, leaves the home for Australia. The mother is left desolate having lost her three sons, for whom she was constantly 'hungry', and having discovered her husband to be a 'hard man'. A relief from all this tragical element is supplied by an English lodger, whom the author has clearly introduced, and who serves also to illustrate the difficulty which the average man has in understanding the commotion and tragedy to which the 'change' has given rise in the Welsh home, where there is 'too much feeling'.[19]

This summary is worth quoting in full because it shows how very alert an intelligent contemporary could immediately be to the range of social, religious and political issues addressed in the play. This was largely because the play carried many of these meanings so openly and so clearly, to the point one might say of positively advertising their presence. In addition to this plain text there was, though, or so I would argue, a socio-political sub-text to the play, which continues to be worth our investigation.

A useful starting point is Francis's own attempt to explain, in *Wales* (Nov. 1913), how and why this sudden appearance of a 'New Welsh Drama' had come about. He referred first to a kind of national awakening, and then to the effects of intermediate and higher education, before adding: 'In the third place, the younger generation, with its dramatists to be, grows up in a system of society where accepted ideas are going through changes . . . In the pressure of industrialism, the old Liberal-Labour attitude of the South is changing into the fiercer front of Socialism.'[20] Francis himself had been raised, a blacksmith's son, in the industrial township of Merthyr, at a time when Lib-Lab had been at full strength. It was also in Merthyr, however, that one of the first dramatic signs of a shift in working-class allegiance appeared with the election of Keir Hardie in 1900.

Before we consider other famous changes that followed in the economic, social and political fields, it is worth mentioning something which could be equally significant to an artist, even if it seems much less tangible to a historian, namely a change of social atmosphere; an alteration, one might say, in barometric pressure ˉin the valleys. Francis's sensitivity to this can not only be deduced from *Change*, it can be conveniently measured in a short paragraph from a piece he wrote for *The Welsh Outlook* about travelling to north Wales to attend the Corwen eisteddfod in 1919. He enjoyed the experience, but was puzzled, he explained, by the unusual pleasure he found himself deriving from staring through his hotel window at the peaceful, convivial crowd of eisteddfodwyr. Eventually, the penny dropped:

> Down in my mind, in all assemblings of the people, there stirs a memory of the old 'mass meetings' in Glamorgan, from which so often came struggle and privation – sometimes soldiery, shootings and death. Those grim crowds had their own characteristic note – a savage undertone breaking into passionate applause or quick, cold laughter, shot with irony and menace. It was the voice of mankind fiercely conscious of its circumstances, caught in the friction between what men would be and what the times have made of them.[21]

This 'characteristic note' of the 'grim crowd' is to be distinctly heard in *Change*, but what is worth noticing at this point is the mixed tone of Francis's remarks; the note of unease which sounds throughout his paragraph. There is unmistakeable sympathy for a work-force driven to extremes, it is true; but there is also, signalled by words like 'savage', 'menace' and 'fiercely', an apprehensiveness at the new spirit of violence that has crept into the attitudes and actions of the men. It is this ambivalence of feeling that governs *Change* and guarantees a complex interplay of points-of-view throughout the play.

J. O. Francis was, it seems, a sensitive, educated man of liberal temperament, who had been an active political Liberal when young.[22] The new labour activism of the immediate pre-war years, with its increasing militancy and class-consciousness, was, he very well knew, the irresistible product of changing social and economic circumstances in the industrial areas. It meant the end of consensus and the beginning of conflict. 'Strife' was a noun which suddenly entered the common vocabulary of the period. The new periodical *The Welsh Outlook*, to which Francis was a regular contributor, discussed the implications of these changes repeatedly, in a style that was outwardly objective, but can now seem to us inwardly disturbed, even obsessive. Emphasis was placed in the editorial of the very first number on the breakdown of traditional values and resulting moral confusion: 'young men and women are bewildered by the conflicting standards of the home, the workshop, the church and the newspaper.' 'Our modern attitudes to the Sabbath, to sport, to the drama are obvious examples of changing values', wrote the editor, before going on, significantly, to attempt to mediate between the old, Liberal, order and the new, emergent order which clearly favoured a different political philosophy: 'Individualism and Socialism are really ways of valuing certain human qualities and placing some higher, some lower, in the scale of honour . . . Industrial unrest is fundamentally an attempt to revalue man and to put a higher price upon him.'[23] Interestingly enough, some publications in the *Welsh Drama Series*, sponsored by *The Welsh Outlook*, carried on their back covers an advertisement for the periodical which listed industrial unrest side by side with the new drama as two contemporary topics the journal prided itself on discussing.

Nonconformity was, of course, another important factor in the changing social equation, and the declining power of the chapels is given prominent attention in *Change*. In a thoughtful article that appeared shortly after the war, Principal Thomas Rees regretted 'the ever-widening cleavage between Nonconformity and Labour in Wales':

> Twenty years ago Welsh Nonconformity practically consisted of one social class and belonged to one political party. Today, we have a sprinkling of peers and millionaires, a large middle-class of professional men and wealthy merchants who resent the increasing demands and

pretensions of the workers, and the workers both in town and country, growing ever more class-conscious, repay the resentment with good interest . . . The government of the churches has passed largely into the hands of the middle class, who are their best financial supporters. We are in danger of becoming, like English Nonconformity, the churches of a bourgeoisie. The more class-conscious section of the workers tends to identify the churches with capitalism, profiteering, oppression and their attendant wrongs and evils.[24]

He saw that the centre of moral authority in society was moving away from the chapels to the new labour organizations, and he attributed this partly to 'the constant stream of English and other immigrants into the industrial districts . . . creating an atmosphere of hostility and antagonism to all religion.'[25] This is very much the view of John Price, the elderly collier in *Change*. With increasing bitterness, he sees his three sons, one by one, lose interest in the chapel, and he blames their defection on the influence of outsiders like Pinkerton, a stranger and socialist troublemaker:

It's men like him are the curse of South Wales today. Who is he, I'd like to know, that he should be made a proper 'god' of? I've been in the valley here now for sixty years. I remember Aberpandy before ever the Powell-Griffiths sank the first pit, and the sheep of Pandy Farm were grazing quiet where the Bryndu Pit is now. And I never so much as heard talk of this fellow Pinkerton till two or three years ago.[26]

As historians have shown, the labour force in the south Wales coalfield increased by over a half between 1900 and 1914, and sixty-three per cent of the newcomers were immigrants from outside Wales.[27]

Although *Change* reads like a coalfield drama, it was claimed, when the play was first produced, that it was based on turbulent events at Llanelli during the national railwaymen's strike in 1911, when two strikers were shot dead. The play's relationship to that incident is, however, slight to say the least, and it would be more useful to regard it as a composite study – a study, that is, of the various factors contributing to the widespread industrial unrest that marked the immediate pre-war period in Britain. Deian Hopkin, the latest historian of the Llanelli disturbances, has in any case pointed out that they were typical of this more general historical phenomenon which included, of course, the Tonypandy 'riots' of 1910. According to Dr Hopkin, the chief causes of this general unrest were 'a rapid growth in trade union membership and activity; a change in the mood of industrial relations accompanied by an erosion in the influence of an established union leadership, and a profound and widespread social crisis.'[28] In its way, *Change* touches on all these issues, with particular reference to 'the element of generational change.'[29]

By the time that *Change* came to be written, the British stage had already shown itself capable of dealing, after a fashion, with the industrial aspects of this 'social crisis'. Galsworthy's *Strife* (1909) was a creditable attempt at sympathetic treatment of both sides to an industrial dispute, and interestingly enough the play was frequently mentioned (alongside predictable references to Ibsen and the Irish theatre) by early reviewers of *Change*. Any broad similarities of theme and structure between the two plays are, however, far less significant in my opinion than the important affinity there seems to be between the socio-political outlook of Galsworthy and of Francis. This unconsciously shared mentalité is, I believe, inscribed in different yet related ways in the form as well as in the content of their respective plays.

The 'politics' of *Strife*, at least as understood by one intelligent contemporary, is beautifully, if unexpectedly, brought out in a piece that appeared in *The Welsh Outlook* for January, 1914.[30] The piece is an extract from a speech by Principal Burrows to University Settlement workers in Cardiff, and the editor of the periodical has added to it the prefatory explanation that it is reproduced because it seems 'so appropriately to crystallise the aims and desires of *The Welsh Outlook*.' The question which the Principal addresses is how to overcome the dangerously growing antagonism between the classes, and the vital first step, as he sees it, is to destroy the stereotyped view each class has of the other, since these caricatures play into the hands of extremists of every colour. The way forward, Burrows argues, was shown when *Strife* was first put on the stage. The decision was then consciously taken not to give Harness, the typical Trade Union official, a red tie. Old Anthony, 'the splendid representative in that very play . . . of the Industrial Autocrat', would, says the Principal, have snorted his contempt at this weak-kneed decision. Agitators, he would have said, need to be clearly branded as such. 'If you realise them as individual human beings, you are in danger of sympathising with them, and your battle for your privileges is half lost already.' But just as Galsworthy refused to caricature the labour activist in Harness, so he refused to travesty the class of owners in his portrayal of Anthony: 'Galsworthy, who has the true dramatic power of seeing both sides of the question, makes him not only upright and a fine fighter, but a kind man to his own family and his immediate dependents.'

Burrows then proceeds to show how, nevertheless, Galsworthy has personified in Anthony all the ruling-class attitudes that, if unmodified, would lead to social catastrophe:

> What determined Anthony's industrial attitude was his deliberate belief that the only way of securing his profits was to keep his men down. Such a man would be suspicious of anything that developed the intellectual side in them. Football would be all right and should be encouraged. It would occupy their minds, and keep them quiet. Debates and classes would be anathema. Above all he would object to a personal intercourse that in his view encouraged sentimentalism in the employing class, blunted their sense of self-interest, and ran across the lines of class solidarity.

This policy of no compromise is, says Burrows, bound to lead to the kind of bloody confrontation seen in Dublin, and could result in bomb attacks such as those perpetrated by anarchists in Barcelona. But thank God, he adds, Britain 'is not yet in fact divided into two opposite hostile camps of rich and poor.' There is only a small section of the labour movement 'which, on the analogy of Continental precedent, preaches the class war on its side, as Anthony and his like preached it on theirs . . . after all, the working classes are English and Welsh like you. Blood is thicker than class.'

Principal Burrows was, then, openly preaching the gospel of moderation, conciliation, and compromise. He took *Strife* as his text, and in so doing managed, it seems to me, to penetrate to the political sub-text of that play, which is almost identical, I would further suggest, to the political sub-text of *Change*. Burrows posited a choice between 'evolution and revolution' which, he argued, society would have to make. In the very next number of the *Welsh Outlook* a letter signed 'One of the Propertyless, Penrhiwceiber' appeared, informing the Principal that 'a Revolution is inevitable (not necessarily a bloody one).'[31] Reform, said the writer, was useless because it would never produce a truly equitable society. Change of that sort was no better than 'feeding a dog with his own tail and then wondering why the animal shows no improvement in its condition.' The correspondent's disagreement with Burrows interestingly included a different reading of the Principal's key text:

> The character of Anthony in Galsworthy's *Strife* is a more honest expression of Capitalism than those who say they sympathise with the working class for improvement, who never let their sympathies decrease

their shekels. Generally the rich will do anything for the worker except
get off his back, knowing if he does he would have to work himself . . .
The only way of abolishing the Class War is to do away with the cause
of it . . . we must establish a Co-operative Commonwealth which I
believe will be the result of organisation and education of the working
people.

Obviously, in this writer's view, Galsworthy's portraits of intran-
sigence appeared true to the realities of the class struggle, while the
dramatist's determination to display these portraits in a disapproving
light seemed part of a well intentioned but totally ineffectual bourgeois
attempt to promote good feelings between two classes each of which
was destined to be the enemy of the other for as long as the capitalist
system lasted.

The clearest attempt made in the Welsh theatre to dissuade the
working class from resorting to militant industrial action and to
persuade workers to trust to the goodwill of the managers rather than
the inflammatory rhetoric of the new breed of union leaders, was
Naunton Davies's *The Human Factor* (1920). Davies was a prosperous
and respected doctor, member of a well-known south Wales family,
who published well over a dozen competent plays during a comparatively short period of time. *The Human Factor* follows events
during an imaginary strike 'in Glamorganshire, in the year 1910.' Urged
on by their unscrupulous leader, James Walford – who is, like
Pinkerton, an Englishman and therefore a meddling, dangerous
interloper – the miners set out to starve their highly principled, decent
and thoroughly careworn manager, John Williams, and his family into
submission. Walford's beguiling talk about the virtues of socialism at
first persuades the upper-middle-class Rhys Morgan, the local Rector's
son, to support the union's struggle. Morgan's dream of social justice is,
however, in reality based on softer sentiments than those of Walford:

> [The workers] may be hot-headed, impetuous, obstinate. Which of us is
> not? It's the Welshman's inheritance; and sometimes our hot Welsh
> blood carries us away. But in your reckoning you are apt to leave out the
> human factor. Once touch our hearts, and the human factor comes
> uppermost . . . [The human factor] is what I call the good desire that lies
> buried in us all – the spark of kindliness that wants only the right touch
> to set it ablaze. It's the quality that sets men as Gods walking, and saves
> the worst of us from utter badness.[32]

As its title suggests, Naunton Davies's play is a demonstration of the
ultimate capacity of this universal power of human kindliness to

produce a panacea for all social evils. The human factor acts as the solvent of all disagreements and disputes, however violent.

By the end of the play Good Heartedness is on liberal (not to say Liberal) display on all sides. Sobered by their abortive attempt to scare the manager's family with an explosion, the penitent men are ready to make their peace with their employer. This unexpected turn of events promises to persuade even the manager's timid wife (once she recovers from her faint) that they are not the 'wild animals' and 'brutes' of her frightened imagination. John Williams's obstinate and provocative pride has been somewhat softened, and even the villainous Walford is shown to be capable of a humane action. Equally important, it seems, to the author, the snobbishness of the Rector and his wife abates sufficiently to allow them to approve of the marriage of their son, Rhys, to the daughter of the *nouveau riche* manager. The original cause of the industrial dispute, which was never very clear, is conveniently forgotten about by all.

Naunton Davies's middle-class view of social and industrial affairs is nowhere more apparent than in the creation and the treatment of the character of Gwilym, described by the author as 'a quaint Welshman, attached to Rhys.' Gwilym is to the new middle class of south Wales what the faithful retainer was to the old aristocracy. He is a loyal, cunning peasant – a true innocent son of the Welsh soil, as Davies no doubt saw him – always ready to use his wiliness to trick the socially insubordinate miners and forever eager to serve his betters with wholehearted obedience. In fact, good old Welsh-speaking Gwilym is the very stuff of the Welsh bourgeois dream of a traditional lower-class that knows its place and respects its superiors.

The Human Factor fully deserves Cecil Price's dismissive description of it as 'a coalfield melodrama', but the social philosophy which underpins it is not so very different from that which underlies J. O. Francis's incomparably better play *Change*. The greater richness and complexity of *Change* is, I would suggest, due not only to the superior talent of Francis as a dramatist, but also to the wider social distribution of his sympathy and the correspondingly heightened quality of his social intelligence. John Price, the old collier, for instance, is a harsh, intolerant and tyrannical man, but his favourite son, Gwilym, is able to see his father as more than a religious bigot, or the 'cantankerous old devil' hated by his brother Lewis:

> It's men and women growing old in a world that doesn't understand them, and that they themselves don't understand . . . the old brigade can

only see that they're losing, and they're bewildered, pressed on all sides
by things that they don't understand. If they argue with you, they get
beaten. Why? Because they've been careful to give you the education
they never had themselves.   (48–9)

Gwilym is, in fact, a kind of *alter ego* for Francis in the play – sickly, a
bit of a poet, and altogether an outsider – and Gwilym's death is at the
very heart of the drama. He is shot by accident as he tries to prevent his
brother, the fiery Lewis, from rallying the men in an effort to repel the
advance of troops sent to protect a train full of blacklegs. The violent
clash between the strikers and the soldiers takes place off stage, but
Francis is notably careful to have the strikers literally cast the first stone
and draw first blood. The action of the soldiers is thus presented as self-
defence and the blame for the murderous consequences is presumed
therefore to lie primarily with the miners. Gwilym appears to die not as
a hero of the class war but as an innocent, sacrificial victim in a scene of
regrettable social violence. The religious overtones of the incident are
not lost on Lewis. Driven almost demented by guilt, he finally accepts
his father's triumphantly merciless judgement on him: he is a Cain who
has slaughtered his gentle brother Abel.

Needless to say, Francis does not himself endorse John Price's
judgement. Indeed, his play is in a profound sense a historical tragedy –
that is a tragedy brought about, as it were, by history. Characters are
shown to be intimately formed, and informed by the values and
circumstances of the place and the period in which they grow to
maturity. Understanding this, Gwilym pleads with his brothers not to
be hard on their father, 'because he doesn't look at things with your
eyes. He can't help himself any more than you. He belongs to the old
valley. At heart he's of the agricultural class – slow, stolid, and
conservative. You, Lewis, you're of a different kind altogether – you've
grown up in modern industry, with no roots in the soil. That's why
you're a rebel. That's why the men of your time are rebels too' (50).
Although he does tend to simplify and to schematize this kind of
perception, Francis is a significant writer precisely because he is capable
in *Change* of understanding and of bringing out the historical aspects
not only of public events but also of private relationships – relationships between individuals and within families.

Nevertheless, after due and admiring notice has been taken of
Francis's self-effacing even-handedness in dealing with his characters
and their sometimes violently differing convictions in *Change*, it is
important also to note that the author does in a quiet way use the

historical tragedy to voice a social hope. The grounds for this hope are articulated by Gwilym early in the play when he says that 'the world needs sacrifice as much as it needs laughter' (49). Gwilym himself becomes the sacrifice which his own Welsh world of industrial conflict and social strife sorely needs. This aspect of the play's meaning was, interestingly, seen by Francis's ally, the controversial Welsh writer W. J. Gruffydd, when *Change* was first performed in Cardiff:

> Those who have essayed this most difficult task of dramatic writing will fully appreciate the author's nice perception of artistic justice in the portrayal of Gwilym, whom the younger generation of rebels against the old conventions are apt to forget, when their turn comes to hold up a mirror to their countrymen. He is just the right dramatic corrective and foil to the rather hard and arid intellectualism which has produced Lewis and John Henry, and which – God forfend that it should ever dominate the rising drama of Wales! Certainly, *Change* is wonderfully free from it.[33]

Gruffydd had clearly realized that Gwilym was the figure representing the author's hopes of conciliation – between Chapel and Labour, between employers and union, between Liberalism and the believers in Socialism and Syndicalism.

Although Francis had a far better understanding than Naunton Davies of the socio-economic reasons for the new unionism, with its emphasis on collective action and solidarity of labour, he still shared the yearning of the educated professional middle class for a world in which individual relationships reigned supreme. Indeed, the very form of the domestic drama which Francis adopted in *Change* was ill suited to the extensive exploration of social living. The world of work which shaped the lives of people in the industrial communities in such a thoroughgoing way, is present in the play only through eloquent comments like the following from Lewis:

> ... there on Bryndu stands the pit that is your master. From the cradle to the grave, it's been holding you in the hollow of its hand. The food you eat, the clothes you wear, the bed you lie in – it's master of them all, aay, almost of the very souls within you! When it gives, it gives with grudging, and when it gives no more, sooner or later, you've got to tighten your belt and see the sorrow writing deep on the faces of the women. But it's not going on for ever, I tell you; and all your cowardice and cant won't serve to save it. (35)

J. O. Francis's play is, therefore, an interesting half-way house between the literature that had used industrial work only as background or

setting to a story, and the 'Welsh industrial novel' which Raymond
Williams has written about so illuminatingly:

> The working society – actual work, actual relations, an actual and
> visibly altered place – is in the industrial novel central . . . because in
> these working communities it is a trivial fantasy to suppose that these
> general and pressing conditions are for long or even at all separable
> from the immediate and the personal . . . The privileged distances of
> another kind of fiction, where people can 'live simply as human beings',
> beyond the pressures and interruptions and accidents of society, are in
> another world or more specifically in another class.[34]

Naunton Davies's play clearly inhabits that other world and is the
product of that other class. As for *Change*, it is so interesting and
powerful because it attempts, with seriousness and intelligence, to
understand the working-class on that class's terms, while still hoping
that class divisions can be transcended and society reunited at the level
of supposedly ordinary, general, human experience.

Since, as Raymond Williams has further shown, even the most
socially aware and sophisticated of the later industrial novelists
experienced problems with devising fictional forms authentically suited
to the working societies they sought to portray, it is hardly surprising to
find that J. O. Francis's play has got its weaknesses in this respect. He
must have been one of the first Welsh writers to treat relations within a
family as a microcosm of the stresses and strains within an industrial
society. This structural device later became a central feature of the
Welsh industrial novel, and was used to particularly powerful effect in
T. Rowland Hughes's *Chwalfa* (1946). But as Raymond Williams has
remarked, 'the difficulty with the insertion of a complex political
struggle into a local family form is that it can quickly become too
selectively exemplary, and then too early limited by exemplary
consonances of personal quality and political correctness' (15). This is
fair comment on Francis's incomplete success in *Change* at managing
'the political projection of a family'.

Central to the play is the plight of woman on the margins of a world,
both of chapel and of work, in relation to which she is made to feel
helpless and passive, being excluded from the crucial decision-making
processes, whether they be deacons' meetings or strikes. The industrial
literature produced in Wales is, in fact, very interesting in its treatment
of this subject. Lewis Jones, for instance, tries to re-empower women by
enlisting them in the active struggle of labour against capitalism in

Cwmardy and *We Live*. Mary, the daughter of an old-style union leader, having inherited her father's tactical shrewdness and determination, becomes one of the architects of the miners' new-style campaigns for control of the mining industry. As if to emphasize her 'feminine' sensitivity and vulnerability, however, in order to prevent her from seeming too 'mannish', Lewis Jones makes her physically frail and tubercular. In *Times Like These*, Gwyn Jones finds a different way of liberating women from the stereotype of an industrial Mrs Greatheart, the longsuffering wife and mother. His Mary, Mary Biesty, refuses her appointed role as striking collier's loyally supportive wife and scandalizes the community by determinedly setting out to better herself, leaving the valley to find lucrative secretarial work first in Newport and later in London. Her progress is suggestively contrasted with the decline of her sister-in-law Olive, a gentle and patient soul who is gradually worn out by poverty and hardship. She dies young of peritonitis in a local hospital that 'was a muddle of kindness and callousness, of devoted service and sheer time-serving, and it was for ever short of money.'[35]

Compared with the two Marys, Francis's Gwen is a somewhat idealized portrait of virtuous and sacrificial motherhood, as his opening description of her indicates: 'a gentle, soft-voiced woman, whose face is very kind and a little sad. Even in her smile there is a certain touch of wistfulness, suggesting some under-life in which memory and emotion have greatest power. She is a well-preserved little woman of sixty, with white hair' (9). Throughout the play she is the vehicle for expressing the pain that comes from first the breakdown and then the virtual destruction of the family. When reviewing the production of *Change* at the New Theatre, Cardiff (May, 1914), Professor Gilbert Norwood responded particularly warmly to this aspect of the performance:

> If there is any element of real permanence, of undisputed greatness, in *Change*, it is this splendid attempt at a most difficult task – the expression of a mother's heart. The contrast between the old generation and the new, which forms the main theme of this drama, is here treated well indeed, yet with no extraordinary power. But the contrast between man and woman, between the father with his memories and prejudices, the sons with their hopes and opinions, on the one side, and the mother with neither prejudices nor opinions, but only blind eternal instincts on the other – this is an achievement indeed.[36]

Norwood's comment is interesting, because it suggests that some members of the middle class derived considerable comfort, in the face of the violence of recent industrial unrest. from contemplating the soothing figure of the eternal mother, reassuringly situated at the very centre (and 'heart') of these otherwise disturbing working-class developments. And Francis's drama does offer some grounds for comfort of this kind. In Gwen's keening, at the very end of the play, can be heard just a hint of the voice of the old mother Maurya, in Synge's *Riders to the Sea*, whose sorrowing is full of a barely suppressed bitterness both at fate and at the wilful, selfish impetuosity of her restless men in their irresponsible yielding to the lure of adventure.

In spite of its limitations and weaknesses, *Change* is clearly one of the outstanding products of this fascinating early period in the development of a twentieth century Welsh literature in English. It deserves better than to be treated by us as it has been – forgotten except as a title to be mentioned in any conscientiously full scholarly survey of the field. When he addressed a gathering at the National Eisteddfod held in Pontypool (August, 1924), J. O. Francis ventured modestly to suggest that 'the progress of the drama in Wales in the last 12 or 15 years in creative achievement was greater than in any other Welsh field of art during the same period.' That is still a tenable point of view, and Francis's own contribution to this 'creative achievement' still awaits proper recognition, more than three-quarters of a century after the first production of *Change*.

2

Writing Glamorgan

The contribution made by Glamorgan to the development of a modern Welsh literature in English has been so immense as to be virtually immeasurable. It could even profitably dispute with Cardiganshire the controversial privilege of being considered the *fons et origo* of this kind of writing. For reasons of convenience, at least, Caradoc Evans may still be treated as the literature's originator, but, as John Harris has shown, the crabbed 'peasants' of *My People* are the product of a migrant imagination.[1] The stories were written in London, but from a point of view which, although geographically much nearer to Evans's west Wales home, was culturally more remote almost than the English metropolis itself. Filled with admiration for the libertarian, egalitarian and fraternal world being dreamed about, if not actually lived, in industrial south Wales, Evans through his parodic Old Testament style put the mark of Cain on a rural society which, by contrast, appeared backward and savagely feudal to him. In his stories Cardiganshire became, as Dylan Iorwerth has wittily put it, a mean and peasant land.[2]

His unfairly notorious style is not a purely literary artefact, however. It is the vivid, livid, linguistic sign of social change felt not as a form of continuity, but as sudden discontinuity. Glamorgan represents the time and place of sundering, while the west stands for everything the other side of a great historical divide. Similarly, whether they be idyllic or satiric in kind, the highly selective, instructively distorted pictures of the rural west produced in the early phases of twentieth-century Glamorgan's English-language literature are the indispensable mirror images fashioned by industrial south Wales inversely to reflect, and to enable it to reflect upon, its own fiercely cherished separate identity.

The following chapter is an attempt to explore, in an undogmatic, fluid and preliminary fashion, some of the ways in which the work of several of the major English-language writers from Glamorgan seems to be variously marked by the experience of separateness. In the body of impressive work that they produced between them can be detected signs

of a central ambivalence of experience similar to that which Octavio
Paz, in his Nobel Prize speech, claimed as a characteristic of South
American writing:

> This consciousness of being separate is a constant feature of our
> spiritual history. Separation is sometimes experienced as a wound that
> makes an internal division, an anguished awareness that invites self-
> examination; at other times it appears as a challenge, a spur that incites
> us to action, to go forth and encounter others and the outside world.[3]

Although Paz's carefully balanced comment usefully reminds us that
the psychological (and creative) consequences of socio-cultural separation are complex, it is equally important to remember that they are
subtle and extend across a spectrum far wider than that covered by his
suggestive duality. In the case of the Glamorgan writers, the condition
of separateness can manifest itself in forms as different as the personal
isolation of Alun Lewis and Rhys Davies, the conviction of solidarity
with a unique society that is found in the novels of Gwyn Thomas, Jack
Jones and Lewis Jones, and the search of Glyn Jones for social and
cultural connectives. It can influence the style, as well as the content of
Dylan Thomas's writing, and may partly account for Vernon Watkins's
passion for friendship. These differences must be emphasized and
respected. But underlying them, and interconnecting them in laby-
rinthine fashion, it seems to me, is the writers' common experience –
simultaneously constructive and destructive, liberating and inhibiting –
of belonging to a place apart; a historical region which was certainly
not assimilable to England, but which could not be integrated into
traditional Wales either. It was therefore doubly separate – set apart on
two counts and on two fronts – and its writers were perhaps
accordingly doubly blessed and doubly cursed.

                                    *   *   *

In *All Things Betray Thee* (1946), Gwyn Thomas so wants to dramatize
the sense of a decisive break with the past, of a radical new departure,
that the novel itself breaks with the naturalistic convention suitable for
patiently tracing the sober complexities of actual historical developments. The author strives to produce, out of an uneasy amalgam of
styles, a heroic fable, a myth of origins suitable for a society he
passionately believes to be unprecedented in Welsh terms. Alan Leigh,
the traditional harpist, comes from a countryside full of 'gutted villages'
into the iron towns of Moonlea where work allows people no time 'to

marvel at the anguish of their slashed root.' His own rural experience makes him at the outset a blithely sardonic conservative: 'There'll be no change in them. They will endure dumbly here as they did elsewhere, a kind of walking dung that doesn't even insist on the traditional privilege of being carried to the furrow.'⁴ By the end, however, experience of an early and abortive attempt at mass struggle leaves him with an altogether different view of human inertia, a view that is at once tempered and tragically intensified by a new idealism. He understands that he is now among people who 'know from the feel of their every day that they are well within the doorway of a changed world.' The harpist hears the new music, but knows, with anguish, that people will be slow to march to it, and that it can be played only on artistic instruments that have not as yet been fashioned.⁵

Although he chose to set his novel in a fictitious early-nineteenth century iron town not a million miles from Merthyr, Gwyn Thomas was actually himself very much the product of the late-nineteenth and early-twentieth century great coal-producing centre of the two Rhondda valleys. Merthyr and Porth may be geographically in close proximity, but they were brought into being at two very different stages in the history of industrialization, and consequently developed into two very different industrial communities. Merthyr was an early, and by and large culturally indigenous industrial settlement, whereas the Rhondda was later, more cosmopolitan, culturally mixed and rapidly radicalized. Jack Jones, a Merthyr writer, registers this in his novel *Black Parade* by having the tearaway Harry pause in trepidation at the thought of having to cross the mountains – the great divide – between the two neighbouring industrial conurbations that are nevertheless so culturally and historically out of step that one is felt to be declining just as the other reaches its zenith: 'Man, it isn't hell you're going to, but to the rich, roaring Rhondda Valleys', urges his friend.⁶ It is the, partly literal, foreign-ness of the Rhondda that Harry, brought up in a distinctively Welsh, and even Welsh-speaking society, jibs at. Merthyr writers themselves have therefore tended to present their relationship to the pre-industrial Welsh past rather differently, emphasizing the continuities as well as the discontinuities that constituted change in their case. (Compare the contemporary cases of the Merthyr historian, Gwyn A. Williams and the Rhondda historian, Dai Smith.) A neat example of this is the difference between Gwyn Thomas's traditional harper, Alan Leigh, whose instruments and songs are rendered archaic and useless by Moonlea, and Jack Jones's Twm Steppwr, the traditional entertainer and singer of folk songs and ballads, who wanders freely back and forth between industrial townships and semi-rural villages. Needless to say, they both also represent the respective authors' divergent views of the industrial writer.

Moreover, by the beginning of this century, the Merthyr–Dowlais area had a sufficiently long and chequered industrial history for Jack Jones to be able to look back, nostalgically, elegiacally, and no doubt fancifully, to its golden age – the only golden age simultaneously to have been an iron age. He even produced what can only paradoxically be called versions of industrial pastoral. The central figure corresponding to the shepherdess is of course the all-sustaining and embracing Mam – whether she be the infinitely tactful, epically long-suffering Saran of *Black Parade*, or Jones's actual mother in *Unfinished Journey*, the autobiography in which he contrives to make his own birth, in 1884, effectively mark the passing of the old pure 'Welsh' order of iron and the dawning of the new, bastardizing system of steel production.[7]

By contrast, Gwyn Thomas's story, full in the Caradoc Evans vein, 'My Fist Upon the Stone', concentrates its hostility on an incestuously intense relationship between a mother and her miner son, which for him epitomizes everything that is repugnant, servile and anti-progressive about the unreconstructed peasant mentality that can persist even among the proletariat.[8] Like Evans, he invents what is a kind of inverted, or anti, pastoral mode primarily in order to define, by opposites, the desirable state of things. In the process, he reveals in practice his commitment to the idea of literature, even comic literature, as a form of impassioned moral polemic – an idea that may well, in his case, ironically have its roots in the very Nonconformist background which he so despised. He would have blown raspberries of laughter at the words of Zoar's minister in *Black Parade*: 'Nonconformity . . . is the only [socially] militant religious body of our times.' Ministers to him were the class enemy, the hypocritical or self-deluding stooges of capitalist owners and managers who used them to keep the industrial workers in thrall.

Gwyn Thomas's Rhondda imagination therefore works best when it is most combative and uncompromisingly adversarial. But the imagination of Glyn Jones, another native of Merthyr, is at once finely discriminating and sympathetically eclectic, gently respectful and yet quietly independent, even subversive. In his work the experience of separateness primarily finds expression through a heightened sense of social contrast (the valley, the city, the village) and of linguistic strangeness. To some extent the different life of the rural past and of Welsh-language culture remains accessible to him, and his visits there, both in fact and in imagination, provide him with a ready source of creative renewal.

By the end of Glyn Jones's novel *The Valley, The City, The Village* (1956), the west Wales village of Llansant becomes the place that sets Trystan, the hero, free both of religion and politics – free to draw and paint. Never directly challenging, let alone repudiating, the established authority of preacher or political leader – indeed even generously acknowledging the faithfulness of his grandmother and uncle to 'the reticent and fastidious puritanism in which they were nurtured', and the minister Mr Hamner's dedication to his calling – Trystan nevertheless turns away from them to art.[9] His 'self-indulgence' is what he, rather guiltily, calls it, associating it with illicit carnality and recalling Glyn Jones's own confessions on the subject:

> This glorying in all
> Created things, the golden sun, the small
> Rain riding in the wind, the silvery shiver
> Of the dawn-touched birches, and the chromium river,
> Innocent itself, has yet calamitous
> And wilful pride for child and famulus.
> And thus I see the point when puritan
> Or mystic poet harried under ban
> Sensual nature, earth, sea and firmament.[10]

In his own case Glyn Jones had (and still in a way has) to endure and defy not a single but a double ban on art such as his – the Nonconformist ban, and the nowadays much more powerful ban imposed by the many in south Wales who will accept art only on politically accommodating terms.

'Indulgence' Trystan may defensively call it, but the quality of the writing frequently shows his choice of art to be something else – a vocation which is at once spiritual and deeply humane, and a unique mode of religious apprehension. It founds its special reverence for life upon an irreverence for the conventionally accepted denominations and assessments of things. The familiar is deconstructed, as in modernist art, in order to be reconstructed in all its wonderful, unpredictable and gratuitous strangeness. 'Above my high head the birds pass and repass, whistling their kitchen hosannas as they seek food, hailing the day. The luxuriant graveyard wall, like a garden set up on its end in the sun, receives twittering the small grain-bearing birds into its tufted foliage' (233). So Glyn Jones himself uses exotic words and tropes to discompose the world, to unsettle it until it tilts at a new angle to the sight. The reader is exhilaratingly introduced to what Georges Bataille called 'the unsuspected delirium of the universe.'

Trystan is a painter, but his love of form and colour is not only conveyed through, it actually stands for, Glyn Jones's feeling for language: he is a writer whose wittily equivocal confession is 'I fancy words'. He is, though, both a nonconformist and a practising Nonconformist, and as such he is permanently troubled by his 'gift for logopoeic dance', that amoral love of the sheer anarchic power of words, which he also attributes to his character Gwydion (named after the sly magician, deceiver and shape-changer): 'He was a dictionary reader, a neologist, an inventor of nicknames, a collector of the technical tricks of the *cywyddwyr*. Any such oddity as an adjective embedded in the middle of a noun delighted him. He wrote poems by dropping water from a pipette on to words in his thesaurus, and by picking, as though from a bran-tub, phrases which he had cut out of a newspaper' (269).

The passage encapsulates Glyn Jones's ambivalent feelings about his, and his close friend Dylan Thomas's relationship to language, and about the whole modernist movement by which they were both profoundly affected. For getting one's historical bearings it is useful, for instance, to remember that Wallace Stevens's 'dandy' volume *Harmonium* was published in 1923, when Glyn Jones was eighteen. But paradoxically it was precisely this interest in international experimental modernism that helped Glyn Jones to reconnect himself, in prose and verse, to the rich Welsh-language tradition, by-passing Nonconformist Wales and relishing instead the panache of the great lords of language, the aristocratic *cywyddwyr* of the Middle Ages who wove words tautly into poetic forms that were a basketry of mental swoopings. In this respect, it's worth remembering that T. Gwynn Jones had, since his audacious breakthrough of 1902, been forging in Welsh a modern literary discourse out of the linguistic and cultural materials of the Middle Ages.

Glyn Jones has admitted that although he has been in Paris and London, what 'rustles/ Oftenest and scentiest through the torpid trees/ Of my brain-pan, is some Merthyr-mothered breeze.' Substitute 'Swansea' for 'Merthyr' and the sentiments, if not the words, could be those of Dylan Thomas. On a recent visit to New York an acquaintance of mine was subjected to truculent interrogation by a taxi-driver: 'Where you from?' 'I'm from Wales.' 'Wales? Say is that anywhere near Swansea?' That is a pithy summary of the outside world's present state of knowledge both of Welsh geography and of Welsh literature; but it could also almost be Dylan Thomas himself speaking. 'This sea town was my world: outside, a *strange* Wales, coal-pitted, mountained, river run, full, so far as I knew, of choirs and sheep and story-book tall hats, moved about its business which was none of mine.'[11] Exaggeration, certainly, but embedded in it are the seeds of a truth which helped determine the way his genius developed. He was that new Welsh phenomenon, a thoroughly provincial writer, and he knew it. He even eventually learned to capitalize on it, and *Portrait of the Artist as a Young Dog* was perhaps the most brilliant result. But at first he resented it, this provincialism, and the resentment was itself a classic symptom of that social condition. Instead of feeling disinherited and deracinated, as he had every right but absolutely no inclination to do, he simply wanted to be closer to what, from his point of view, seemed to be the cultivated centre of things; and his self-consciously avant-garde adolescent poetry was his passport to sophistication. In this sense his provincialism was the very making of his genius, as his genius in turn was the making of him socially. That famous early reference to himself as the Rimbaud of Cwmdonkin Drive rings exactly true.

Through his writing he completed the journey begun by his Welsh-speaking Carmarthenshire father – the journey up, out and away from one culture, first to the peripheries and then to the very artistic centre of another. He is the mesmeric Lloyd George of modern Welsh letters, except that he did not have to attempt to unite in himself two disparate cultures. Behind him lay not Cricieth but weird and wonderful Llanstephan, where cousin Gwilym spouted colourful Welsh gibberish in the high Nonconformist preaching style in an old barn, and Uncle Jim, like a demented fox, ate pigs raw. Generously imbued by its Welshness with an inexhaustible strangeness, the whole farm as portrayed in the *Portrait* is a splendid adventure playground for the ebullient young imagination, and as such is the wild Welsh west counterpart of cowboy-haunted, suburban Cwmdonkin Park. Later, with all traces of the actual indigenous and unpalatable culture now erased, this corner of rural Carmarthenshire became, in 'Fern Hill', the simply enchanted country of childhood, just as in the thirties it obligingly served as a surrealist landscape moulded to fit the contours of the subconscious.

In his poetry, the complex social and cultural materials of a specific historical period are turned into a view of the world as forever governed by nature's cyclical processes. Cataclysmic change, of an unmistakably cultural, social, economic and political kind, was the dominant reality of south Wales life between the Wars. It is what accounted for the difference between Gwilym Marles and Dylan Marlais Thomas and for the immense cultural distance between Fernhill and Cwmdonkin Drive, Uplands, Swansea. It is what caused a Gwyn Thomas to devise a new form of art, capable of portraying the human face of desolating socio-economic processes. But in Dylan Thomas's poetry, eternal natural processes still reign supreme, and the individual, both in his biological and psychological aspects, is helplessly subject to them. 'The force that through the green fuse drives the flower/ Drives my green age.'[12] The irony is that, for all the modernist organicist stylistics that accompanied this philosophy, for all the modern anthropology and modish pagan religiosity associated with it, this is still close kin to the 'peasant' view of life that Gwyn Thomas railed against, resurgent here in insular, insulated suburban Swansea. 'The back of our dumbness will have been broken and it must have been a granite sort of spine while it lasted', says Alan Leigh: but Dylan Thomas is 'dumb to tell' not only 'the crooked rose/ My youth is bent by the same wintry fever', but of 'the silicotic roses, and lilies pale as gas', which the metallurgical and coal industries had combined to produce in the neighbouring Swansea valley. Yet only a few years earlier, and a bare half-dozen miles away from Dylan Thomas's 'seaside town', the effects of those industries on Alltwen, Pontardawe produced, in Gwenallt, one of the greatest Welsh writers of the industrial experience.

Two poems – one by Gwenallt, the other by Dylan Thomas – when placed side by side bring out very clearly the difference between their respective cultural situations as writers. In 'The Dead' Gwenallt, having turned fifty, recalls 'The people and surroundings that made him what he is.'[13] He does not speak simply as an insider to the community in which he was raised – in fact the poem is one where he specifically looks back, having moved on and away – but he does establish how the society has remained inside him, in very complex ways, and 'the steel ropes' that tether him are evidence that an industrial township can attach itself to one's affections every bit as tenaciously as a rural village.

Gwenallt explores the disparity between the surface conduct and conventions of his society and the underlying realities. A child's play is interrupted by an ominous cough; in the decorous Bibled parlour lies a corpse obscenely turned to cinders; women carrying coal are carrying 'a bucketful of death'. His tropes are all metaphors, insisting on the literal truth, as it were, of what is being 'figuratively' said. Gwenallt's sensitive, visionary imagination seems to be creating an angry, almost Blakean, picture of a suppressed reality that is grossly at odds with his society's Christian acceptance of things. He emphasizes the savage, arbitrary violence that characterizes this humanly-constructed system of exploitation. He depicts this social hell as unnatural yet man-made. Then at the very end he pulls back and sees in these social conditions the pain that is endemic to the human condition, and at that concluding point he speaks not only an behalf of his society's suffering but also in praise and affirmation of the Christian spirit with which that suffering was borne. The poem therefore ends with Gwenallt fully reconciled to and identified with, all the qualities, both of resistance and of acceptance, his society had so movingly embodied.

Dylan Thomas's 'After the Funeral: In Memory of Ann Jones' is very different. Crucial to the poem is Thomas's acknowledgement that his mode of writing is totally out of keeping with its subject: 'this for her is a monstrous image blindly/ Magnified out of praise.'[14] He justifies this by representing himself as the celebrator of those qualities in Ann that were hidden from her society, and maybe even from the old woman herself. He thus turns his poem into a dramatically subversive, anti-social piece. Indeed it is useful to think of it as a poem written to compete with the minister – the voice of official praise ('mule praises, brays') which is mocked at the beginning of the poem. This public, social eulogy is what the poem is written against, and is intended to replace, and as the poem reaches its histrionically self-conscious climax, Thomas, a bardic priest, invokes Ann's qualities in terms that are vaguely religious, but defiantly heterodox. He detaches her from her drab, repressed Nonconformist background and transforms her into a kind of pagan priestess of nature and of love. She becomes his *alter ego*, the counterpart of that Rimbaud of Cwmdonkin Drive who was militantly bohemian, anti-social, believing only in the sacredness of the untamed imagination and in the liberating energies of language. 'After the Funeral' is also a triumphant vindication, after a fashion, of D. J. Thomas's policy of distancing himself and his family from the inhibitingly conservative 'Welsh' Wales of his own boyhood.

There are a number of reasons – ranging from a cossetted child's cherished feelings of helplessness, through his wish to shock the Nonconformists and shatter their 'providential', prudishly antisexual view of the world, to his rejection of politics – why Dylan Thomas adopted the philosophy of natural generation and decay. But they cannot be properly explored here, nor would they in any case account for what, through great poetry, he managed to make of it all. It is, though, interesting to note that Thomas and his great Swansea friend, Vernon Watkins, simultaneously meet and part precisely here, in this shared view of life as process. 'Over Sir John's Hill,/ The hawk on fire hangs still', writes Thomas in a marvellous poem acknowledging the ambivalent power which, in Shakespeare's words, both cheers and checks life. Watkins, in contrast, is inclined to notice only how 'sheer over this the kestrel ruin hangs'.[15] His poetry flows from an imagination wounded by the way in which 'Ruin now love's shadow be/ Following him, destroyingly', as Shelley put it.[16] 'I sang in my chains like the sea', declaims Thomas in an image that recognizes his creative dependence upon the non-human forces which constrain his life. Watkins, though, sees only mutability's depredations, wherever 'Time's seething wash its hungry groan renews.'

Vernon Watkins's vocation as poet is to anticipate in imagination the restoration of all things that will occur at the end of time: his poetry will 'reconcile what death divided/ And knock the breath out of the sea.' Like the artists who 'stun[ned] the rock with vision' in order to produce the superb prehistoric cave-drawings, he responds to the world's fleeting beauty, 'making the skilled hand run,/ A hunter, spearlike' to catch it in full flight (148–9). But he will never be reconciled or subdued to the flux of the temporal order. In his poems he appears in a double aspect – as a spiritually implacable Niobe, who will not be comforted until eternity makes full reparation for all of life's endless anguish of loss (165–70): and as a heron, 'that time-killing bird', who 'fixes eyes on stillness' beyond 'the water's moods' (287), and all the flying world (176). Interestingly, this is the image he chooses for his friend in 'A True Picture Restored: Memories of Dylan Thomas' – an image of the heron that is subtly altered from 'the elegiac fisherbird' who 'stabs and paddles' in 'Over Sir John's Hill' (286–9).

Watkins was, of course, the author of 'Ballad of the Outer Dark', along with its wonderful sister poem of the Mari Lwyd. In one sense, the dark is the clamorous realm of the unquiet dead, those ultimate victims of life's transience who cannot rest and will not let Watkins rest until he has found a place for them in the economy of his completed spiritual vision. 'Unless I make that melody,/ How can the dead have rest?' is the question in 'The Feather' which helps explain the sonorous ritual music of his poetry (120). But elsewhere the anarchic sea reminds him that 'no ghost is truly laid/ But spinning on a dolphin's eye will turn,/ Turn, turn, till all things are re-made' (126). As the tide turns, and the world turns, so the dead turn in their graves, fearful of being consigned to oblivion. The lines are powerful testimony to Vernon Watkin's terror of mutability.

Apollonian art must, Nietzsche predicted, 'always triumph first over titans, kill monsters, and overcome the sombre contemplation of actuality, the intense susceptibility to suffering.'[17] In Watkins's words, his poetry must be felt to be deeply 'rooted in loss' before it can blossom into spiritual affirmation (167). But that is precisely where it not infrequently fails, perhaps because the poet feared too close an engagement, and trial of strength, with the powers, both within him and without, that made for disorder. The poem 'Niobe' gives us some inkling of what might have been, had he risked it (165–70). As for his self-enfeebling tendency as a poet to contemplate the world's painful mutability only in the most rhetorically general of terms, there could well be understandable personal reasons for such a habit, bearing in mind the breakdown he seems to have suffered in his youth. In his homage to 'Yeats in Dublin' – a poem which pays Yeats the compliment of beautifully imitating his late style – he quotes the master as complaining that his materialistic contemporaries 'try/ To substitute psychology/ For the naked sky/ Of metaphysical movement' (64). But reading Watkins's collected poems one is left with the suspicion that future critics may well want to refer 'the metaphysical movement' of his poetry to the psychology of the poet.

In any case, his Neoplatonic metaphysics didn't serve him too well as a writer. 'I stamp my feet on the earth whenever they would force me into the clouds', said that most canny of Transcendentalists, Henry Thoreau. Perhaps Vernon Watkins didn't stamp his feet enough. Robert Frost, too, knew what he was doing when he climbed birches only to bend them down to the ground, and found (both as boy and as poet) that it was 'good both going and coming back.'[18] But Watkins preferred to take Zacchaeus as his model, the tax-gatherer who climbed a tree, like Jacob's ladder, from the mundane to the eternal plane, and rested there (143–6). His hero Yeats knew that poetry came from the dialogue between the appetitive worldly self and the soul. But there seems at times insufficient fleshliness, or carnality, in Vernon Watkins's verse to allow the miracle of incarnation, in which he clearly believed, convincingly to happen in the poetry itself. Consequently the lines in his weaker poems 'elongate a thin nothing: a long, grey, weeping sausage', as Dylan Thomas acutely remarked. 'All the words are lovely, but they *seem* so *chosen*, not struck out. I can see the sensitive picking of words, but none of the strong, inevitable pulling that makes a poem an event, a happening, an action perhaps, not a still-life . . . They seem . . . to come out of the nostalgia of literature.'[19] And yet there are also dazzling passages that suggest what an undeveloped gift for sensuousness he possessed: 'Lizards on dry stone; gipsy-bright nasturtiums/ Burning through round leaves, twining out in torch-buds.'

There is a limited but nevertheless important sense in which Vernon Watkins's vision of things could be that of a socially and culturally displaced person. The son of Welsh-speaking parents, he was raised in a deliberately Anglicized, middle-class home that isolated him both from the original family background (poignantly revisited in the poem 'Returning to Goleufryn') and from much of his social environment – which was in any case constantly changing as his father, a bank manager, was moved from branch to branch. Watkins was sent away to English public school at Repton, where he spent several Edenic years that ill-equipped him for his next social incarnation, as trainee bank-clerk in the hard commercial world of Cardiff during the thirties. It's hardly surprising that he should eventually, following a nervous breakdown, have taken steps to use his talented imagination to provide himself with a carefully controlled environment and mental life-support system.

First, he homed in not on a community but on a corner of his native Glamorgan landscape, the Gower peninsula, whose nakedly elemental features allowed him to bring his internal anxieties into clear external focus, by providing him with the symbolic language through which he articulated his feelings of instability, and 'conquered uncertainty.' He settled on Pennard cliffs, in 'a house facing the sea', while his job in a Swansea bank became the safe anchorage to which he regularly returned every morning after each night's mental voyaging. Second, he constructed for himself an alternative community – of family, friends, and fellow-artists – not held together by any given social structure, or even ties of blood, but built by the elective 'affinities' and 'fidelities' which he celebrated in several of the most protectively loving and tenderly admiring poems written in English. (Indeed perhaps his only equal as a poet of sensitive concern for others is the Coleridge who was similarly deprived of family and home at a critically early age.)

Third, his 'friendships' came to span, and so to transcend, time, as his soul elected its own society from writers of other countries, other languages, other ages. Artists throughout the centuries who shared his belief in art's hieratic, sacred power to redeem the fallen world, lost in time, seemed to him to constitute an invisible church of true believers to which, following perhaps Eliot, perhaps Kathleen Raine, he gave the name 'tradition'. Its Welsh name and manifestation was 'Taliesin' – Vernon Watkins, like Glyn Jones, choosing to circumvent the recent and contemporary Wales of philistine Nonconformity in order to connect himself with a distant period when it was supposedly recognized that, as David Jones put it, 'Ars was inalienable from Man and Man from Ars', while the artist was an indefatigable hunter of spiritual forms, through all their endlessly mutating material manifestations.[20] 'It is the form', said Watkins of his poetry, 'speaking against the false forms it cast out' (311).

What going away to Repton did to Vernon Watkins, the transfer to Cowbridge Grammar School accomplished for Alun Lewis: it was not so much the cause as the drastic fulfilment and finalization of the process of separation from his native society.[21] The eventual result was that rather detached sense of attachment which is beautifully conveyed in the opening lines of the poem 'The Mountain over Aberdare' – very much a place poem, but written by a partly displaced person, who approaches the valley scene only circumspectly, by degrees, and for all his tender concern for it, remains perched outside. Not that Alun Lewis had ever been a fully integrated part of that mining community. Although born in Cwmaman and later moving only to neighbouring Aberdare, he was born to parents who were slightly removed by education, by background (in his mother's case), and by inclination from their immediate neighbourhood. From them he inherited not only contrasting temperaments, which he found difficult to reconcile in himself, but also a secularized version of the Nonconformist temper. Unfortunately this, too, came to him in a form that divided him against himself. Ever conscious of his responsibility, as man and as artist, to his fellow-men, he was also deeply imbued with a sense of his obligations to himself – the duty of self-knowledge and self-realization. At first he felt this only as a freedom and escape from what was claustrophobic in his social environment. But later it became a form of imprisonment which left him 'locked in uneasy conflict with the unwinking/ Inscrutable demon of self-knowledge.'[22] Lewis's writing became a (sometimes vicious) form of self-investigation, even self-interrogation, since 'he would take no respite from the immaculate Gestapo of his brain.' He may well have been too devastatingly honest for his own good, ultimately defenceless against the seething contents of his own mind. Yet this personal disability was the very quality which made him a superb writer of journals, steely in his resolve to censor nothing, quicksilver in his imagination, quickfire in his notations, slow to force an ideological shape on ever-burgeoning impressions.

During the late thirties, when 'the world reverberated destruction', his personal unease strangely reflected the social and political unrest of the time, depressions answering Depression, inwardly simmering just as Europe was nearing the boil. 'The perversions of Hitler had affected me less profoundly than my own destructive impulses', he admitted in a remark that darkly illuminates *Raiders' Dawn* (1942).[23] Part of his personal problem was his society's failure to provide him with a guiding image of the artist and any satisfactory account of his function. This is one of the great themes of Welsh writing in English during this period. Glyn Jones's Trystan, Gwyn Thomas's Alan Leigh, Dylan Thomas's 'Rimbaud', and Vernon Watkins's Taliesin – they all tell the same story. Moreover that same society also failed to supply him – as it failed to provide Dylan Thomas and the fictional Trystan – with a language for understanding those aspects of himself from which, he suspected, the impulse to write came. Therefore he set about forging his own poetic language to explore his own baffling nature: 'The white brain crossing/ The frontiers of darkness/ To darkness and always/ Darkness pursuing' (39). His sober fear of violence and his sensual love of it, his domesticated and his darkly wild selves, are all concentrated in the callow yet quite remarkable poetry of *Raiders' Dawn*, a first collection whose turbulent, and occasionally turgid, sexuality recalls the early Dylan Thomas. Sex is repeatedly linked to violence as well as being contrasted to it: 'Through the trembling blue the golden porpoise plunged' (53). His central ambivalence of feeling on this subject is richly caught in these lines from 'The Madman':

> Exultantly he drives his screaming pinnace
> Through the clashing ocean of love.
> His dripping keel cleaves deep. And snow-white birds
> Wheel round and round his prow.
>
> Yet all the storm is but a lover's gesture,
> The glittering constellations are his seed,
> His mast, a rose tree softly lapped in leaf,
> Sucks up the salt sap of his timeless grief. (86)

Part of Lewis abhorred the devastation of war and celebrated the talismanic power of love to safeguard his beloved Gweno and himself from the destructive forces inside and outside the self: 'Death the wild beast is uncaught, untamed' but 'Our soul withstands the terror' (45). But another part of him came perversely alive *in extremis*: crisis heightened his sensibility and sharpened the sensuality of his response to the world: 'When the raving tuskèd boar/ Gored the sensual innocent,/ The goddess heard it squeal and roar/ In pride of blood on Venus' mount' (40–41).

Life away in England in the army heightened his sense of his Welshness. He was fascinated by the complex human ramifications of English class distinctions, particularly as these were preserved in the relations between officers, NCOs and other ranks. This became a leading theme in his incomparable short stories. His eventual passage to India, though, brought with it much more unsettling and un-manageable revelations. Alun Lewis never recovered from the shock of his exposure to the land and its people – the unimaginable scale of it, 'the nihilist persistence of the sun'.[24] Like the bou-oum of the Marabar caves in Mrs Moore's ears in *A Passage to India*, sun and land combined to render senseless the whole vocabulary he had used to make sense of life – the radical liberalism, socialism, humanism and humanitarianism which had been his valuable Welsh social inheritance from childhood. Even 'the warm pacts of the flesh', he found, could be 'betrayed' (67). The *laissez faire* spoke directly and fatefully to the darkness in his subterranean self which had always threatened to sap his will to persist. But at least, in the interval before the end came, he was able to put his poetry to new and transforming use, bringing that terrible darkness to unavailing light.

No other Welsh writer was equipped to keep up with Alun Lewis in his unique spiritual travels, but had he only known it, his early plight, as a beginning writer in the thirties, was a common one. What should he write? What did being a writer mean and entail? Who was he writing for? Where could he get his works published? It was Rhys Davies who most ruthlessly diagnosed the situation, simplifying the problem until he was able to solve it with conspicuous official success. Since the mass readership lay outside Wales, Welsh material would have to be properly processed and marketed accordingly, and served to stereotyped taste if necessary – never mind how unappetizing or unhealthy the resulting food might be for native Welsh consumers. One has, though, to resist the temptation to describe the prolific Davies simply as the slick fast-food merchant of this literature. His is a more complicated and artistically deserving case, precisely because at his rare best he was able to have it both ways – selling his books worldwide but without selling his society short.

The secret of that success is perhaps to be found in Davies's original position in valleys' society. A grocer's son, he was a *petit bourgeois* among proletarians, and therefore naturally saw Rhondda life from a different, if limited angle – an angle that was both unusually acute and distorting. The acuteness is there in the way he lights upon unexpected corners of the accepted social field, picking out for instance the collier's wife, uncomplaining slave to the whims and appetites of her six hulking sons and gorilla of a husband, who keeps her frustrated feminity separate and virginal by investing 'in a wonderful white silk night-gown', which she lovingly lays by for her own laying-out when she's dead.[25] Defiantly unorthodox people, with an unquenchable imagination, attract the attention of the semi-outsider Davies, particularly when they succeed in releasing the sexual energies he is convinced have been buried under coal and chapel. And is it a coincidence that tradesmen so often play the part of a fifth-column in the writings of this shopkeeper's son? Shops supply the glittering good(ie)s that secretly incite the shadow self to rebellion. But unfortunately, Rhys Davies also possesses vices inherent in his virtues as a writer. In his stories he felt himself to be practising a 'privately elegant craft',[26] and can in turn be felt to be demonstrating his aesthetic mastery of a social world which his superior class position, and perhaps an inherent dandyism, helped him to regard as exploitable material. There is about him sometimes something of the manipulativeness of his character, Mrs Vines, whose secret delight it is to spy on the lower-class young man who is her tenant.[27]

But what, after all, should a south Wales writer's relationship have been to his social material? And did it entail new adaptations of existing fictional methods? No one, for instance, better registered the molten fluidity of life in the industrial townships than did Jack Jones, yet he found it difficult to construct fictional forms corresponding to the new moulds into which this life was being poured. Neither in the Welsh-language nor in the English-language literature of the past could he find the exact formal correlatives for his experience, but his imagination was unable to answer the challenge of this double separation and settled instead for approximate solutions. The insanitary conditions, the colourful characters, the tough sinews of community, the resilience of the family unit, the eruptive and disruptive energies at work – these features of industrialization are crammed into his authentically detailed novels. Yet although he himself moved restlessly from one party to another throughout his life in search of a clarifying political philosophy, his novels continued to operate primarily on the level of picturesque spectacle and picaresque adventure. It is almost as though he were imitating his adored mother, who used to allow the local fleapit theatre to use her furniture as props, in return for a free pass for her children and herself. 'There wasn't much in our house, but what there was they were welcome to it in return for a free pass for our mam and us children. We lived so close, mam and us children could deliver the furniture required, and collect it after the performance.'[28] In his fiction, Jack Jones, too, is something of an old-style actor manager, or greathearted theatrical producer of Merthyr history, turning his personal experiences into a splendidly histrionic and emotionally vivid performance.

Lewis Jones, in his two novels *Cwmardy* and *We Live*, set out, conversely, to show how the very consciousness of men and women, and their relationships one to another, were being re-formed by these devastatingly new social and economic conditions. Big Jim the miner, and his son Len, feel themselves reacting, even on top of the mountain, 'to the palpitating throb of the pit engines that came to them from below'.[29] Jim is stirred to an awareness of how proudly suited to a life of challengingly hard labour is his magnificent physique. Only slowly is he drawn into using his inarticulate strength on behalf of the workers in their struggle with capitalist owners and managers. Len, on the other hand, a physically slighter and nervously intense character, feels the palpitation of the pit engines sending tremors of foreboding through him – fears not only of sadly commonplace disasters like explosions, but also of the mine's sinister domination of every public and private aspect of valleys life. He determines to test his own, intellectual, strength against that of the pit, developing his nervous imagination into a sensitive instrument for analysing and counteracting the exploitative system centred on the mines. It is quickly clear to Len that only by combining in a disciplined and organized way can the workers effectively resist – but for them to see this requires a revolutionary process of re-education, through experience and patient teaching. Lewis Jones describes the coming into being of this new outlook, and its repeated testing in action that refines and develops it. He is at his most original when he devises fictional means of conveying the great surface drama, the inner social necessity, and the complex psychology of these emerging mass labour movements.

Writing about industrialization also meant fictional innovation in Gwyn Thomas's case. Born and bred a member of a mining family in Porth, he knew, not through considered intellectual analysis but by 'the feel of [his] every day' that in his Rhondda was a new kind of society, demanding new social, economic, and political remedies, and equally demanding a new kind of literature to render it truthfully. Raymond Williams has suggestively argued that Thomas devised a style that allowed him to speak not only for but from his people, inventing a fiction that worked like a play for communal voices and that was choric in character. It should be noted, though, that Thomas was also, however reluctantly and unhappily, an Oxford man, who placed his sophistication at the service of his Porth community. He was at his best in the novels, novellas and stories of the forties, written primarily about the thirties. At his most remarkable he was capable of producing what, in a different context, he called 'inward growing mirages' that fantastically corresponded to the grotesque and monstrous features of life during the Depression years.[30] But from the beginning he found it difficult to devise a complete fictional structure that would comfortably accommodate his style, so that many of his stories, let alone his novels, remind one of his character Ben, whose wife set out to knit him a trim black tie but only succeeded in producing a shape that 'practically covered his whole chest. Ben explained that his wife,while strong on such items as meat pies, was not very good as a tie-maker, but the rest of us thought that Ben's wife, while knitting this tie, must have let her eyes stray on to a pullover pattern.'[31]

His narrators are not first generation inhabitants of the industrial valleys, they're second generation, aware of 'life threatening to get on top of [them] like some great lusting animal' but correspondingly equipped to cope. In fact, this association of rapacious socio-economic power with a brutal animal sexuality bordering on rape is a central theme of *Oscar*, where the great pig of a man who owns a mountain on which a lucrative coalmine is being operated is notorious for his crude, unceremonious womanizing:

> 'Did he jump on you?' I dropped Oscar to ask the question clearly. I was interested in Oscar's antics.
> 'Near as hell to jumping. First, he got me a bit drunk. Then he got me in here. Next thing I know I think the whole bloody roof has come down on me. What gives him the right? That's what I'd like to know.'

'He owns a mountain. He can jump on that and he thinks there's nobody as important as a mountain.'[32]

In an autobiographical talk, two years before his death, Gwyn Thomas, recalling the inter-war years, admitted that 'the plight of women in that time of dark philogenetic romps and squalors is something from which I still turn my mind.'[33] But in some of his best work sexual relations are disturbingly seen as being intimately connected to the dynamics of power within a society. No wonder he ends his talk by recalling the occasion when he took his old schoolteacher, a fierce and indomitable fighter for social justice, to see an opera for just about the first time in the old man's life: 'He asked me, "What's it about then, this *Rigoletto*?" I tried to explain. "*Rigoletto* is a deformed jester, whose daughter is seduced by his master, who is a libertine and a scoundrel." "Who is this master?" he asked. "The Duke of Mantua," I said. "See what I mean?" he asked. "They are at it all the time." ' (*The Subsidence Factor*, 16) And the reference to opera is appropriate, because Thomas's own work has got its operatic features – its elaborately mannered language, its showpiece arias, its air of melodrama. Even the owner of the local Italian café in *The Dark Philosophers* rejoices in the name of Idomeneo Faracci. But then, as Thomas noted, music in a great variety of forms – from gazooka playing to grand benefit concerts – was the great popular art-form of the valleys during his youth. 'There must have been more solo singers in the Rhondda of the 1920s than in any place outside formal centres of musical expression. It was as if people realised that normal speech was quite inadequate to describe what had happened to them' (*The Subsidence Factor*, 11).

Gwyn Thomas's protagonists are Rhondda street-wise, knowing, and sardonically proud of it: 'Boy, you know so little of life, life must be hurt to find anybody knowing so little of it', as one of his characters says to another. Yet running through the stories there is also a strong vein of innocence – the idealism of what late in life he referred to as 'the frank political enthusiasm and social evangelism' of the thirties.[34] *Oscar* and 'Where My Dark Lover Lies' are particularly impressive – works in which he seems to have evolved what might be described as a Rhondda Expressionist style of writing, perfectly suited to conveying the deranged social phantasmagoria of the Depression period. And in *The Dark Philosophers* he captured the full, ambivalent flavour of his people's talkativeness – their incorrigible impulse to put so much of themselves into words. On the one hand words were prized as the precious tools of social engineering: they used them to cross-examine their experiences, determined not to accept the 'received' opinions of their self-appointed social superiors, intent on reaching and resting only on bedrock. On the other hand they also, as Gwyn Thomas percipiently remarked, 'wrap[ped] [themselves] up in words like a mummy with bandages . . . . I guess it comes from being defeated so often. When you get kicked around so much of the time, words must be a good sort of dope.' At his weakest, he, too, was a willing addict. By the fifties, the English reading public was losing its taste for the dark intensity that marked the comedy in his best writing, and so it encouraged him to limit his range to what was more palatably Welsh. 'The less saintly of us', he later astutely remarked, 'throw away half our talent in making for ourselves a credible public image' (*Artists in Wales*, 78). Perhaps that could serve as the sad half of his own epitaph. Saddest of all, south Wales itself betrayed him, mutating after the war into a materialistic society he found it impossible to make any serious sense of. Eventually, therefore (to borrow another of his irresistible phrases) 'his buffoonery became a mere entertainment, and ceased to be an inner lining of existence.'

*   *   *

So rich and diverse is this English-language literature of Glamorgan that it is fortunately guaranteed to confound any attempt to comprehend it and to account for it under a single simple rubric. All this chapter has endeavoured to do is to isolate what appears to be, in Octavio Paz's words, 'a constant feature of the spiritual history' of these writers, without overlooking the density and irreducible specificity of each of their separate cases and individual achievements. But of course, Glamorgan writing did not end with Gwyn Thomas, nor did it conclude with the disappearance of Glamorgan itself off the local government map. Over the past thirty years the region has continued to produce many of the best English-language authors of contemporary Wales, but their work confirms them to be the product of socio-cultural circumstances significantly different from those that so distinctively and decisively formed their predecessors. In fact the sense of separateness that haunts many of them most is precisely the sense of being separated from the past of their own community, as can be seen from the work of two of the oldest and most distinguished of them – work which also, incidentally, suggests that for all the social changes post-War Glamorgan has seen, the Merthyr-Rhondda axis still holds strong.

In his stories, Pontypridd-born Alun Richards is one of the sharpest chroniclers of post-industrial south Wales and a splendidly comic, satiric, yet affectionate exploiter of the richness and diversity of the social material produced by its cosmopolitan mix.[35] The preceding generation of writers has been as much a hindrance as a help in his case: his stories engage with several of the cherished myths its coal society had helped fuel. Richards delights in valleys speech – sharp, forthright, vivid, even fantastic – and his stylized rendering of it stays closer to the original in rhythm and in idiom than does that of, say, Gwyn Thomas. Behind the bravura performance of a valleys born and bred character like Elmyra Mouth, however, there lies a lot of bravado, since hers is a decaying community, no longer tightly clustered around the pit but an aimless part of the far-flung Cardiff commuter belt. For Elmyra, sophisticated cosmopolitan Cardiff is Sin City, full of foreigners from other parts of Wales who congregate at the BBC, where her placid husband Davie travels to work as a lowly technician:

> Wasn't it full of strangers? Glamorgan people lost out all the way along the line. You seldom came across anybody from the valleys, or Cardiff even, just the *in* Welshy-Welsh, catarrhal BA'd North Walians down for what they could get; Ministers' sons from everywhere, and girls from farms by the look of them, legs like bottles, all sitting around endlessly in the canteen, heads bent together and the hum of gossip rising like steam above a football crowd. (*The Former Miss Merthyr Tydfil and other stories*, 232)

For all her pride in her toughness, Elmyra just isn't equipped to cope with this scandalously suave enemy and her fears and frustrations give rise to desperate fantasies.

Being a professional writer, Alun Richards has frequently been forced to turn his back on Welsh materials in his search for a living, as have other contemporary writers like Leslie Norris. 'I live in England, seem English' writes Norris, 'hammocked in comfort'[36] in Sussex for years but now primarily residing in Utah. Yet he has repeatedly returned in poetry to his elegiacally appreciative memories of his childhood in declining pre-war Merthyr, when life there was flaring up in a final burst of vitality among 'the charred hills' and where 'we stared over the scraped hill to luscious England' (*Selected Poems*, 64). His is an un-Rhondda-like memory of industrial energy and dereliction which is gentled by the nearby presence of Nature. In 'A Small War' he remembers 'Climbing from Merthyr through the dew of August mornings/ When I was a centaur cyclist' (96) escaping to the freedom of the Brecon Beacons; in 'Water' he celebrates visits to his relatives' farm, overlooking the town, where 'On hot summer mornings my aunt set glasses/ On a low wall outside the farmhouse' (*Selected Poems*, 52); and in his latest collection, *The Sea in the Desert*, he still recalls idyllic summer bathing in the bend of the river, just beyond the town: 'It was a known world then. / We lived in it, we made it/ with our voices.'[37] In fact, all of Norris's subtle ruminations on water, stones, trees, grass, birds and other features of the natural environment from England to the States are an organic development of his early Merthyr experiences. His young imagination seems to have been alerted, and sensitized, to creaturely life by the contrast between it and the harshness of the working environment. This is brought out beautifully in 'Barn Owl', as the softly frail beauty of the bird the boys have found is protectively registered by the colliers:

> Men from the pits, their own childhood
> Spent waste in the crippling earth,
> Held him gently, brought him mice
> From the wealth of our riddled tenements,
> Saw that we understood his tenderness,
> His tiny body under its puffed quilt,
> Then left us alone. We called him Snowy.
>
> (*Selected Poems*, 76)

The unexpected suggestion of a rhyme between 'tenderness' and 'tenements' is eloquent with what Norris has discovered – a surprising and warming human sensitivity in the most harshly unpromising of circumstances. It reverses the feelings expressed in his (presumably autobiographical) story 'Lurchers', where a small boy who has spent his earliest years on his grandfather's farm on the outskirts of Merthyr, shares the old man's contempt for 'a community which did not live directly, as we did, by what it produced':

> We believed completely that the rest of society was in some sense an immoral growth, a parasite like mistletoe, hanging without purpose from the great oak of our work. At such times we would look with pride at our dogs, seeing them as symbols of those puritan qualities we admired; they were staunch, loyal, infinitely hard-working, shy – like us – and sometimes sullen with strangers. And yet, although I loved my grandfather's sheepdogs and could work Bob myself, I did not want one of my own. I yearned for another kind of dog altogether – a long, silent hunter, a dog outside the law. I wanted a lurcher.[38]

It would be interesting to investigate the sheepdog and the lurcher aspects of Norris's work – his guilt, for instance, at enjoying the spectacle of the fight in which Billy Rose was 'Ripped across both his eyes' (*Selected Poems*, 20).

In Leslie Norris's poetry about his early environment, there is sometimes, perhaps, the danger that he will grow too comfortable with recollection, too wryly practised a producer of gentle plangencies, and too consciously rapt a story-teller. Indeed it's noticeable that when he attempted a rendering into English of Gwenallt's 'Y Meirwon' (The Dead) he chose to leave out that searing phrase we have already noticed Gwenallt used to describe his invincibly strong, yet tortured sense of belonging to a place and to its people. Compare the opening of his version with Conran's more faithful translation:

(a) Conran:

With his fiftieth birthday behind him, a man sees with fair clarity
  The people and surroundings that made him what he is,
And the steel ropes that tether me strongest to these things
  In a village of the South, are the graves in two cemeteries.[39]

(b) Norris:

Reaching fifty, a man has time to recognise
His ordinary humanity, the common echoes
In his own voice. And I think with compassion
Of the graves of friends who died . . . .   (*Selected Poems*, 67)

The raw edge to Gwenallt's words, the grim baldness of his expression and the driving energy of his rhetoric, are replaced in Norris's version by nicely modulated, measured and modest phrases that universalize rather wistfully where Gwenallt particularizes, passionately. The difference is of interest because it helps us define the experience of belonging that permeates much of Norris's writing. As he has put it in 'A Small War', 'the great battle-cries/ Do not arouse me. I keep short boundaries holy,/ Those my eyes have recognised and my heart has known/ As welcome' (*Selected Poems*, 96). The statement attracted self-righteously censorious attention from some when the poem was first published, because it was written at a time when campaigns were being bravely and vigorously mounted to save vital aspects of Welsh culture. Norris's announcement that 'I would not fight for Wales . . . Nor would I fight for her language' (*Selected Poems*, 96) was therefore understandably unpopular with activists. It is worth noting, however, that the statements are made in the context of Norris's memories (that recur elsewhere in his writing) of childhood friends who were killed in the Second World War, as 'they circled the spitting sky above Europe' (*Selected Poems*, 96). That second of the Great Wars was very much in Norris's mind when he insisted that 'It's the small wars I understand', and this early wartime background explains a lot about Norris's style and stance – his haunted awareness of death, his poignant sense of mutability, his dislike of grand rhetoric and of large, loud gestures. Moreover, the thirties that older writers like Gwyn Thomas naturally remembered as the grim time of the Depression were for Norris simply the Edenic years of childhood: 'I'm glad I had my boyhood before the war, before the '39 war that is. I'm glad I knew the world when it was innocent and golden and that I grew up in a tiny country whose borders had been trampled over so often that they had been meaningless for centuries.'[40]

What Alun Richards and Leslie Norris have, then, in common – and what sets them apart from their predecessors – is the habit of using the industrial Glamorgan of their past, of their youth, to calibrate the very different experiences of the present, although the result in the one case is frequently a social satire that cuts both ways while the result in the other is often elegy. Like that of the writers of the previous generation, their work is rooted in the experience of separation, and their feelings about their situation are deeply ambivalent; but their real predicament – and it is one that is shared by the talented generation of writers junior to them – is that they are faced with 'an old south Wales that is starting a New.'[41]

3

The Two Aluns

And all sway forward on the dangerous flood
Of history that never sleeps or dies,
And, held one moment, burns the hand.

(W. H. Auden, 'To a Writer on his birthday')

At the very beginning of Emyr Humphreys's novel, *Open Secrets*, the heroine, Amy, lightly touches her sleeping husband, John Cilydd, on the shoulder, in order to bring him out of the nightmare that is clearly oppressing him. And once he is awake, she gently sympathizes with his attempts to rid himself of his terrible apparitions:

> 'All over Europe people are having nightmares', she said. 'No question about that . . .'
> Cilydd became intent on recalling images, conjuring them up before his eyes.
> 'Cattle trucks. An endless train of cattle trucks. On the line from Rouen to the Western Front. Only families this time as well as soldiers . . . It was a strange effect . . . As if the Front was also moving closer. There was no way a collision could be avoided and yet no way of knowing what would happen.'[1]

John Cilydd has been returning, in dream, to his experiences as a front-line soldier during the First World War. And that is not surprising, since *Open Secrets* begins during those nerve racking months leading up to the outbreak of the Second World War. Sensitive to the omens of coming catastrophe, John Cilydd's troubled mind involuntarily exhumes images from the past that grimly foreshadow what is to come.

Indeed, together with the novel *An Absolute Hero*, which precedes it in the series, *Open Secrets* succeeds in capturing, with disturbing intensity, the threatening atmosphere of the late thirties, a period full of a sense of brooding disaster. Modern retrospect amply confirms what so many felt at the time: that this was a fateful period in the history of most of the countries of Europe. As one reads novels such as these, it is therefore natural to wonder whether any other writers from Wales have succeeded in capturing the international tension of those years. And the answer, as far as I can see, is that it is to be felt most powerfully and poignantly in the poetry of the two Aluns.

The Welsh-language writer, Alun Llywelyn-Williams was born in 1913: his namesake, Alun Lewis, two years later. They were raised within a few miles of each other, since the former was a native of Cardiff and the latter spent his childhood in Cwmaman, near Aberdare. Moreover, in the fullness of time, their respective first volumes of poetry were published with again a gap of two years, coincidentally, separating the one from the other – except that this time it was the younger man who was first off the mark. Alun Lewis's *Raiders' Dawn* appeared in 1942, followed in 1944 by Alun Llywelyn-Williams's *Cerddi, 1934–1942* (Poems, 1934–1942). What is interesting is the extent to which these young poets, although writing in two very different languages, unconsciously shared a single tormented intuition of what Auden called 'gradual ruin spreading like a stain.'[2]

As Alun Llywelyn-Williams explained years later, he felt closer, when a young man, to Anglo-Welsh writers than he did to Welsh-language writers, because it was writers like Rhys Davies, Glyn Jones and Jack Jones who had best portrayed those industrial and urban areas of Wales to which he himself belonged. Moreover, although his parents were Welsh speaking, he had grown up speaking English and associating Welsh with the stifling atmosphere of chapel.[3] He acquired a fuller knowledge of Welsh only very grudgingly as a teenager, at the express insistence of his father. Then, as he unexpectedly grew to love the language, so too he began to chafe at what he believed to be the failure of writers to modernize Welsh by using it to address contemporary issues. In particular he deplored their failure to chronicle the Depression years, and his feelings on this issue may well have been augmented by guilt. He was, after all, a scion of the privileged classes: a doctor's son, brought up in Cardiff, who had been well protected against the poverty he occasionally glimpsed haunting the street-corners even of comfortable, suburban Roath.

Alun Lewis was similarly distanced from the hardship experienced by working people in his native valley. At the age of eleven he had won a scholarship that took him away from home to study at the famous old grammar school in distant Cowbridge.[4] And although he was the son of a schoolmaster, not of a miner, the transfer to genteel Cowbridge still involved a shocking change of scene for a small valleys boy. Moreover it meant that, socially speaking, he could never go home again: he had been removed, once and for all, from his original social milieu. This detachment from his early background formed an important aspect of all his later urgent attachment to it; witness the famous occasion, in 'The Mountain over Aberdare', when he looks down from the hilltop on the mining township below. His glance is simultaneously informed by an empathic understanding of the life of the community, and disciplined by a wider intellectual perspective. If his position partly signifies his inability to be completely *of* the valley and its people, it also indicates his responsibility both to mediate his community to the world beyond and to see it in a wider social context.

Interestingly enough, Alun Llywelyn-Williams also places himself on the top of an eminence overlooking his native region in number eleven of his *Poems*. From that objectifying distance he sees the curtain rising on 'the dramas of the comfortable hearths', and listens to the 'delight of the malleable multitudes' who are 'emptyheadedly loitering under the dazzling lights of the streets.' Devoid of sympathy for them, he reaches, in his own sardonic and aloof way, the elevated point of view already noted in Alun Lewis's poem. He rises above the narrow outlook of his self-absorbed society, in order to keep an eye on events elsewhere upon which, he knows, the future of that society depends. He surveys the social landscape of Europe, noting in particular the ominous implications for Wales of the Civil War in Spain:

> Away over the sea, the splendid museum
> is being violently plundered, and the stars are angered by the drone of planes;
> listen to the wail of our struggle, and the people of Spain
> mourning the sweeping away of their withered loved ones.[5]

Like Alun Lewis, Alun Llywelyn-Williams realizes that the chief lesson taught by the thirties is that life in Wales can be understood only with reference to the wider social, economic and political scene of which it is, inextricably, a part. There is no corner of Wales, however remote, that is not helplessly subject to processes set in train elsewhere. The most ominous example of this, for Alun Llywelyn-Williams, is the invasive power of the technology of modern war. 'There is for us no such easy escape', he writes, 'as the desired fortresses of yesterday –/ We now can perish on the beloved slopes of Snowdon itself' (*Cerddi*, 12). Indeed, among his best poems are those in which his imagination fearlessly explores the implications of that chilling perception. He is then capable

of producing verse that is akin, in atmosphere, and also on occasions in
style, to W. H. Auden's terrifying poem, 'The Quarry'.

> O what is that sound which so thrills the ear
>   Down in the valley drumming, drumming?
> Only the scarlet soldiers, dear,
>   The soldiers coming.[6]

One such piece is the third poem in his collection, where a familiar spot
metamorphoses into a sinister landscape, full of threat:

> Once again, the land must be secretly examined
> in case of conspiracy in the distant mountain,
> of sniping from the ditches, from the windows of the houses,
> and of whispering on half-alive hearths.   (*Cerddi*, 16)

This is a chilling picture of the paranoia that grips the mind when
everything that used to be stable and dependable has undergone a
terrifying mutation. Similar episodes of nightmarish transfiguration
occur in Alun Lewis's poetry. Even the stars come to resemble
'warriors' nodding crests', and in the silence of night, 'the moon-mad
darkness ripples,/ Making the terrified watchdogs rattle their chains
and bark.'[7] Both poets are prey to unsettlingly vague feelings of unease
and find it difficult to distinguish friend clearly from foe. As Alun
Llywelyn-Williams puts it, 'it's said that war has broken out/ but our
enemy has not yet been identified' (*Cerddi*, 15).

Both poets also register, with a start, that they are subject to, and
could well become victims of, powers that are beyond their control and,
furthermore, beyond their comprehension. They experience recent
history as a predatory monster. In 'Postscript for Gweno', Alun Lewis
gathers all his experience of the hopelessness of the thirties into a single
suggestive image. He speaks of inhabiting 'the mad tormented valley/
Where blood and hunger rally/ And Death the wild beast is uncaught,
untamed' (*Raiders' Dawn*, 45). Civilization is threatened by the 'lust of
the impudent monster' in Alun Llywelyn-Williams's poetry: 'Friend, we
cannot stay/ and see the wolf roaming the streets of Cardiff' (*Cerddi*,
12). But his greatest fear is of the raid that can come so unexpectedly
from the air, the 'hidden death in the cloud'. His poems refer repeatedly
to the sly, deadly incursions of the bomber, a threat that had been fixed
in people's minds ever since Guernica had been bombed to destruction
in 1936. Less than a year later, Alun Llywelyn-Williams imagined he
saw 'the shadow of its steel wings/ flitting across the slopes of Snowdon'

(*Cerddi*, 14). He had fully grasped how mercilessly penetrative this new weapon could be, how it bypassed conventional defences and reached into the most innocent, remote and defenceless corners of the country. This was, therefore, for him the most complete and powerful symbol of the terrors the sophisticated technology of modern war brought in its train. And Alun Lewis agreed with him. The very title of his first volume, *Raiders' Dawn*, refers to the nightmare of an evening air-raid and of the devastation that dawn reveals. Moreover, his poem 'Destruction' captures the fearful drama of a night-attack:

> And now the impersonal drone of death
> Trembles the throbbing night, the bombers swoop,
> The sky is ripped like sacking with a scream.
> The viaduct no longer spans the stream.   (*Raiders' Dawn*, 90)

It's clear, then, that during the phoney war the minds of both poets were haunted by the same fear and that it entered deeply into their imaginations. Many years after the war had ended Alun Llywelyn-Williams recalled the feelings he'd had as the conflict approached, and it is probable that Alun Lewis, had he lived, would have broadly approved of this passage:

> Quite early on in the thirties, the danger of another war became daily more apparent, and for those of us who remembered something of the first world war and who had no reason to disbelieve Baldwin's glib assurance that the bomber would always get through, a second world war meant quite literally the end of European civilization as we knew it. I certainly was firmly convinced, and so I believe were many of my contemporaries, that we were a generation facing certain and total annihilation. And there seemed to be a dreadful inevitability about it. The triumphant forward march of fascism in Europe and the criminal ineptitude of government in Britain and France served only to underline the truth of the Marxist dictum that capitalism would encompass its own destruction. I was not a pacifist, but it was impossible to regard with enthusiasm the prospect of having to fight fascism in defence of a corrupt social order in which I could not acquiesce and in a struggle which could only lead to the total devastation of all the protagonists. The poetry I attempted to wrest from this sorry state of affairs immediately before and during the years of war was a poetry of despair, my own personal despair, my despair for Wales helplessly entangled in the cataclysm, and my despair for the whole of human civilization.[8]

These comments help account for the rich ambivalence of the feelings expressed in the fourteenth poem in his collection. At the beginning of the piece he is filled with foreboding, sensing 'the fear that's abroad, and the shadow of massacre'; then he notes that 'the corrupt society is dying, dying,/ to the tune of grief and woe and the last groan'; and the poem concludes with his realization that the old order will probably have to be violently destroyed before 'a purer city' can arise in its place (*Cerddi*, 22).

*   *   *

Is it possible, Alun Llywelyn-Williams wondered in 1973, for a man to write effective poetry when he's full of alarm and despondency? He was, very modestly, of the opinion that the poems he himself had written before and during the Second World War were not of a high standard. But he praised the work of First World War writers, and referred admiringly to the great, archaic poetry of Llywarch Hen.[9] That reference to the ancient Welsh poetry of war is particularly interesting in view of the fact that both he and Alun Lewis had included poems about the 'men of Catraeth' in their first published collections.

It was in 1938 that Sir Ifor Williams's magisterial scholarly edition of *Canu Aneirin* first appeared, and it seems that the grand epic style and the elegiac tone of the poetry quickly caught the imagination of young poets who sensed that they too were shortly to face death. One could almost suggest that they discovered, in Aneirin's work, an ancient native Welsh literary tradition adequate for expressing the experiences of war. Perhaps this helped them set their own confusion of feelings in some kind of order as the Second World War approached. In the process they could almost be said to have inaugurated a modern Welsh literary tradition, since Anthony Conran, when he came to commemorate the young Welsh soldiers who were burned to death under decks on the ironically named *Sir Galahad* during the Falklands War, also adopted Aneirin's poem as a model for his modern elegy. His use of *The Gododdin* allowed him to mingle heroic with mock-heroic in bringing out the obscene disparity between patriotic rhetoric and violent reality, and the peculiarly modern character of the soldiers' heroism, as they moved towards 'the Malvinas of their destiny'. The whole, magnificent piece is, in fact, a marvellously inventive and effective blend of the modes of writing of Aneirin and of Ezra Pound – a notable example of how a resourceful, consciously artful, use of the materials of ancient literary tradition can give rise, in Wales, to a very distinctive kind of modernist writing:

Men went to Catraeth. The luxury liner
For three weeks feasted them.
They remembered easy ovations,
Our boys, splendid in courage.
For three weeks the albatross roads,
Passwords of dolphin and petrel,
Practised their obedience
Where the killer whales gathered,
Where the monotonous seas yelped.
Though they went to church with their standards
Raw death has them garnished.[10]

The whole piece gives the faint, but deliberate, impression of being a translation – it is imbued with a calculated roughness, an awkwardness even, that suggests the presence in the background of an ur-poem which the modern poem seems simultaneously to reveal and to obscure. In other words, Conran's poem is constructed to resemble a palimpsest, where we sense the ghostly presence of words behind words and of ancient experience which is both consonant with and at odds with modern experience. Much of the power of Conran's poem comes from this fitting misfit between present and past.

Aneirin was, of course, one of the 'men of the north', a native of the old Cumbria that stretched from present-day southern Scotland down through what is now northern England. It is therefore appropriate that a Scottish poet should have been one of the first to appreciate Sir Ifor's monumental edition, and to respond to it in poetry. Hugh MacDiarmid's piece 'On Reading Professor Ifor Williams's "Canu Aneurin" [*sic*] in Difficult Days' appeared in the August, 1938 number of *Wales*. It deals with the consolation the Scot found in remembering and reaffirming the ancient links between Wales and Scotland, at a time when all the 'major' European powers were arming for battle. MacDiarmid is reminded, in Aneirin's poem, of the unremitting, invisible struggle of small countries for justice and survival, in the face of the great states' arrogant and violent assertion of their military might. It was after all the very same 'History' that had raised 'the vast military empires of the shark/And the tiger', as Auden put it, that had established 'the robin's plucky canton.'[11] MacDiarmid thought he heard the song of the robin in Aneirin's poem:

Between two European journeys of Neville Chamberlain's
And two important speeches of Herr Hitler's
I return to the Taliesin and Llywarch Hen poems,

Full of *hiraeth*, of angry revolt
Against the tyranny of fact . . .

Aneurin stays me with mosses
And comforts me with lichens
In the winter-bound wood of the world today,
Where the gaunt branches rattle like gallows bones.[12]

The poem supplies an excellent example of the imaginative sustenance poets could find in Aneirin's poetry as war loomed. But since each poet of course came to Aneirin not only in the general spirit of the times but also from the direction of his own very personal concerns, it is interesting to distinguish between the uses made of Y *Gododdin* by Alun Lewis and Alun Llywelyn-Williams.

Although Alun Lewis could neither speak Welsh nor read it, it could be that his imagination was temporarily stirred by the general excitement Sir Ifor's edition caused at the time in intellectual circles; or perhaps he – and possibly Alun Llywelyn-Williams, too – had read David Jones's *In Parenthesis* which was first published in 1937, a work which made substantial use of material from Y *Gododdin*. At least he was moved, for some reason, to capture in English something of the character of the old Welsh poetry, and he gave his piece the suggestive title 'The Defeated: for Wales'. (In 1937 Auden concluded his poem on Spain with the lines 'We are left alone with our day, and the time is short, and/ History to the defeated/ May say alas but cannot help or pardon.' [*Poetry of the Thirties*, 136]) Lewis's warriors leave for the Catraeth of their destined defeat with as much stoicism as steel in their hearts: 'Our courage is an old legend./ We left the fields of our fathers./ Fate was our foeman.' It will be remembered that W. H. Auden, when a young student at Oxford, was inspired by Tolkien's lectures on Anglo-Saxon poetry to write in a corresponding alliterative way. It seems that Welsh poetry very briefly affected Alun Lewis in a similar fashion, exciting his imagination and awakening him to new forms of expression. Since he himself increasingly felt his life was controlled by remote, impersonal powers, he was instinctively drawn to the view that life sought a kind of release in extinction:

Oh! dark are we whose greed for life
Was a green slash in our eyes
And in our darkness we are wise,

Forgetting honour, valour, fame,
In this darkness whence we came.

                                        (*Raiders' Dawn*, 29)

Alun Lewis felt the pull of the fateful attractions of darkness
throughout his life, and it is possible he succumbed to them in the end.
But his feeling for the ultimate potency of the dark also made him
exceptionally, tenderly regardful of 'how weak and little is the light,' as
Edward Thomas put it: 'All the universe of sight,/ Love and delight,/
Before the might,/ If you love it not, of night.'[13] So Alun Lewis could
poignantly notice how 'summer blossoms break above my head/ With
all the unbearable beauty of the dead' (25).

Indeed, when Alun Llywelyn Williams reviewed Alun Lewis's
posthumous volume *Letters from India* in 1947, he selected for
comment a passage that plucks out the heart of Lewis's mysterious,
paradoxical relationship with death: 'Death doesn't fascinate me half
as powerfully as life: . . . I turn insatiably to more and more life . . .
Death is the great mystery, who can ignore him? But I don't seek him.
Oh no – only I would like to "place" him.' And in the same review,
published four years after Alun Lewis's death, Llywelyn-Williams
writes feelingly – with all the intensely mixed emotion of a survivor –
about the work of authors killed in the war: 'A critic of the verse written
during the second world war might well be pardoned for exercising a
certain caution in assessing the work of poets whose untimely death in
such tragic circumstances inevitably makes them loom abnormally heroic
through the sacrificial mist, like the men who marched to Catraeth.'[14]

Almost ten years earlier, in 1938, Alun Llywelyn-Williams too had
been uncertain what Fate had in store for him. It was then, in that mood
of ominous unease, that he turned to Y *Gododdin*, expressing surprise
(and perhaps experiencing dismay) at the discovery that 'there is no
grave,/ in the embrace of the sullen moorlands/ for the three hundred
who left the feast so blithely.' Within a few lines, however, this bitter
regret turns into its opposite – a positive rejoicing that those young
soldiers had been seized and removed cleanly, in the very prime of life,
instead of being condemned to 'a long decay . . . in the damp lap of the
moorlands' (*Cerddi*, 17). In their very different ways, therefore, both
Aluns use the story of the men of Catraeth to help them come to terms
with the evil of their own times, and to express the feelings of a generation
of men 'exploded by necessity', as Kenneth Allott graphically put it.[15]

*   *   *

It was, perhaps, in their experience of love that these two poets most sharply felt the pain of their situation. 'Under each starry leafless tree', wrote Alun Lewis, 'Lovers lie in ecstasy,/ While over every trembling thing/ Orion's sword hangs glittering' (*Raiders' Dawn*, 66). Orion's sword becomes the sword of Damocles in these lines which seem to suggest not only the overlordship of Fate but also the turbid feelings of sexual frustration that fill Lewis's early poems. Instead of being directed outwards, towards an object of desire, his sexual passion frequently turns back on itself, harming both body and mind: 'in this blood-soaked forest of disease/ Where wolfish men lie scorched and black/ And corpses sag against the trees/And love's dark roots writhe back// Like snakes into the scorching earth' (*Raiders' Dawn*, 25). There the landscape of torment seems to be both political and sexual – seems indeed to be showing the effects on man's intimate personal life of the public disorder of the thirties.

Sometimes, then, it is suggested that the disturbances of the times are reflected in the sterile passional life of the poet – 'I who am agonized by thought/ And war and love' (*Raiders' Dawn*, 18). At other times his relationship with his lover is contrasted with the madness of the surrounding world:

> For you abide,
> A singing rib within my dreaming side;
> You always stay,
> And in the mad tormented valley
> Where blood and hunger rally
> And Death the wild beast is uncaught, untamed,
> Our soul withstands the terror
> And has its quiet honour
> Among the glittering stars your voices named.
>
> (*Raiders' Dawn*, 45)

This defiant view of love as sanctuary, as a cosmically endorsed refuge for the couple's sanity, and humanity, is touching when, as C. Day Lewis wrote at the time, 'The innocent wing is soon shot down/ And private stars fade in the blood-red dawn/ Where two worlds strive.'[16]

Alun Lewis was too fine and subtle – and honest – a psychologist, however, to rest content for long with such a simple contrast between the private and the public realms, between love and war. He understood, and admitted, that violence had the power to ignite the imagination and to incite the senses to a disturbing pitch of discrimination – as Wilfred Owen had shown in several of his most memorable poems. This perception produced, in 'Raiders' Dawn', an image that is instinct with ambiguity:

> Blue necklace left
> On a charred chair
> Tells that Beauty
> Was startled there.   (*Raiders' Dawn*, 15)

If ordinary, normal beauty has here been startled out of the land of the living, then another, more fearful beauty, has taken its place – the unexpectedly awesome beauty that the bombing 'produced' as it were, and that is manifest in the sensually rich contrast between the blue necklace and the black chair. That is why Alun Lewis is able, at times, to identify with the words spoken by the dancer in one of his poems:

> 'Our love was always ringed with dread
> Of death,' the lovely dancer said,
> 'And so I danced for his delight
> And scorched the blackened core of night
> With passion bright,' the dancer said.
>   (*Raiders' Dawn*, 65)

One of the poems in the collection *Raiders' Dawn* is called 'Odi et Amo', and the Latin title encapsulates the ambivalence that enters into Alun Lewis's feelings on almost every occasion in the book when he's dealing with love, or with war, or with the complex of interconnections between love and war.

The same explosive mixture of feelings is not to be found in Alun Llywelyn-Williams's poetry. Where Alun Lewis is drawn, or perhaps driven, to paradox, the other Alun prefers to observe a clear distinction between 'two irreconcilable worlds' (*Cerddi*, 28) – of peace and war, of love and hate.

> Since Death is at hand, with his grim visage,
> be brave, my darling, don't weep for what's to come;
> it can never destroy the precious exultation of love
> that we've snatched from the grasp of his everlasting terrors.
> Let us ignore the secret scowl of the grave – what does it matter
> Whether we find there paradise or perfect sleep?
> We've been privileged to know the overwhelming surges of the bounded
>   seas
> in the urges of the flesh and the freshness of its passions.

As we've seen from the example of Alun Lewis, this was, understandably, a favourite topos of the poets of the period, and Llywelyn-
Williams's treatment of it compares favourably with the best English
examples, such as Louis MacNeice's 'Meeting Point':

> The bell was silent in the air
> Holding its inverted poise –
> Between the clang and clang a flower,
> A brazen calyx of no noise:
> The bell was silent in the air.
>
> The camels crossed the miles of sand
> That stretched around the cups and plates;
> The desert was their own, they planned
> To portion out the stars and dates:
> The camels crossed the miles of sand.
>
> Time was away and somewhere else.
> The waiter did not come, the clock
> Forgot them and the radio waltz
> Came out like water from a rock:
> Time was away and somewhere else.[17]

Here, as in Alun Llywelyn-Williams's poem, the magical potency, the
spiritual mystery and miracle, of love stands out in dramatic relief when
set against the dark background of the period.

It may well be that Alun Llywelyn-Williams loses out somewhat as a
poet, compared to Alun Lewis, because he is so reluctant to take risks;
to descend into the dark cellars of his mind. But then he also has a
corresponding advantage over Lewis in that he is in full, conscious
control of his alert intelligence, and this cool self-possession and self-
discipline allows him to be, when he chooses, bitingly ironic:

> Under the kindly mountain, that nursed the peace
> of the golden summers, and the long, lovely afternoons,
> we hurl explosive death, experiment in preparation
> for the bitter game and its lame conclusion.   (*Cerddi*, 37)

There is no lack of underlying passion in his poems, but he is always in
perfect command of his mind and his medium, so much so that it is
impossible to read his poetry without being struck by the classical
restraint of its style and its epigrammatic quality:

The songs of yesterday'll be sung no more, no more,
over baby's cradle or in a young lad's prank;
drowned out by the finale of a chorus of steel,
the aircraft's callous raid, the mad rush of a tank.

(*Cerddi*, 30)

The difference in style between the two poets is, then, very evident and very important. But it should be noted that this arises from something deeper than two contrasting temperaments. Each of the poets was dependent on the resources made available to him by the literary culture in which he was working. Both men were actively interested in the products of literary modernism, especially the poetry of Eliot, Yeats and Auden. Indeed, Yeats's influence is everywhere to be seen in Lewis's impassioned attempts to grapple with – and thus to get to grips with – his own nature. And the example of Auden and others had clearly been instrumental in enabling Alun Llywelyn-Williams to break free from the sickly romanticism that, in his opinion, was the curse of contemporary Welsh-language culture.

Yet, in the last analysis, the style he developed did not resemble that of the great modern masters. What we can now, in retrospect, see is that he was, instead, inspired by them to recognize and to acquire for his own writing the strengths of the classical Welsh poetic tradition. His own distinctive, creative, achievement came from his success in combining the vigorous colloquial simplicity of the *Canu Rhydd* (the poetry not written in the strict meters) with the richly compressed style of writing characteristic of the *Canu Caeth* (cynghanedd poetry).

* * *

'Wars kill poets; they do not make them', Alun Llywelyn-Williams noted tersely in his 1947 review of Alun Lewis's posthumous volume, *Letters from India*. That sorrowful and penetrating essay remains one of the best short discussions on record of the work of a poet who did not live to fulfil his immense promise. The reviewer undoubtedly reached the very heart of a dark mystery when he wrote: 'The letters read like a chronicle of a pilgrimage undertaken in search of a fatal secret. The strange thing about the book is the impression it gives of the inevitability of the final result.' And maybe he inadvertently revealed the impulses that lay at the very heart of his own being as a poet when he added: '[An] all-embracing curiosity for life, and the contrary need for solitude and peace – that is at once the mark and the burden of a poet.' But, he generously went on, 'only a poet on the true road to greatness feels it as deeply as Alun Lewis did; and expresses it so cogently.'[18]

Alun Llywelyn-Williams noted that Alun Lewis had failed to make contact with the native culture of India. But then, he added, 'that, of course, is not in the least surprising. It can have been no more possible to establish in India a living contact from within the army than it was in occupied Germany or in the war-torn countries of the Western allies.' It's an interesting observation that seems to invite us to consider the poems that stemmed from his own military service overseas (in Europe) alongside the poems Alun Lewis wrote in India that appeared in *Ha! Ha! Among the Trumpets*. It's worth following this hint, even while recognizing that it can of course lead only to limited insights into the wartime poetry of both these writers; and the most economical way of pursuing Alun Llywelyn-Williams's point is to examine one poem by each of them.

'On a Visit' is a poem based, presumably, on an experience Alun Llywelyn-Williams had towards the end of the war, while serving on the continent with the Royal Welch Fusiliers. Written in the first person, it relates how, years ago, he had come upon a great house standing on the sunlit slope of a valley 'steep and secret with quiet pine-trees.' Reluctantly admitted by the scrupulously courteous owner, a Baron, he was shown the house's war-wound – room upon room whose windows had been removed by bomb-blast so that 'the east wind stung/ and vomited snowflakes onto carpet and/ mirror and chest'. But insufficiently chastened by this image of devastation he had insisted, in an inexplicable spirit of perversity, on being led to the living-room. Taken there by his visibly discomfited host, he warmed to the homely signs he saw of decent, civilized living: the elderly wife seated near the generous fire, the firelight intermittently illuminating a picture of Christ on the wall, a handsome piano piled high with copies of classical music. Seeing Liszt and Chopin lying side by side he'd been moved to enthuse, praising music's power to cross national frontiers and to bring peoples together. But he'd stopped abruptly upon seeing the tears gathering in the woman's eyes, 'like a lake filling up with stars'. He'd realized, too late, that the piano reminded this couple of their lost son. Embarrassed then by his guest's embarrassment, the host had asked forgiveness for such 'discourteous bearing', and had explained 'we do not wish to share our pain with anyone.' All three had then stood silent, 'till the man turned to the piano as though challenging its power':

> For a moment, he sat there, humbly praying
> before seeking the tune: then the graceful music flowed
> from his hand, prelude and dance and song so

bitterly sad, so carelessly cheerful and gentle and full of
mercy until the sound blended into a communion
where angels walked, healing our hurt and setting free
our captive hours.[19]

Read in the light of the remark Alun Llywelyn-Williams made in his
review, this poem can be understood as dramatizing the difficulties of
making 'living contact', during wartime, even with those in the
occupied territories who are one's natural allies. Implicit in the poem –
and a crucial factor in the whole drama – is the narrator's status as an
officer in the liberating army. He unconsciously trades on his authority
when he insists on gaining admittance to his host's living-room, the last
refuge of private, domestic feelings. And in the process he is, of course,
taking unfair advantage of the code of aristocratic courtesy by which
the Baron is bound. As the pattern of the poem makes clear, the result is
an intrusion into the life of the family that is as violent, as damaging, as
destructive, as the bomb-blast. The supposed 'ally' suddenly, in the
ignorance of his arrogance, becomes the enemy. It may well be that in
this incident we are being shown the kind of wartime experience that
caused Alun Llywelyn-Williams's outlook to change in the way he
himself elsewhere described. In his poem on 'Remembering the
Thirties' he recalled his pre-war certainty that he, an enlightened
socialist, was on the side of the angels who were fighting the evil empire
of capitalism: 'For this we were born,/ to confidence in the destruction
of false idols.' But he emerged from the war with the very different
conviction that he was essentially no different from the enemy – that
human nature was always piebald.

> The saving grace was the discovery in war, in the midst of its evil
> destructiveness, of the astonishing power of the human spirit to survive
> and to triumph. What the war really gave me, I suppose, was a salutary
> direct experience of human suffering and folly of which I had hitherto
> been a mere passive observer, and a realisation that they are inherent in
> the human condition everywhere at all times. They are prerequisite and
> inescapable conditions for the exercise of love and compassion, for our
> awareness of joy and our attainment of wisdom, because good and evil
> are inextricably intermingled. Ideologies, and political systems, even
> forms of religion, are propitiary ephemeral supports in the face of forces
> that transcend time and space, but poetry though it can't attempt any
> solutions to the eternal paradox of human life can at least celebrate its
> mystery and its magic and articulate our occasional glimpses of
> universal truth.[20]

At the end of 'On a Visit' music is shown as performing the pseudo-religious office here ascribed to poetry, and in the process it becomes a form of redemptive communion between the visitor and his 'hosts'. Living contact has occurred, against all the odds. It is as if the original situation had been turned inside out: strangers from different cultures, brought together initially by the most inauspicious of circumstances, and relating to each other at first only in unfortunate, blundering ways, are eventually joined together in a moment of genuine mutuality. Moreover this ambivalent aspect of the whole story is inscribed from the beginning in the style of the poem. It is written as if the events recalled were almost a dream, and it is written in a distanced way in a style of discourse that is formal, dignified, courteous. On one level this style of presentation can be said to encode the spirit of elaborate, defensive-cum-aggressive *politesse* that governs most of the 'visit'. But on another level the style enacts the inner meaning of the story; bringing out its ritualistic, ceremonial aspects; showing it to be a vision, an initiation into a state of deeper psychological and spiritual under-standing. The style therefore speaks to us of Dante, of *The Mabinogion*, of strange meetings that are simultaneously ancient and modern.

Alun Llywelyn-Williams would not have needed to search for long before discovering examples, in his review copy of *Letters from India*, of Alun Lewis's rueful failure to make living contact with the native culture. In the very first letter from India that is collected in that volume, he describes a visit he paid to a tiny Buddhist shrine, near a 'steep granite scarp that was so like home.' 'I stood by Buddha for a long time, trying to understand. But it was no good. I only knew that it was closed to me as long as I was a fussy little officer sahib with a hundred unimportant jobs on his mind'.[21] Early in his stay he intuited the people's resentment, and at one point he told Gweno sadly: 'I wish I had come here as a doctor, teacher, social worker: anything but a soldier. It's not nice being a soldier in India.' (*Letters*, 68) His enforced detachment from the human scene helped him concentrate his attention on the landscape, which he sometimes captured with Lawrentian vividness, in bold blocks of fierce colour:

> When I was leaving Karachi, one of the instructors said to me, 'You're the most selfish man I've ever met, Lewis. You think the war exists for you to write books about it.' I didn't deny it, though it's all wrong. I hadn't the strength to explain what is instinctive and categorical in me, the need to experience. The writing is only a proof of the sincerity of the experience, that's all.

And the country is so beautiful now, the rich crops and the long fields of yellow sunflowers and red currant flowers and the peasants look so well and fertile, too. The rains make the burning cruel earth into a green gentleness of fruit and leaf. Soon it will all dry up again. I dread the long dry merciless months ahead. (*Letters*, 67)

There was a part of him content, as he put it, to 'watch the Marco Polo wonders of ordinary life' (*Letters*, 60). But not for long. He was, from personal conviction that had grown straight out of his cultural background, not a wonder-voyager but a lifelong traveller after meaning.

The invincible strangeness of India affected him in many ways, and he fashioned it into several different emotional shapes in his poetry, some of them very complicated. But one of his shortest and simplest poems on this theme is also one of his best. It is here reproduced in full:

The Peasants

The dwarf barefooted, chanting
Behind the oxen by the lake,
Stepping lightly and lazily among the thorntrees
Dusky and dazed with sunlight, half awake;

The women breaking stones upon the highway,
Walking erect with burdens on their heads,
One body growing in another body,
Creation touching verminous straw beds.

Across scorched hills and trampled crops
The soldiers straggle by.
History staggers in their wake.
The peasants watch them die.[22]

In their calm air of dealing with the eternal, immutable verities, the two opening stanzas recall Hardy's famous paean to what is permanent: 'In Time of the Breaking of Nations'. But of course Hardy identifies with what lasts, whereas Alun Lewis feels dwarfed and threatened by it. The prepositions in the poem map out the mental landscape. In the first two stanzas they are used mostly to interconnect the humans and their environment, to place people comfortably in their native setting. Then comes that word 'Across', which changes the whole physical and cultural perspective, signifying the migrant soldiers' exclusion from the inner life of the country they are condemned, by war, to traverse. The verbs spell out the same message. After the timeless present participles of the first stanzas comes the short-lived-present tense of the last verse. The present participle is the tense of 'Creation' itself, an open-ended, seamlessly continuous state of existence; the present tense is, in sharp contrast, the tense of the transient 'History' of European presumption. After all, the very colour of the Indian's being is, as it were, a gift from the remorseless sun that saps the soldiers' strength. At home 'among the thorntrees' the dwarf is 'dusky and dazed with sunlight, half awake'.

*   *   *

Alun Llywelyn-Williams's sympathetic review of *Letters from India* is proof positive, it seems to me, that the two poets were kindred spirits, although they never met. During the course of his review, the author corrected the impression some people had had that Alun Lewis had contributed to *Tir Newydd*, (New Land), the literary magazine edited by Alun Llywelyn-Williams from 1935 to 1939. 'This is unfortunately not true – how I wish it were: the short stories that appeared in the periodical under the name of Alun Lewis were the work of another writer of the same name.'[23] His regret was mainly due, no doubt, to a feeling that Welsh-language literature would have benefited enormously from Alun Lewis's genius. But there is also a note of personal loss in his comment. Perhaps he felt that the work of this Welshman who did not speak Welsh was, after all, closer to his heart than much of the writing of his Welsh-language contemporaries.

Certainly Alun Llywelyn-Williams tended, throughout his career, to be severe in his criticism of Welsh-language writers who seemed to him not to respond in their work to those social and political pressures he and Alun Lewis were so aware of in their poetry. As editor of *Tir Newydd*, during the thirties, he made several very controversial pronouncements, accusing young poets of using Welsh to escape from contemporary realities, and of ignoring the crisis of their times:

> In our time, more perhaps than in any other previous age, the relevance of poetry, and even indeed the very justification for poetry, is inseparable from its sensitivity to contemporary life, for the simple reason that those universal experiences that have ever been the subject of poetry have suddenly, and for the first time, been embodied in the unequivocal and urgent shapes of the present age. The whole culture and civilization of Europe is in imminent danger: man's moral nature goes in fear of his scientific capabilities; the values and the power of religion must be reassessed, with particular reference to the Christian

faith; the whole social system, including commerce and industry and international politics, is rapidly proceeding towards disaster and calls out for reform. Let no one think that these are merely academic questions. They are of the utmost importance to each and every individual. Moroever, if they are to be solved, they demand the personal attentions of each one of us. They are therefore of immense importance to every poet – and yet there is scarcely an echo of all these problems in the contemporary poetry of Wales.[24]

Forty years later he made a similar point, with specific reference this time to the failure of Welsh poets to respond to the Second World War. 'In the first war, in Wales, T. Gwynn Jones mythologised his reaction. I could only offer a direct affirmation of my own experience as a combatant. Most Welsh language poets of my generation ignored the whole business as though it had nothing to do with them, or with Wales – a negative reaction which was surely very strange even for civilians.'[25]

It's no wonder, then, that he felt drawn to the work of Alun Lewis, and we today owe a great debt of gratitude to the two Aluns who between them ensured that the literatures of Wales did after all bear memorable witness to life during an extraordinary period of modern history.

4

Flintshire and the regional weather forecast

In a recently published essay Seamus Heaney recalls the period when he, then a young lad growing up in Northern Ireland, used to listen reverently to the BBC's 'Regional Forecast', sonorously read in cultured English.[1] 'Something was temporarily relinquished' in the listener, and 'a harking towards an elsewhere occurred' as local talk about 'a drying day or a growthy day' was temporarily replaced by the radio-speak of 'bright intervals' and 'cold fronts'. In this early experience of contrasting discourses the mature Heaney now discovers an adumbration of the challenge confronting him as an Irish writer:

> If our forefathers had not then advanced as deeply into certitude and as far beyond the linguistic pale as the ones I have heard since in the United States saying that 'Today our forecast calls for snow', they had nevertheless begun to interpose between ourselves and the evidence of our senses a version of the meteorological reality which weakened the sureness of our grip on our own experience. The weather forecast succeeded in establishing itself in competition with the actual weather.
>
> Even so, as readers and writers, we continue to regard with admiration those who would resist this situation, who refuse to accede to what the forecast calls for and persist in an effort to invent an idiom that will expose us to what exactly it was we experienced. When this happens . . . we have raised our subcultural status to cultural power. (11–12)

How does the Welsh author writing in English respond to the regional weather forecast? Any attempt at a complete answer is bound to raise a storm, so let me confine myself to a few innocent remarks about two texts. One is *A Toy Epic*, which deals with three boys growing up in Flintshire during the thirties. The other is a play set 'In the living-room of a house in Glansarno, a small village in a remote Welsh countryside.' If you are Welsh, you will know exactly where you are here – you are in England. By that I mean that this is an outsider's view of Wales as a single homogeneous region, a social organism as primitive and as simple as an amoeba. We have here a made-to-measure image of Wales, designed to fit exactly into the limited space available for it in the Great British mentality. But the play in question is, of course, *The Corn is Green*, based on Emlyn Williams's experience of growing into manhood near the Newmarket (Trelawnyd) where Emyr Humphreys spent his childhood some fifteen years later. The two works therefore positively invite comparison, promising us insights into the different terms in which two writers construct, and so construe, the 'same' region.[2]

*   *   *

The Corn is Green is a collier's rags-to-educational-riches story: a Welsh *Pygmalion*, but with a reversal of gender roles, so that the man becomes the pupil and the woman becomes the teacher. Morgan Evans, an inarticulate young Welsh and Welsh-speaking collier, is saved from a lifetime of degrading labour down the mine by a formidable English bluestocking, Miss Moffat. Recognizing his exceptional talent, she dedicates her own considerable abilities as a schoolmistress, and as a disciplinarian, to preparing him for Oxford. Eventually he secures an interview there, but is warned by Miss Moffat on his return not to set his heart on obtaining a place, because that will make failure totally unsupportable. Morgan is appalled by her advice:

> [In Oxford] the words came pouring out of me – all the words that I had learnt and written down and never spoken – I suppose I was talking nonsense, but I was at least holding a conversation! I suddenly realised that I had never done it before – I had never been *able* to do it. [*With a strong Welsh accent*] 'How are you, Morgan? Nice day, Mr Jones! Not bad for the harvest!' – a vocabulary of twenty words; all the thoughts that you have given to me were being stored away as if they were always going to be useless – locked up and rotting away. (81)

This is cliché gone theatrical, and cliché itself is only a half-truth that is given the full treatment. What is missing from the scene is a sense of there being a whole complex of feelings from which Morgan's mind understandably escapes, under the pressure of circumstances, into a temporarily simple passion of love for Oxford and of hate for home. What Emlyn Williams has in fact done is to make sure that he and his London audience are on the same wavelength, by tuning in to the regional forecast. Ever since the Blue Books Report of 1847, the English had viewed the Welsh as a sub-literate people in dire need of English education.

But if this is the regional weather forecast, then what were local weather conditions really like at that time? Here we need to bear in mind that the play stands in a significant relationship to two quite different periods. Insofar as it is set around the turn of the century and loosely based on Emlyn Williams's own experiences, it is useful to compare it with *George*, the first volume of his autobiography.[3] But the play was written and produced in 1938, when some sections of the English middle class had been thoroughly alarmed by what seemed to them to be the desperate political radicalism of the south Wales miners. *The Corn is Green* is designed to allay those fears – fears with which Emlyn Williams could himself, perhaps, sympathize, at least in part. Although he had spent several years of his childhood in the vicinity of the Parlwr Du/ Point of Ayr colliery, he was still an outsider to the industrial world of work, as he revealed very honestly and effectively in one episode in *George*. After his family had moved to live near Wrexham, Emlyn Williams, then a gifted young County School boy, had occasion to visit Summers' steelworks, where his father was by that time working:

> . . . like a stray insect I scuttled through a vast streetless city of black sheds, interminable rumbling walls, swivelling cranes, belching chimneys, wagons snarling along rails. I ought to have been excited by the pervasive all-powerful activity, but apart from pleasure that my father was part of the machine-metropolis, I was conscious only of ruthlessness. I stumbled upon Dad's shed; though we both knew that I was expected, I was as proud and puzzled to see him as he was to see me. He introduced me to his mate Mr Hughes from Flint, whose son Ivor was due at Holywell County School in a year's time. 'Well', said Dad to him, 'this is the boy!' I realised, with a swelling of the heart, why the cuttings were so grimy: privately and in good taste, he was beginning to boast about me. (176–7)

Williams ends by 'walking out of the money-making cauldron', glad 'of the mute estuary night; if that was life, I wanted no part of it.' Sympathy with the plight of those who worked under such conditions, an association of heavy industry with an impulse to escape, a feeling of unease at the alien, threatening, power of the world into which he had innocently stumbled – all of these emotions, and more, are there in disguised form in *The Corn is Green*, in his ambivalent depiction of the mining background.

Fredric Jameson has spoken of the 'political unconscious' of a text, and this is a useful phrase when considering the 'plot' of *The Corn is*

Green.[4] The choice of a literally coal-black miner is of course central to
the whole process. Needless to say the miners are as ready to sing as if
they were auditioning for a part in *Proud Valley*. And they're not the
only songsters. Bessy, the Cockney sparrow, seduces Morgan by
singing a song to him in Welsh – a song she's learnt specially for the
occasion, knowing how partial the Welsh are to singing. Emlyn
Williams uses stereotypes in his capacity as mediator between the
working class and the middle class. He draws a picture suggesting that
what the exploited working class primarily need is better social
opportunities, in the form of an education that will allow them to
progress upwards until they're assimilated into established society. It's
a picture that eases class tension and that minimizes class conflict.
Hence the mine-owners are represented by a basically good-hearted
squire, at whose anachronistic social prejudices we can all laugh. In
fact, he sprays prejudice, with genial impartiality, in all directions –
covering miners, women and the Welsh language, with equal gusto. As
for the heroine of the story, Miss Moffat, she is an admirable member of
the eccentric, philanthropic, progressive wing of the English middle
class.

Miss Moffat it is who supplies the play with its stirring political
climax. 'You have brains, shrewdness, eloquence, imagination and
enough personality', she tells Morgan, 'and Oxford will give you
enough of the graces.'

MORGAN: For what?
MISS MOFFAT: [*simply*]: Enough to become a great statesman of our
country. [*After a pause, as he stares at her.*] It needn't be just politics – it
could be more, much, much more – it could be . . . for a future nation to
be proud of . . . P'raps I'm mad, I dunno. (95)

There are shades, here, of Lloyd George, the young Emlyn Williams's
hero. And the Welsh wizard can stand for all those people – artists and
writers prominent among them – whose great delight in life has been to
read the regional weather forecast for Wales from London in a Welsh
accent.

It is interesting to note that Lloyd George is the great adversary with
whom Emyr Humphreys has wrestled all his creative life. According to
Humphreys, Lloyd George's career was the outcome of 'all the fateful
choices Welsh nonconformity had made during the nineteenth-
century.' He triumphed 'for the benefit of the twentieth-century model

Welshman, of which he was the shining prototype.'⁵ With Lloyd
George, what Emyr Humphreys acidly called 'the Arthurian vision of
history', with its unhealthy emphasis on the dutiful part Wales has
played in the making of Great Britain, reached its triumphant climax.
But if Lloyd George is close to being the fascinating villain of modern
Welsh history, in Emyr Humphreys's version of events, he is even closer
to being the charismatic – and appropriately histrionic – hero of
modern Wales for Emlyn Williams. Lloyd George seems, indeed, to
have acted as a kind of role-model for the aspiring actor – so much so,
that one is left idly speculating whether the title of his autobiography,
George, was chosen with the Welsh wizard in mind! What is certain is
that Lloyd George is mentioned no fewer than seven times during the
course of that book – if one includes an amusing occasion when
Williams comes across a horse of that name. And following a nervous
breakdown at Oxford, the young Emlyn Williams actually spent an
obviously delightful period acting as tutor to Megan Lloyd George at
Cricieth – an engagement that culminated in a meeting with the Great
Man himself.

The ringing affirmation of Wales's Britishness at the end of *The Corn
is Green* takes on a new significance when we remember that, two years
before the play was first performed, nationalists had made a dramatic
gesture that had, however briefly, caught the public imagination
throughout Wales. The burning at Penyberth had been an action in
defence of everything that made Wales different from England, with
particular reference to the language. Emlyn Williams had been raised a
Welsh speaker, but with language, as with class, he chooses to play the
role of conciliator in *The Corn is Green*. The plot makes the transition
from one culture to another seem relatively troublefree and completely
desirable, in the name of personal development and social progress. On
the one hand he tends to depict Welsh as the lively but limited local
patois of a generally backward people. Here is old Tom, an ancient
character who is virtually monoglot:

MISS RONBERRY [*nervously*]: Is there anything *you* would like to know,
Mr Tom?
OLD TOM: Where iss Shakespeare?
MISS RONBERRY: Where? . . . Shakespeare, Mr Tom, was a very great
writer.
OLD TOM: Writer? Like the Bible?
MISS RONBERRY: Like the Bible.

OLD TOM [*looking at her doubtfully*]: Dear me, and me thinkin' the man was a place. [*Following the others, muttering sadly*] If I iss been born fifty years later, I iss been top of the class. (38–9)

For Old Tom read Uncle Tom, perhaps. On the other hand, Emlyn Williams also satirizes those who are contemptuously dismissive of Welsh. They are, though, presented only as being comically ignorant – a mode of presentation which allows him to tackle the problem at a suitably superficial level. Here is the Squire addressing a Welsh boy: 'Oh yes – well, come here where I can see you, eh? . . . [*As Idwal advances fearfully round his chair.*] Now, boy, how old are you, or whatever the Chinese is for it?' (6) Prejudice, certainly, but displaying its ignorance so cheerfully that there is, as it were, no harm in it.

The difference between this and the bitter reality of what is called 'the language question' is strikingly emphasized when we look at what happened when Emlyn Williams, in the fifties, publicly encountered a real-life 'squire', with strong views on the Welsh language. The October, 1958 issue of the magazine *Wales* included an article by the eminent anthropologist Lord Raglan, who cast what purported to be the coolly dispassionate, analytical eye of the professional anthropologist over Wales. The result was pronouncements like the following:

> Most of the speakers of Welsh are . . . illiterate or semi-literate, but there are a few thousand people who have learnt to speak the literary language, and who make a regular cult of it.
> . . . The Welsh language is . . . used for at least three undesirable purposes, to conceal the results of scholarship, to try to lower the standards of official competence, and, worst of all, to create enmity where none existed, [that is by stirring up] hatred of England among the more ignorant Welsh.
> . . . [Nationalists] and the Welsh Board of Education . . . wish the people of Wales to live not in the present but in a fictitious druidical past, and therefore persuade or compel them to waste their time and restrict their opportunities by studying the moribund Welsh language. It will be a happy day for Wales when that language finally takes its proper place – on the bookshelves of the scholars.[6]

Incensed by the ignoble lord's article, Emlyn Williams wrote a reply for the next number of *Wales*, beginning as follows: 'My blood has never boiled – perhaps it doesn't belong to the right group – but when I finished reading Lord Raglan's article . . . I was conscious of a low but steady simmer; I can still hear it. It's getting steadier.' The whole piece is

written in consciously urbane, elegantly measured language. He and
Raglan meet on equal ground – on elaborately English terms, one might
say, of icy courtesy, polite irony and barbed wit. They are clearly both
true Brits – punctiliously pukka. Emlyn Williams will have no truck
with vulgar nationalism: 'Oxford and London have been very good to
me.' And he assures his adversary that 'we are all proud that an ancestor
of the Queen should have been a Tudor.' The Britishness of his response
to Raglan is worth noting, because it is consistent with the regional
outlook that is inscribed in *The Corn is Green*. But of course his fellow
Brit. , Raglan, has departed from the script. He's shown the ugly,
xenophobic side of the Anglo-centric British character. And, in
replying, Emlyn Williams is forced to reveal aspects of his early
background that are carefully suppressed, or else deliberately distorted,
in the play.[7]

For instance, he reveals that his Welsh-language upbringing had
actively helped him acquire other languages. 'Welsh being etym-
ologically the most individual language in Europe, this has given to me,
and to countless others . . . a priceless training for learning languages
without which I, for one, could never have secured entry to an English
university and thence to the world.' This is a relationship between
Welsh Wales and 'the world' (confirmed in *George*) which is the
opposite to that portrayed through Morgan's progress to Oxford in
The Corn is Green. Moreover, Williams is hurt into sarcasm by
Raglan's ignorant remarks about Welsh-speaking illiterates. The
English origins of the surname Williams was, he writes, 'explained to
me by my illiterate mother (her language was Welsh, hence she was
illiterate – I am quoting his lordship).' As for Taid and Nain, 'the whole
job-lot qualify, straight away as pretty well 100 per cent illiterates. My
maternal grandfather could recite most mellifluously from The Song of
Solomon, and from poems by Ceiriog as sweetly elegiac as "Lycidas";
but alas, he did it in Welsh.' Here, then, we glimpse a separate,
sophisticated people's culture in Welsh, of a kind and quality never
hinted at in *The Corn is Green*. Although one should in fairness add
that Emlyn Williams had not himself benefited from such a culture. As
he himself significantly notes in *George*, 'I used to hear of Bands of
Hope, Penny Readings and Eisteddfodau – festivals of competitive
singing and reciting – but Glanrafon was so remote that I never went'
(43–4).

The Raglan–Williams exchange highlights several different forms of
the ideology of Britishness. Lord Raglan sees Wales as well on its way to

being perfectly assimilated to a Britain synonymous with England. He believes it to be enough for Wales to retain only the minor local differences that characterize an English region. Emlyn Williams is then forced by the bigotry of Raglan's Britishness to celebrate the language and the culture that have historically differentiated Wales very sharply from England. This could lead to a picture of Britain very different from Raglan's – a Britain of radically different, yet politically equal regions, of which England would be only one, alongside Wales, Scotland and Ireland.

In fact, Wales's relationship to England is examined in *George* in terms very different from those that govern the story in *The Corn is Green*. An interesting case in point is the mention made of O. M. Edwards in the autobiography. '"O. M. Edwards",' says Emlyn Williams's father, 'with a sigh of repletion, and joining his fine fingers in thought, "bettered himself from nothing, but with a careful Welsh mother like your own and his father a God-fearing farmer of the old school"' (124). Here, then, is an example of local-boy-made-good which is instructively different from the version of that myth offered us in *The Corn is Green*. Whereas young Morgan Evans goes to Oxford in order to escape his background and to turn his back on Wales, O. M. Edwards, in that mythologized version of his career so lovingly embraced by the Welsh *gwerin* of the turn of the century, took Oxford by storm only in order thereafter to devote all his energies and talents to the celebration of the virtues of his background and to the patriotic service of his native country.

Elsewhere in *George* there is a fascinating description of O. M. Edwards's brother. John Morgan Edwards was headmaster of Holywell County School during Emlyn Williams's time there, but although he was a Balliol graduate, like his more famous brother, 'Oxford had in no whit chafed at his edges and he remained imperviously Welsh, with the dry common sense of his farmer ancestors' (123). Emlyn Williams gives a marvellous description, both sympathetic and comic, of the headmaster's performance at the School's Prize Day:

> ... the partitions of the Hall were stacked away and the whole Sunday-bested school squeezed in, opposite an audience of Governors and Parents. The staff were Sunday-bested too, as much on trial as their pupils had ever been; Miss Cooke and Mr Boyer wore shimmering purplish plumage. The Boss, even more bedecked, rose like an unwilling taurine sacrifice to deliver his Report, and rising changed from a fine figure of a country Head into an outsize schoolboy at a viva, wrestling –

before a Board of parents – with a foreign tongue in which he knew, with every word he uttered, that he was losing marks. Edwards Minor (M.A.Oxon) was doomed from the start. The pupils who had sat through this before looked sideways with a soundless schoolboy groan, but poor J. M. hated it as much as they did, he was Father Making a Fool of Himself. 'Whereas hereto-before the poss-ition of a catering school – er I mean a school catering for a mixed poppilation, in North W-W . . . (a dead parent-watching pause: 'Winnipeg' whispers Totty) Wales, in the avenues which we explore we turn out s-s-s . . . ('Sausages' whispers Totty) standards ass high ass any . . .'(127)

In this splendid passage of sympathetic identification with a Welsh-speaker's stutteringly inadequate attempts to master the master-tongue, Emlyn Williams displays a quality of understanding of the social complexities of the situation which is markedly superior to his treatment of the subject in *The Corn is Green*. In the play, English becomes the great liberator of native Welsh intelligence, the facilitator of understanding, whereas in this passage English is seen as a foreign, colonial tongue that can turn intelligent men into seeming fools. The strength of *George* is that it can show us both these aspects of the linguistic situation. The weakness of *The Corn is Green* is that it cannot.

*   *   *

Emlyn Williams's reply to Lord Raglan appears on pages 16–20 of *Wales*. On the very next page, by enticing coincidence, there begins an extract from Emyr Humphreys's 'forthcoming' novel *A Toy Epic*. The chapter printed is 'A Death in the Street' – one of the sections in the novel where the condition of Wales is not under review. But to pass from the Emlyn Williams article to the Emyr Humphreys extract is, in my experience, to be struck by a difference in style which is very revealing. Williams speaks in his prose like an elocution teacher – which reminds us that *The Corn is Green* is essentially a play about acquiring polished, educated English. He adopts an arch, mannered, histrion-ically eloquent style. No wonder that in his article he exults in 'a vowel-control which we Welsh find to be the envy of North-country or Cockney friends who have also had to storm the citadel of the Queen's English (the same vowel-control which was to prove not exactly a handicap to the oratorical career of Lloyd George).' Emyr Humphreys writes in a plain manner, avoiding any egregious features that identify it as Welsh. This is his anti-regionalism operative at the level of language.

He normalizes the life of his locality, thereby reproducing the unconscious view of a native that life in those parts is unremarkable. It is the Welsh equivalent of Barthes's 'white writing' or 'writing degree zero' – a style of writing that passes itself off as artlessly 'normal' or 'natural'. And as Emyr Humphreys has gone on writing, the impulse, which is as much political as artistic, to use a language that irons out lilt and bleaches the colour out of Welsh saying has grown increasingly strong. This can be seen as one of his most important contributions to the development of a mature, independent, non-regional English-language literature in Wales. It has helped accomplish what Seamus Heaney has called 'a Ptolemaic revolution': 'while a literary centre in which the provinces revolve around the centre is demonstrably a Copernican one, the task of talent is to reverse things to a Ptolemaic condition. The writer must re-envisage the region as the original point.'[8]

It is tempting at this point to make a simple, decisive contrast: to depict Emlyn Williams as an unfortunate Copernican, and to praise Emyr Humphreys as a perfect Ptolemist. In other words, it would be easy to argue that just as regionalism is the bane of *The Corn is Green*, so an awareness of Wales as a self-validating and self-sufficient culture is the invincible strength of *A Toy Epic*. But the break with regionalism can never be as clean and simple, or as creatively empowering, as that, as Seamus Heaney reminds us in the essay which is my constant point of reference:

> It is necessary to beware of too easy an assumption that the breaking of political bonds necessarily and successfully issues in the forging of a new literary idiom; in such enterprises of renewal, it is likely that a conflict of interest will arise between the imaginative and the activist wings . . . Now the forecast will certainly be broadcast in local accents, but the message may remain equally puzzling and askew. 'Our forecast calls for the Irish language, hydroelectric power and knee-length gym-frocks.' 'Our forecast calls for communal farms and wedding parties at the mausoleum.'

As I see it, *A Toy Epic* is very much an 'enterprise of renewal', and it does indeed bear the marks of a conflict of interests between the imaginative and the activist 'wings' of Emyr Humphreys's highly politicized mind. This is most evident when, following his political 'conversion', Michael's mind becomes obligingly receptive to the author's own beliefs. Michael proposes to live, and if necessary to die, for Wales. 'Young as I am, through this certainty of purpose, wisdom has at last been made available to me. If I live to be a hundred, I shall never have a richer purpose, a better vision, and never a wisdom so pure and certain, so free from sadness and regret' (99). Emyr Humphreys certainly captures here the pompous earnestness of a self-centred adolescent, but unfortunately his detached, ironic view of Michael goes only skin deep. From this point in the novel onwards Michael becomes the authorized consciousness, and the two other voices – those of Albie and Iorwerth – are to some extent subordinated to his. This is a pity, because the strength of the novel lies in the rich polyphony of its different voices, the multiple narrative structure that allowed Emyr Humphreys to articulate some of the cultural complexities of the background from which he himself came.

Emyr Humphreys's own native region is, of course, Rhyl and its hinterland, and the first novel he published, *The Little Kingdom* (1946), begins with a view from a vantage-point near Rhyl which also tells us a great deal about Humphreys's mature view of his home territory. A farmer, Richard Bloyd, gazes 'across the water', where he sees 'the Wirral emerg[ing] from the early morning mist; become once more a solid and substantial rich-green sea-girt land, speckled with red-roofed houses.'[9] The scene suggests an England that is a sight for sore Welsh eyes; a realm of magic, enticingly prosperous and magnetically, majestically strong. Ever since Tudor times (as Humphreys would put it), this England has been a powerful kingdom of the Welsh mind, a myth controlling consciousness. Emyr Humphreys grew up in a region where this myth was palpable – where the physical proximity of England meant that the power and attraction of Englishness was a fact of life as solid and substantial as the Wirral is to Bloyd. The novelist can usefully be thought of as a product of the border county of Flintshire, and like other writers raised in border country he has an ingrained sensitivity to cultural contrasts. In Raymond Williams's case this kind of background perhaps helped make him a dispassionate inquisitor of social structures, as well as a lifelong searcher after community. In the young Emyr Humphreys's case it meant his Welshness was never simply and unproblematically given; rather, it was a potential for identity he first painfully discovered and then deliberately chose to realize. This awareness of Welshness as a cultural condition constantly needing to be as it were won, or redeemed, from Englishness has been at the heart of virtually everything Humphreys has ever written. In this respect his native region could be said to have made him a novelist ideally equipped to portray a Wales that has throughout this century increasingly come to resemble one large border country. 'Ynom mae y clawdd' ('Offa's Dyke is within us') wrote Bryan Martin Davies recently, after settling near the border, not far from Emyr Humphreys's childhood haunts.[10]

A Toy Epic is, both in a geographical and a metaphorical sense, a border novel. It traces the growth to manhood of three boys – Michael, Iowerth and Albie – who come from contrasting backgrounds. Albie is a town boy, Anglicized son of Welsh-speaking parents, who identifies very much with the working-class to which his bus-driver father belongs. Iorwerth is raised on a farm in the rural heartland of decaying Welsh Nonconformity. Michael is a son of the rectory, looked after by a maid, and able but reluctant to speak Welsh because as a child he's picked up the social vibes that tell him it's vulgar and silly. Now it seems to me that any Welsh reader will immediately, instinctively, experience such a book as a social *Gestalt* – as a single, intricate, indivisible image corresponding to the internal design of Welsh society. And indeed reviewers in Wales reacted to it in this way, when it was first published. Writing in Welsh, John Gwilym Jones described it as offering 'a cross-section of Welsh society.'[11] Gwyn Thomas, in a private letter to the author, said he 'would rate it the most moving book about our people I have ever read.'[12]

But the reaction in England was instructively different. Reviewers there either praised the technique, or treated the novel as a *Bildungsroman*. 'It is a story of schooldays in Wales', said the *Telegraph*. 'It tells the story of three boys growing up in Wales', according to the *Sunday Times*; and the *Church Times* recommended it as 'a novel written on the theme of adolescence with great and virtuous economy.' Note that Wales is treated as if it were merely the location of the action, a location that is made to seem extrinsic rather than intrinsic to the business of growing up – which is mentioned as if it were always and everywhere the same. Reviewers did mention that 'the boys have very different backgrounds – a country parsonage, a seaside town and a small farm.' But they clearly failed to understand how these fit together and amount to a single coherent social picture. The difference between the English and the Welsh responses to *A Toy Epic* is, I think, very revealing. It shows that the novel is an insider job – a view of Wales *by* someone who knows it from the inside, written *for* those who know it from the inside. Inherent in the narrative pattern of the novel is a structural analysis of Welsh society during the thirties – arising from an understanding of the historically grounded structure of oppositions and correlations that characterized that society.

The writing is consistently informed by a supple, acute and attentive social intelligence. Take, for example, the scene where the three boys go to the County School for the first time to sit the entrance scholarship examination. The Welsh-speaking farmboy, Iorwerth, is the most distressed of the three. 'Oh, the minutes of pain and apprehension, pain in the stomach sitting in a large, strange, yellow desk, in a strange well-windowed yellow room' (40). The implacable foreignness of his surroundings is conveyed by the sequence of repeated words that stake out the social experience that's fencing him in. A gowned teacher enquires authoritatively: '"Who wanted this paper in Welsh?" He looks around, eyebrows and paper raised.' The use of zeugma allows the author to bring out the highly charged inner meaning of the physical gesture. 'I, Iorwerth, suddenly remember, it seems the last moment, that I had been told that I did. In the room my arm alone is raised.' The assonantal link between 'eyebrows' and the word 'I' suggests the way Iorwerth is suddenly made to re-view and to re-experience himself in the moment of this encounter. He is bewildered into painfully new self-awareness, and so names himself anew – 'I, Iorwerth' – at the same time realizing that in this company his very name marks him down as a curiosity, a Welsh-speaker. The verbal paralleling of 'raised paper' with 'raised hand' highlights the way he is forced, shamingly, to identify himself in a public action that immediately singles him out and sets him apart.

These self-reflexive aspects of the style subtly render the torments of Iorwerth's precocious self-consciousness, in a tortuous monologue that contrasts poignantly but also comically with Michael's blithe one-liner. 'The English paper was easy, said Michael, and I wrote a lot about Long John Silver' (40). The untroubled boyishness of Michael's mind is captured in the blurted, unguarded exclamatoriness of his sentence, which is very much in the spirit of the English schoolboy books he has read. The conjunction 'and' runs two potentially self-contained grammatical sentences together into a single helter-skelter of impulsive feeling. There is transparent relief here, certainly, at finding the feared exam easy. But there is also genuine unconscious testimony to the transporting power of English children's literature. Elsewhere in the novel Emyr Humphreys makes it plain that this literature is not innocent universal romance – that it is ideologically loaded, both in terms of its class origin and its specifically English provenance. But here he recognizes the power of this literature to excite, stimulate and thus develop the young imagination – a power conspicuously lacking in the pious missionary tracts with which the Welsh language tries to satisfy young minds.

Paraphrasing Raymond Williams we might say that society in Wales must be taken at its full weight before there can be any significant form in English known as 'the Welsh novel' – as distinct from regional literature. This passage from *A Toy Epic* shows us what it's like to be alive to the way life in Wales generates its own closed system of meanings, central to which has been, during this century, the interplay between the two cultures. Emyr Humphreys is determined to explore the habits of mind and the social preoccupations that characterize the Welsh in their dealings with each other. So his novel proceeds to deal, on native grounds, with the conflicts that not only provided the structure of Welsh life but were woven into its very fabric during the thirties – chapel versus church; nonconformity and labour; industrial townships and rural life; the language-difference with resultant *Kultur-kampf*; and so on. These are all investigated at the point at which they enter into people's lives and colour their relationships. Above all, they are treated as constituents of individual consciousness and features of personality. Consequently, individual consciousness becomes the site of social conflict.

Emily Dickinson once famously wrote about 'internal difference,/ Where the Meanings, are'.[13] Wrench her phrase completely out of context, and it seems to me to be very apt for my present purpose. The meaning of modern Wales is inseparable from Wales's internal differences. Indeed one could almost say that Wales is held together by its differences – those differences that matter so passionately and peculiarly to us, that they baffle outsiders. The business of the authentically Welsh writer is to honour those differences by taking them seriously, on their own terms – in short, by recognizing their significance. Emyr Humphreys does that. Emlyn Williams, in *The Corn is Green*, does not.

5

A Corner of Wales

'I was brought up in a broad valley in one of the four corners of Wales.'[1] From the very beginning, *A Toy Epic* puts itself firmly on the Welsh map. Indeed it fills out that map, by reaffirming the Welshness of a part of Wales that tends to be overlooked whenever the Welsh construct a mental image of their country. The other three corners leap instantly to mind, at least in the form of the outdated stereotypes by which many continue to take their national bearings. The industrialized proletarian South, the rural West, the craggy fastness of the North-West are familiar fixed points of reference. But the North-East of Wales has never captured the public, or the literary imagination. It remains an unknown quantity, an unexplored locality the character of whose Welshness seems to be undecided, even problematic. As such, it is a region eminently available for use by a writer who wants to dispense with stereotypes in order to discover and develop more accurate views of the Welsh scene.

And of course it goes without saying that Emyr Humphreys was himself born and raised in this neglected corner. There is indeed a good, close fit between the fictional landscape of *A Toy Epic*, spreading from secluded inland valley down to the brash seaside holiday resort of Llanelw, and the actual geography of the novelist's home patch, which extended from inland, upland Trelawnyd to coastal Rhyl and Prestatyn. There is also no doubt an intimate, if intricate relationship between the growing pains suffered by Michael and his friends and Emyr Humphreys's own experiences of growing up. But if *A Toy Epic* is therefore partly a sympathetic study of the milieu that originally made him, it is also in part a record of what he subsequently made of that milieu, in the light of the fire lit by Saunders Lewis and his nationalist companions at Penyberth, Llŷn, in 1936.[2]

Emyr Humphreys's imagination was kindled by that fire. He was a non-Welsh-speaking sixth-former in Rhyl County School at the time, and just beginning to be excited by what Saunders Lewis had written in

English about eighteenth-century Welsh literature.[3] This discovery of a rich Welsh culture which had hitherto been concealed from him, took on a sharply political significance following the burning by Plaid Cymru members of a training school to teach aerial bombing which an imperious London government had insisted on establishing in the Llŷn peninsula, in spite of virtually unanimous Wales-wide opposition. For Emyr Humphreys the fire highlighted Wales's colonial status. Thereafter he could not fail to see the signs of socio-political subservience wherever he looked, and *A Toy Epic* is a re-reading of his own early background in these revealing terms. In particular it shows how pitifully common was the experience of culture-shame, a state of mind in which the Welsh language came to be regarded as a badge of social inferiority. In their different yet related ways, both the maid Mary and Michael's mother contrive to Anglicize the boy pretty thoroughly. As for Albie, well his full name, Albert Jones, shows him to be a strange cultural hybrid – his commonplace Welsh surname being preceded and dignified by the name of imperial Victoria's beloved spouse. Moreover the 'Cambrian Avenue' in which his council house is situated is a comically grandiose Victorian street-name redolent of English attempts to add a patronizingly Latinate glamour and a patina of antiquity to the humble Welsh word 'Cymru'. His simple, good-natured father Dick is a closet Welsh speaker, happy to use the familiar language on the sly, as if indulging in a forbidden vice, when Iorwerth comes to stay. But his status-conscious mother, no doubt remembering the time she spent 'in service' as a skivvy, is determined that Albie shall not be, like her, a member of the Welsh-speaking under-class. The pity of it is that the mother's socially induced culture-shame is changed into a disabling condition of cultural deprivation and historical ignorance in the case of her son, who simply does not know where on earth he is.

It was Saunders Lewis who, through his written work and his public actions, saved the young Emyr Humphreys from a similar fate. Lewis enabled him to put the Trelawnyd–Rhyl area on the map by making him see it as one of the 'four corners of Wales'. Emyr Humphreys was able to get his bearings by seeing his own locality in relation to the rest of Wales and by understanding it in terms of Welsh history. In the process he discovered that his native Flintshire had already produced two outstanding Welsh novelists in Daniel Owen and E. Tegla Davies, and that discovery was very important to his own development as a writer.[4] As can be inferred from *A Toy Epic*, Emyr Humphreys was from the beginning very interested in the experimental fictional

techniques of modernist writers like Joyce, Lawrence, Woolf and
Faulkner. But he also identified with what he came to term the 'North
Wales school of writers'. Prominent among them was the great fiction
writer Kate Roberts, who, although she was a native of Caernarfonshire
in the north-west corner of Wales, spent the last years of her long life,
until her death in 1985, living and writing in Emyr Humphreys's north-
east corner of the country.[5] In the essay on 'The Welsh Novel' that he
published in *Lleufer* a few years after *A Toy Epic* appeared, Emyr
Humphreys emphasized that in north Wales a deeply traditional
'peasant' culture had modulated by the end of the nineteenth-century
into a conservative middle-class way of life with the chapels at its
centre.[6] This ethos produced novels of high moral seriousness that,
after the fashion of Bunyan's *Pilgrim's Progress* and William Williams's
eighteenth-century poem of spiritual conversion, *Theomemphus*,
examined the frequently tormented condition of the individual soul.[7] It
can easily be seen that *A Toy Epic* is itself a novel that translates this
tradition into modern, largely secular terms, as it traces the soul-
searching and soul-making psychological development of three young
men, each of whom undergoes some kind of conversion experience, and
each of whom unconsciously (or consciously in Iorwerth's case)
patterns his life on the religious model, thinking in terms of a 'vocation',
a 'destiny' and so on.

   In that same *Lleufer* article Emyr Humphreys also contrasted the
north-Wales novels with the English-language novels associated with
another corner of Wales, namely the south-east. There the new
cosmopolitan society of the industrial valleys produced, from the
thirties onwards, a colourfully picaresque and panoramic fiction suited
to the varied and rapidly changing world the writers knew. Appreciative though he is of the verve and brio of their work, Emyr Humphreys
has always had reservations about their achievement. They seem to him
to be dissipating their talents in a form of verbal exhibitionism that is
not infrequently calculated to catch the ear of the English. 'In this
respect', he once laughingly observed,

> I thank God that I was born a north-Walian and I don't have the golden
> endless eloquence of the south-Walians, so that being economical comes
> natural! In my writing I try to use as few words as possible, because this
> is one way of partially reflecting the great glories of the epigram-
> matically terse Welsh poetic tradition as opposed to the oral tradition
> which lies behind the south Wales style, where the flourishing of many
> words is considered to be the acme of 'the bard'.[8]

The concise yet lyrical style of writing in *A Toy Epic*, upon which many reviewers commented very favourably when the novel first appeared, was partly a style deliberately adopted by the author in conscious opposition to the flamboyant manner of writers from the south-east corner of Wales, which to the ignorant outside world had come to seem quintessentially Welsh. An alternative, corrective, definition of 'Welshness' is therefore implicit in the very style, as well as in the subject-matter of *A Toy Epic*.

One corner of Wales remains to be mentioned, and that is the south-west. This is the region diametrically opposite on the map to the north-east in which *A Toy Epic* is set, and a similarly oblique relationship exists between the novel and that other classic of boyhood and adolescence, Dylan Thomas's *Portrait of the Artist as a Young Dog*, which for the most part is set in the author's home town of Swansea.[9] The *Portrait* is very much a charmingly provincial work that sets out to capture the somewhat naïve flavour of life in a part of Wales regarded as being a remote and backward corner of a London-orientated Britain. In that respect, the contrast with *A Toy Epic*, which is resolutely Welsh in its terms of reference, could not be more marked. But what the two works have in common is the highly charged atmosphere of the period in which they are both set – the inter-war period of the twenties and thirties. Both works, having been written either during or after the Second World War, are salvage operations mounted by the imagination, attempts to reclaim a lost personal and social world, and this process of historical recovery gives point and lends poignancy to both narratives. But here again they meet only to differ, with the *Portrait* being keyed to the fantasies of private life, while in *A Toy Epic* personal affairs are ultimately inseparable from the social problems, economic difficulties, class tensions, spiritual crises and political ideologies of a whole society at a clearly given point in its history.

It is in particular seen, with the benefit of hindsight, to be a society over which the coming war casts an ever darkening shadow. The County School days of the three boys in *A Toy Epic* begins with a mention of the 'faded sepia' photograph on the wall of pupils killed in the 1914–18 war, 'boys in uniform, with sad surprised faces' (50): and they end with the news of the young airman Jac Owen's death and with newspaper reports of troops massing for an armed offensive. The book constantly gives the impression of lives helpless before the might of historical forces, an impresssion that is ironically confirmed by Michael's innocently confident belief that he will be able to fight the war on his own terms. Fate bears down on the boys as remorselessly as the bus which heedlessly pushes Michael's car into the ditch at the novel's close. There are also eerie symmetries in the narrative that suggest confinement and hint at the inescapable. The car's collision with the bus is, for example, anticipated very early in the novel when Albie's father comes home one day shaken by the near-miss he has had with a car that came racing towards his bus.

The war is not only, however, a catastrophe visited from without upon a peaceful society. It is in part a climactic expression of the tension and violence that is intermittently felt to inhere in that society. It is, for instance, noticeable that soldiers are sent to break up the 1926 strike in which Albie's father is involved; and Iorwerth's visit, just before the war, to the bigoted barber who wants to line all nationalists up against the wall and shoot them, leads to a prophetically nightmarish vision of the violently intolerant little man, '[swollen] into the shape of a Monster of Unreason able to crush whole streets of cities under his blind merciless boot' (105). Moreover, Iorwerth's timid life has its own fearful symmetry. Shortly after leaving the barber's shop his apprehensive eye notices the confectionary shop where the 'shining steel arms' of the sweet-making machine, 'twist the stiff toffee' (109). It reminds us of the gaily rattling, chattering hay-chaffer which tore off and chewed up one of Iorwerth's fingers in the barn when he was a little boy.

*   *   *

'I was brought up in a broad valley in one of the four corners of Wales. On fine days from my bedroom window I saw the sea curve under the mountains in the bottom right-hand corner of the window frame' (17). The short outward journey from secluded inland community to sophisticated seaside resort takes on considerable significance in another Emyr Humphreys novel, *Flesh and Blood*, but it most clearly serves as a *rite de passage* in *A Toy Epic*.[10] Iorwerth and Michael step out of the confining frame of their young boyhood when they step on board the bus that carries them to the entrance scholarship exam in Llanelw. 'I stand alone and put my hand out proudly to the big-nosed bus', says Iorwerth. 'Obediently it stops.' Up until then the bus has come to the village and gone in its own mysterious time, just as the boys have been usually subject to events rather than directing them. For them to stop the bus is therefore to take a big step forward into a different relationship with the world.

The episode clearly marks a new stage in the development of Michael and Iorwerth, and the novel is itself of course no more than a sequence of such stages in the growth to maturity of the three boys. In a biological sense that process is as simply predetermined and predictable as Iorwerth's 'calf-like' growth 'from the semi-twilight of the darkened kitchen to the sharp light of the empty front garden' (17). Indeed the progress of the boys is repeatedly associated with the imagery of light and dark. But as the novel proceeds, this imagery is increasingly used to qualify, rather than to endorse, the initial impression that young humans grow as simply as young calves, or as a 'leaf opens like a baby's fist and grows towards the sun' (38).

'As I ran from the shade of the entry into the May sunshine trapped in our small square back garden, said Albie, Mrs Blackwell came hurrying up the entry, her shoes untied, her coat open, and out of breath' (28). The passage reminds us of Iorwerth's movement from kitchen twilight to garden sunlight, and so makes us note the decisive influence that the different social environments, of ninety-acre farm and cramped council-house estate, have on the development of the boys' contrasting personalities. Nevertheless the universal characteristics of the several inescapable phases of physical and mental development, from the first sensuous apprehension of the world in infancy ('crumbs lying white and edible near me on the floor' [17]) to the complicated narcissism of adolescence, are sensitively registered in *A Toy Epic*. Also carefully traced is the way in which a sense of selfhood evolves, partly through an inner dynamic and partly through the contribution of external and environmental factors. Initially it is the relationship with parents and neighbourhood that matters, then later the choice of friends and the general influence of one's peer-group proves decisive. But always and throughout the process of becoming a person is fraught with difficulties, and *A Toy Epic* implies that all three boys end up with personalities that are less than complete, owing to stunted emotional growth and arrested development.

Albie is the one who is most clearly seen to suffer, riddled as he is with anxieties that are the product of his basic social insecurity. Rock solid though his parents' genuinely unconditional love for him may be, it is still undermined by Albie's early, permanently unsettling intuition that family life is at the mercy of some remote, capricious power – the 'them' his father defers to and grumbles about, to whom his father owes the borrowed authority of his peaked cap, and with whom the bus-driver comes into bloody conflict only to be put in his place even by his own unsympathetic wife. One of the most powerful scenes in the novel is the one where a pitifully bewildered Albie is dragged by the hand into the suffocating middle of a crowd of strikers. Mounting panic causes him to faint. Traumatized by the primitive agony of self-annihilation which is at the heart of such experiences, he constructs a false self as a defence against a threateningly unpredictable environment.[11] He becomes compliant in order not to be exposed and conspicuously conforms to parental and institutional expectations. He cultivates obedience, affects composure, and becomes precociously adult, at the expense of feelings within him which are never allowed to contribute, in the normal way, towards the process of gradual maturation. It is these unintegrated feelings that are brought disastrously into play by his relationship with Frida during what, for Albie, is bound to be an exceptionally confusing adolescence.

It is clear, then, that an environmental deficiency which is specifically social in character, has an intimate effect on Albie's development. Accordingly his opening description of his surroundings eventually takes on an ominous double significance: 'At three and a half I played in the cul-de-sac, and numbers 13, 14, 15, 16, 17 and 18 stood on guard about me, watching me with square indifferent eyes' (17). The phrase 'stood guard about me' allows initially for the possibility of the houses being Albie's protective guardians: but his possessive later use, in adolescence, of prison-imagery, alerts us to the likelihood that these houses are seen as warders who had already imprisoned his tender embryonic ego.

In Albie's young eyes his house is merely a number virtually indistinguishable from other numbers, but Iorwerth Hughes is known from the beginning in his neighbourhood as 'Iorwerth Maesgwyn'. The family farm is indeed central to his identity, and therein perhaps lies his problem. Iorwerth's naturally timorous character shrinks from any robust, educative contact with the world beyond Maesgwyn where his father and mother are veritable icons of dependability, sitting one each side of the fire in winter 'like two figures on a Christmas card' (32). But even on the farm he is not fully protected from the world's malice, and his innocent wish to share the 'ecstasy' of the chaffing machine results in a physical maiming which also scars him mentally for life. Iorwerth accordingly develops an imagination for disaster, and a dread, in the Kierkegaardian sense, of violence – that is, it both fascinates and appalls him.

On occasions his neurosis endows him with visionary powers. He it is who foresees the carnage to come, when he imagines Jac Owen's body floating 'on the water like a dead fish' (107). And it is he who gains a vision of the casual brutality of modern town life in the form of an imagined glimpse of a boy cyclist caught on the turn by a car and catapulted acrobatically through the air into another car. Prone always to identify with the victims of violence, Iorwerth puts himself in the dying boy's place: 'I drown, I swirl like seaweed in my own thick red blood' (57). The sensation of being overwhelmed by a deluge comes to each of the three boys at some point in their young lives and is expressive of a whole period's vague but persistent sense of impending catastrophe. But the threat of drowning is particularly real to Iorwerth, to whom life on the farm is like being brought up 'at the headquarters of Noah, in an anchored ark' (17).

His fearful mind takes refuge in reassuringly familiar religious beliefs and in early adolescence he seeks the sanctuary of a parentally approved 'vocation'. Like Albie he develops a false self in order to cope with everything that is threatening both in the external world and in the internal world of his own turbulent feelings. Consequently his genuine capacity for goodness becomes distorted into a nervously censorious priggishness. However, whereas Albie suffers from an instability in his social surroundings, Iorwerth suffers instead from an excessive stability in his over-protective family background. Unfortunately this background does not fail him or frustrate him, as in a sense he actually needs it to, if he is to grow less totally trusting of it and therefore less totally dependent upon it. He is never led on to the perception that a relatively (rather than an absolutely) dependable family circle and a relatively (rather than a totally) undependable wider world are both part of a single indivisible continuum of normal human experience. Consequently he is quite unable to handle those shocks and disappointments that eventually come close to 'home', like his father's terminal illness and his girlfriend Dilys's flirtation with his best friend Michael.

As for Michael, he has problems of his own, although it is perhaps his distinctive self-possession that first attracts attention. His privileged social background provides him with an inbuilt confidence, and he is on easy terms with authority because he could, after all, 'watch the parson in his white and distant surplice, with the inward knowledge that I could sit on his knee and even put my finger inside his hard gleaming collar' (18). Yet while he relishes the advantages that come with social

superiority he also successfully rebels against his strict moral background without ever really losing his father's favour. In the village
school Wil Ifor, the biggest troublemaker, becomes his friend, and then
later he loves to slink off from the County School in the company of the
bullying delinquent, Jac Owen. He offends his father repeatedly and
quarrels with him outright over matters of faith. But having in these
ways emphatically established his independence (as Iorwerth and Albie
clearly fail to do) he is reconciled to his father in his late teens on terms
that promise to be solid and lasting.

In all these respects Michael's development would seem to be
admirably normal and successful, so in what way exactly can his
personality, in its final form, be said to be deficient? It is Albie's
unappreciated girlfriend Ann who spells it out, in characteristically
forthright fashion, at the very end of the novel: 'really you know, deep
down, he's a very cold person. He treats people as if they were all the
same, all objects, all . . . oh, I don't know how to put it. I'm not clever'
(118). 'Clever' psychologists have in fact coined a term to describe
personalities of Michael's sort. They call them 'schizoid' and draw
attention to the difficulties such people have in experiencing normal,
humanly appropriate emotions. They are essentially detached and
isolated individuals, and tend to regard others as their intellectual
inferiors, fit only for exploitative manipulation. Indeed, a passion for
ideas, accompanied by an arrogant pride in intellect tends to be a
schizoid characteristic and Michael's obsession, towards the end of the
novel, with the ideology of nationalism conforms precisely to type. So
does his earlier sense of his own hollowness and his conviction that life
is nothing but a succession of roles and masks.[12]

A schizoid disorder is generally supposed to originate in a disturbance in a child's relationship to its mother, and it is noticeable that
Michael's mother is both a cooler and an appreciably weaker presence
in the novel than are the mothers of the other two boys. Here again
there are social factors to be considered. Hyper-anxious as she is about
observing the manners of the English middle-class, Michael's 'well-
bred' mother is always respectably reserved, avoids any display of
maternal feelings, and employs a maid to look after the children. 'In the
garden', Michael suggestively remarks, 'my mother always wore
gloves' (18): there is similarly no flesh-warmth and no intimate sense of
touch in her relationships with her children. Even her anger is cold, as
Michael indicates when he recalls what happened on the horrifying
occasion in his early boyhood when she discovered that he had misspent

most of the money she had entrusted to his care: 'I . . . knew that my father was not in the house and that my mother disliked scenes' (35).

As the three boys grow up together, each chooses one of the others as his model of perfection, believing his friend to be possessed of wonderful strength precisely where he secretly feels himself to be weakest. So they are joined together in a neurotically intimate circle of elective friendship, with Albie admiring Michael's charming self-possession, Michael covertly envious of Iorwerth's warmth and 'goodness', and Iorwerth attracted to Albie's worldly sophistication. Moreover each one develops a 'crush' on the other, as the awakening sexuality of early adolescence gives an intensely physical aspect to these complex interrelationships. And since these friendships are the outgrowth and confirmation of established features of the boys' innermost personalities, then they are the template of all their later friendships. So, for instance, Albie's infatuation with the coolly self-confident Frida replicates his earlier fascination with Michael. And following the end of his affair with Frida it is to Michael that Albie returns, wishing that Ann and the others were not there so that he could discuss his problems with the friend who is also, in a sense, his *alter ego*.

A Toy Epic therefore shows us human growth under a complex double aspect. On the one hand it shows us the remarkable distance that is covered in a relatively short space of time, as infants grow up, and as the boys move from the restricted world of childhood into the immense world of adult experience – from the valley to Llanelw, and beyond to Chester, to Oxford, and in the direction of an ominously sensed Europe. On the other hand it shows us how the pattern and pace of personal growth is prescribed at a very early stage by one's primary relationship with one's parents and one's immediate environment: 'I was brought up in a broad valley . . . My name is Michael' (17). The whole history of Michael's identity can indeed be read in that single opening statement.

And since the main subject of *A Toy Epic* is the mysterious process of constant change that constitutes the inner dynamic of human personality, it is appropriate that one of the books studied by the boys at County School should be Ovid's *Metamorphoses*. In the form of marvellously baroque myths of fabulous transformations, that book provides insights into the endless fluidity of the passional life that lies at the very heart of human existence. Since it deals primarily with sexual psychology, and with what Ovid calls 'the strange mutations of love', his book has a particular applicability to adolescence. Indeed Michael's adolescent imagination inhabits a troubling world that is similar both to Ovid's and to that of the Welsh *Mabinogion*: 'I know that I am on the threshold of a world governed by inscrutable forces and in the deepest forest of this new continent lies a bright fountain, the source of beauty and horror, of a new joy and a new sadness, of perpetual unrest' (71). Metamorphosis is not, however, an experience confined to adolescence, and insofar as it implies a perception of both personal and communal life as involving endless change it is perhaps the figure that governs the whole of *A Toy Epic*. Emyr Humphreys could well have taken for epigraph the lines that open *The Metamorphoses*: 'Now I shall tell of things that change, new being/ Out of old: since you, O Gods, created/ Mutable arts and gifts, give me the voice/ To tell the shifting story of the world'.[13]

*   *   *

'So Jac Owen became an unlikely Icarus', thinks Iorwerth, marvelling at the way the school bully has metamorphosed into an airforce hero (107). People do, after all, change with changing circumstances, and *A Toy Epic* is very much a novel not only about changing selves but about a changed and changing world. A startled and incredulous Albie notices the stealthy appearance of houses 'in the very spaces where the grey donkeys from the seashore ate thistles and nettles during our first years at school' (61–2). But whereas Albie can hardly believe his eyes, Iorwerth can, from an early age, feel change in his very bones, just as the painful joints of a rheumatic can feel every change in the weather. Because, in spite of his unshakeable family background, Iorwerth is clearly the child of a disappearing culture – the rural, Welsh-speaking, chapel-based way of life that is in rapid decline throughout the time he is growing up. And although he attempts to carry on the Non-conformist tradition, he is doomed to fail, because a great culture-shift has denied him the very resources that are needed to combat social change. In this context, too, his maiming seems to be symbolically appropriate.

The novel provides us with several powerful images of Iorwerth's shortcomings in his capacity of heir to a culture. When he carries food out to his father, who is 'wield[ing] his bill-hook with ardent pleasure' as he practises the ancient skilled craft of hedging, the delicate little boy is 'well wrapped up' against the cold (21). Much later, during his father's illness, Iorwerth takes over the running of the farm, only to be overrun by the work. He lacks the authority needed to keep the labourer Jacob Tŷ Draw under control by cutting short the tales he endlessly spins and getting him and Llew back to the fields. Iorwerth just is not up to the game his father is so accustomed to playing.

Moreover in the recent past a toper like Jacob would never have been allowed near the farm. But now 'experienced hands are very hard to get. The young men are turning their backs on the land, going off to work in the seaside resorts or the big towns in England' (92–3). Nor are they entirely to blame, as the rural under-class live in a state of chronic poverty such as the town proletariat can scarcely even imagine. Iorwerth remembers the air of hopelessness that seemed to seep out of the very walls of Wil Ifor's house. That is why he cannot understand why Albie should complain about the hardship of the urban working class.

Albie's father, who is also Wil Ifor's uncle Dick, was one of those who left the country in search of better conditions, and so Albie too is the child of social change, a child of the working class. He is also the means by which his parents hope to bring about a further change in the family's social condition. Education is the ladder of social advancement, and Albie's mother 'sees in her vision a divine system of education select me for praise and distinction out of the side streets and the council houses, and save me from becoming an errand boy and cycling down blind alleys' (44). It is significant that the terms used here are a secularized version of the old religious language. The Calvinistic culture from which Albie's family no doubt originally came, had, it will be remembered, traditionally employed a highly sophisticated theological terminology of personal election and salvation through grace.

But in the secularized Welsh world of the thirties the making of the soul was becoming more the work of the school than of the chapel. No wonder that when he boards the bus bound for County School, Iorwerth is attired like a little latter-day pilgrim. 'I have a satchel on my back which contains my lunch, a ruler, pencils, a pen and a bottle of ink' (39). Already the education system has divided the local community and thereby destroyed it. It has promoted and transported Michael and Iorwerth to a distant County School and left a sulky Wil Ifor and other 'failures' to rot in the village. It is against this aspect of his schooling that Albie, for so long the anxious conformist, eventually reacts. Under the guidance of Marxism he tries, at least in imagination, to re-establish a sense of common cause, or class solidarity, with the 'errand boy' from whom his mother was so anxious to separate him. Sadly he ends up cycling down a 'blind alley' himself – the victim of the system which he had confusedly tried to challenge, destroyed by the conflict between conformist and rebel in his own divided personality. Frida is cruelly right when she taunts him with the barbed accusation that he is a working class conservative and a *petit bourgeois* proletarian.

Iorwerth also falls victim to the system, but in a different way. To Iorwerth's bewilderment, the supervisor smirks when the boy asks to be allowed to sit the entrance scholarship paper in his native Welsh. The country lad is as yet too naïve to realize that the state education system is the instrument deliberately used by the English government since the end of the nineteenth century to Anglicize the whole culture of the country – with the active collaboration of Welsh people who had been made ashamed of their supposed social backwardness. 'Bechgyn', says the mocking word over the boys' entrance to Llanrhos County School. It means 'boys' but could be better translated by a sentence echoing the inscription over the gates of Dante's hell: 'Abandon hope all ye Welsh speakers who enter here.' Once he is alerted to his danger, Iorwerth, like Albie, tries to protect himself from the worst influence of the school regime. As an alternative, though, he has only the superannuated culture of the chapel upon which to call, and as the preacher's sermon on the Deluge most clearly shows, it has deteriorated into a culture that appeals only to those who feel they have been defeated by history.

'We are enchanted, transfigured', says Iorwerth of the experience of listening to the spiritual histrionics of the preacher famous for his eloquence. They are metamorphosed, and transported to 'a world woven by his voice' (87). The sermon is of the type known as a 'jeremiad', which prophesies that doom will befall the people because they have left the God of their fathers and gone whoring after strange gods. The preacher likens the condition of Wales and its 'diseased twentieth-century culture' to the state of Babylon at the time of Noah, when life in 'the cities of the plains' was so decadent and corrupt that God in his wrath sent a Flood to drown the whole earth. But the jeremiad is simultaneously a terrifying and a consoling form of address.[14] Although it threatens, it does so in terms that suggest a remedy is still to be found in a return to the old traditional ways. It allows the deepest fears and anxieties of a bewildered people to surface in apocalyptic visions, yet reassures them that it is the enemy, the powerful oppressor, the rulers of the earth, the unredeemed who will suffer and that the chosen people will indeed be ultimately saved.

In style, the old preacher's sermon is a throw-back to those of the famous 1904 revival, a Wales-wide phenomenon which, as Emyr

Humphreys explained in *The Taliesin Tradition*, 'can be variously interpreted as the last desperate gesture of a people aware in their subconscious mind that their age-old faith was leaving them, or the first of a series of twentieth-century identity crises.'[15] Iorwerth is stirred and comforted by an address which is, in more senses than one, delivered in his own language. After all, hasn't the Bible been to him what tales of schoolboy adventure were to Michael – the book of wonders upon which his starving young imagination eagerly fed? Has he not even consoled himself in school that he was 'the Israelite in Babylon'? (67)

Iorwerth is not alone in thinking of Llanelw as a kind of Sodom or Gomorrah – as being one of the latter-day 'cities of the plains.' The very name of the place is revealing. It may have been based on 'Llanelwy', the Welsh name for St Asaph, the cathedral town a few miles from Trelawnyd [Newmarket] and Rhyl. But by pointed contrast the word 'Llanelw' literally means the 'Church of profit', a place-name well suited to the cynically commercialized 'Pleasureland' that the coastal resort sets out to be. It offers the boys all the excitements, enticements and entanglements of a restlessly sophisticated, rootless, provincial town. It packs people together but does not bind them into a community, although it may awaken in some, like Albie, a rudimentary awareness of belonging to a single exploited 'class'. Iorwerth notices 'the washing of various households almost touching each other, one man's wet shirt rubbing against his neighbour's vest' (55). It also easily blinds people to the reality of the world in which they're living: so Iorwerth fails actually to see the accident in which the cyclist is killed because 'at the precise moment my eyes were intent on a pyramid of glistening bottles of jam in a grocer's window' (57). Meanwhile the exciting disaster of 'a car flying over the precipice' (56) which he had enjoyed as fantasy in the warm darkness of the cinema, is being metamorphosed, behind his back and in 'the harsh light of the afternoon', into the real-life disaster of a boy being 'knocked . . . through the air against a stationary car by the opposite pavement' (57).

'*From fire and brimstone, from the doomed city, fly!*' sings Michael in mock preacherly tones towards the end of the book (113). But as the final chapter is designed to show, there is no ready escape route available for any of the boys. When Albie despairingly discovers that for him 'all roads led back to Llanelw', he is unwittingly speaking for his friends as well, in spite of Michael's determination to save Iorwerth 'from the new Nineveh that skirts the innocent sands. He must not be among the crowd I once saw in a dream, streaming into Llanelw on the

eve of its destruction, in pursuit of green money rolling. As they entered
the city they were consumed in a green fire' (117). There are echoes here
of those sinister places mentioned in Bunynan's *Pilgrim's Progress* –
'Vanity Fair' and the 'City of Destruction'.

Escape by means of retreat into the supposedly idyllic country of the
past is what the boys attempt in the last chapter. Their break for
freedom is also a search for paradise, but all they find is evidence of the
Fall, within them, between them and around them. They attempt to re-
enter a supposedly innocent world of childhood – Michael 'imitates a
child counting out' as the others scatter in the game of hide-and-seek
(114). As he climbs towards the martello tower (a relic of a past war)
Iorwerth looks forward to recovering his early valley-perspective on
life, believing that 'we shall have a wonderful view of the coast' (112).
Instead, Les and Albie fall to quarrelling about what features of
Llanelw they can see at this distance. ' "I'm not mistaken," says Albie.
"I know every stone of the old Sodom only too well" ' (113). All roads
do indeed lead back to Llanelw, and the only hope is to find not a retreat
from the town, but a way through it and beyond it.

*   *   *

'I shall dedicate myself to the country whose beauties about me I always
linger over now, with loyal eyes. And to people like Iorwerth who
among us all is its most direct heir. In reality he is a potent symbol,
because with all his naïve innocence, he represents the soul of Wales for
me' (116–17). He may do so for Michael, but the author does not
encourage us to share that perception. In *A Toy Epic* it is the three boys
together who are 'a potent symbol of Wales'. And they are so by virtue
of their different social backgrounds and by virtue of that incom-
pleteness in each of their characters that has already been remarked
upon. In their relationships they experience and exemplify the cultural
divisions, the language problems and the social tensions that are the sad
legacy of recent Welsh history, and which have inhibited the development of a strong and coherent sense of national identity. As the cases of
Albie and Iorwerth particularly show, it is only by somehow finding
common ground between them that the Welsh-language and English-
language cultures of Wales can hope to recover from the serious
deprivation each suffers through its isolation from the other. Yet as the
example of the two boys also shows, communication across a cultural
divide is as desperately difficult as it is desperately necessary.

'To him I am strange and foreign', says Iorwerth forlornly of Albie
(54). Although he is a boy living in a north Wales seaside resort, Albie is

clearly a product of the same historical process that brought industrial south Wales into being. His family has moved only the few miles from valley to coast, but in so doing it has undergone the same trauma of passage from one culture to another that countless families from rural west Wales experienced when they journeyed east in search of work, first to the Merthyr district and then to the roaring Rhondda valleys.[16] Like so many of them, Albie has been virtually forced to lose contact with the unique culture sustained for more than fifteen hundred years by the Welsh language. What he has gained in compensation is an embryonic sense of class, as opposed to national identity. However he has yet to learn that class-consciousness is not the supra-national, transcultural phenomenon that his Marxist reading has represented it as being. He needs to communicate with Iorwerth in order to realize exactly what is at issue, at this fateful historical juncture, for a Welshman such as himself. Equally, though, Iorwerth needs to connect with Albie if the culture to which he belongs is to have a place in the modern Wales. Yet to recognize this is also to realize that this was precisely the alliance that failed to form in the thirties, the period in which the novel is set.

The relationship between Iorwerth and Albie is, therefore, in its modest way, a kind of microcosm of recent Welsh history. It would, though, be a mistake to suppose that *A Toy Epic* mirrors only the situation as Emyr Humphreys believed it to be in the thirties. Rather it mirrors in addition the situation in Wales as Emyr Humphreys saw it in the fifties – that is in the period in which the novel was actually completed.[17] This is clear from the *Lleufer* article alrady referred to. There Humphreys argues there are two cultures in Wales, conservative Welsh-speaking and progressive English-speaking, which he broadly associates with the north and the south of Wales respectively. 'The time has come', he goes on,

> to call on the Old Wales to save the New Wales and in the process to save itself . . . Without contact with life in the South, there is a danger that the culture of the North will become a mere fossil. Without roots, and lacking all connection with the traditional North, Glamorgan may well spew all the energy of its valleys into the anonymous mid-Atlantic . . . Wales must take advantage of the special relationship existing between the North and the South. Out of this Thesis and Antithesis a Synthesis can be created for the future.'[18]

It is this 'special relationship' that Emyr Humphreys in a way explores via the relationship between Iorwerth and Albie.

It is through Michael, though, that the condition of Wales is most openly addressed in *A Toy Epic* and Emyr Humphreys and Michael evidently have a great deal in common. Both, for instance, experienced a conversion to a nationalist faith at much the same age. They are pretty well agreed too in their analysis of the Welsh problem. Yet it is imperative, when considering Michael, to recall Roland Mathias's perceptive observation that in his work Emyr Humphreys subjects his own convictions to particularly searching critical examination.[19]

Michael's background should be carefully borne in mind. He is raised in an Anglican rectory, and Anglicanism has for several centuries led a kind of double-life in Wales. With the growth of Welsh Nonconformity in the eighteenth and nineteenth centuries, Anglicanism became increasingly regarded as a foreign presence whose privileged status as the state church came under such pressure that eventually the Church in Wales was officially disestablished in 1914. Moreover Anglicanism enthusiastically collaborated with the new, state-controlled education system's programme of Anglicization in Wales. Church schools, such as the one in which Michael and Iorwerth are taught, and for that matter the one in which Emyr Humphreys's own father had been a headmaster, were usually either indifferent or hostile to the native language.

On the other hand, eccentric Anglican clerics had, as Emyr Humphreys emphasizes in his interpretion of Welsh history, *The Taliesin Tradition*, been from time to time the unlikely preservers and custodians of Welsh culture, particularly during the 'dark ages' of the eighteenth century.[20] And it was precisely the kind of scholarly antiquarian interest in the Welsh past that Michael's father displays that made them such providentially effective benefactors of Welsh culture. So in a sense these two different and conflicting aspects of Welsh Anglicanism could be said to be disputing possession of Michael's young imagination, until the issue is eventually decided by his commitment to nationalism.

Such a 'conversion experience' was not uncharacteristic of artists and intellectuals in Wales during the inter-war period – Saunders Lewis himself read English at Liverpool University before the critical state of Wales was brought home to him with the clarifying force of revelation and with the urgency of a clarion call to action. Michael is also typical of the period not only in that his political nationalism derives from a prior cultural concern, but also in that his imagination is fired by a twelfth-century poem by Hywel ap Owain Gwynedd. In other words his passion is not for the Liberal–Nonconformist Wales that Iorwerth represents, nor for the proletarian and proto-socialist Wales to which Albie belongs, but rather for an ancient 'aristocratic' Wales whose golden age was the Middle Ages. The first stirrings of his cultural awakening are felt at Penmon, and this is clearly significant since Penmon was the subject of a famous poem by T. Gwynn Jones, written in the great, intricate *cynghanedd* tradition that itself stretches back virtually unbroken to the early Middle Ages, and to an even earlier period. The majestic verbal, visual and spiritual culture of the Welsh Middle Ages is itself the subject of this poem, in which T. Gwynn Jones imagines the old Abbey walls resuming their form – 'Rich craft, its portal and door,/ Slender its marble towers:/ Heaven for the weak its hall,/ And holy every chamber.'[21]

In addition to being the work of one of the greatest of modern Welsh poets, 'Penmon' is also addressed to one of the greatest of this century's Welsh men-of-letters, W. J. Gruffydd.[22] Therefore in a sense Michael could be said to join the fraternity of nationalist artists, scholars and intellectuals when he undergoes his 'Penmon experience'. He participates in their liberating and exhilarating discovery of a Wales whose cultural achievements are far more impressive and historically extensive than most of the Welsh imagine.[23] He thereby realizes that it is not Wales that is 'narrow' but rather his own ignorantly limited conception of his country. But his education is not complete until he visits the political conference and recalls 'the history and significance of the castle.'[24] Then his vision grows militant, as he realizes that in order to survive not only will Wales have to resist current historical forces, she may also have to mount a counter-attack and take history by storm. This allows him to see how it is at bottom the defeated condition of the Welsh that has made fatalists of Albie and Iorwerth. They cannot believe that they possess the power to influence events. Of course, as has already been noted, by emphasizing the inexorable drift towards war the novel has itself to an extent confirmed the two boys' intuition of immediate helplessnesss. But it clearly repudiates Albie's whimpering, self-pitying cry: 'we are like ants with the hob-nailed boot of Fate always hovering just above our heads as we crawl over the ant-heap of History' (120). *A Toy Epic* recognizes the long-term relevance of Michael's observation that 'History is only made by those who are ready to make it' (103).

The first lesson to learn, Michael continues, 'is to accept the burden of being utterly alone' (103). Emyr Humphreys has himself many times deplored the craven clubbability of the Welsh, and has admired the principled and visionary stand of a fearless nonconformist like Saunders Lewis who, as R. S. Thomas has put it, 'dared [us] to grow old and bitter as he.'[25] Nevertheless in *A Toy Epic* Michael's isolationist stance does give cause for concern, even perhaps for alarm. It is here that the social implications of his 'schizoid' character become evident. For one thing, he has no real or realistic sense of solidarity with the very culture he professes to be protecting. His view of Iorwerth as 'the soul of Wales' is a sentimental lie, and his contemptuous dismissal of Dilys is the other side of the same false coin: 'In spite of her beauty and attractiveness the horizon of her mind was as limited and as rigid as the polished wooden rail that hemmed in the deacon's dais in her father's chapel' (116).

In the second place, Michael's heroic isolationism is presented as being morally suspect. It is tainted by egotism and exhibits megalomaniac tendencies. With his delight in 'discipline' and his fantasy of offering strong leadership, Michael is the stuff of which the authoritarian followers of the fascist right were made in the thirties. The cut on the cheek he acquires in the car accident and which he believes is Fate's way of issuing him with a challenge, is curiously reminiscent of the sinister duelling scar that indicated aristocratic young Germans had been 'blooded'.

It would be a serious mistake, though, to suppose that by the end of the novel Michael has turned villain. No, he is rather a disturbed and disturbing young man whose impending tragedy is not only a personal but also a national, historical tragedy. He illustrates the fate that can befall the intellectual who tries, in necessarily lonely defiance of his people's historically-induced apathy, to confront them with a challengingly truthful, undeniably accurate image of Wales. And he is surely perceived by the novel as being right in his convictions that only by searching the past can Wales discover the key to its future.

Behind this perception lies a discovery Emyr Humphreys made when the bombing school was burned – the discovery that modern Wales (as represented in *A Toy Epic* by Albie, Iorwerth and Michael) had for too long been prevailed upon to ignore its own history, and was consequently ignorant of its true condition. In *A Toy Epic* the myopic vision of officially sanctioned history is quietly suggested by 'the walls of Llanrhos County School' which are 'eloquent with its short history' (50). The walls commemorate only councillors, aldermen, clergymen, the young men killed in the First World War, and the pupils who have distinguished themselves academically. This is a perfect image of the establishment view of recent Welsh history. By contrast one remembers the stone walls of the old mill visited by the young people at the end of *A Toy Epic*, where 'hundreds of initials and names are scrawled over the patches of white-washed plaster' (115). They represent the unrecorded lives and disregarded history of an anonymous people.

The novel does not, however, seek to imply that a single, unchallengeable account of the whole of Welsh history remains some day to be written. Instead it allows for the possibility of there being many different, sometimes complementary and occasionally competing, versions of the past as viewed from a Welsh perspective. Michael's father traces the beginnings of modern Wales back (as Emyr Humphreys is himself fond of doing) to late Roman times. On the other hand the charismatic preacher at Iorwerth's chapel can see the time of the Roman occupation only as one of several periods of profane history, as opposed to the sacred centuries of Nonconformist influence in Wales. Iorwerth's father dreams of completing the second volume of his 'history of Calvinistic Methodism in the north of the county', a fervent member of his own denomination to the last (32). These are all rudimentary attempts to fashion a Welsh historiography in the face on the one hand of a vast popular ignorance of the past, and on the other of the temptation to indulge in an anti-historical millennarianism – a favourite recourse of the defeated. So Iorwerth dreams 'of my kingdom to come' and even Michael has to beware of a similar temptation.

One of the ways of reintroducing the nation to its own history is through providing it with conscientiously historical but compellingly imaginative fictions. Emyr Humphreys has devoted most of his long writing life to doing precisely that. Indeed it can now perhaps be seen that *A Toy Epic* is itself intended to function as at least an *aide-mémoire* for a nation. 'The struggle of man against power is the struggle of memory against forgetting' wrote Milan Kundera. In that sense *A Toy Epic* is very much Emyr Humphreys's unforgettable contribution to Wales's continuing struggle for survival.

*   *   *

When he reviewed the novel in the *New Statesman* on its first appearance in 1958, Maurice Richardson nervously assured his readers: 'There is a little Welsh Nationalism in *A Toy Epic*, but nothing untoward. This is a novel of adolescence.' He may have rather missed the point of the work, but he was perceptive when he praised its 'contrapuntal form' and appreciated the way it succeeded 'in communicating a strong sense of the passage of time and change' during the 'nodal period' of adolescence.[26] It would, though, be more true to say that *A Toy Epic* reproduces for us several significantly different experiences of Time. So, for instance, at the end of a frenzied day spent sitting the entrance-scholarship paper in the town County School, Iorwerth returns home at the regular evening milking time on the farm, and has to reacclimatize to his father's slow, deliberate way of doing things: 'Will I never learn', the boy wonders, 'to take my time, assured of my memory, skill, and above all, the abundance of time?' (47) Of course he never will learn, because he belongs to a generation which is condemned to live at an altogether different pace. No wonder Michael's new watch thuds on his wrist 'like a giant pulse' (41) as he applies his excited mind to the difficult task of answering the arithmetic paper.

Moreover, a child's sense of time is totally different from an adolescent's. In some of the early sections of *A Toy Epic* several different occasions are unconsciously run together in a small boy's mind to form a single composite scene which is a kind of summation of what 'home' means to him. For example in the section in Chapter One when Albie recalls his father coming home for tea, it is clear on reflection that two or more separate occasions have been compressed together to produce the conversation that occurs between his entry and his departure. At the other extreme are those occasions in adolescence when the youngsters begin to contrast their former with their present selves. In the case of Albie this happens at the beginning of Chapter Seven when he blushes at the memory of his earlier infatuation with Michael. Time takes on a completely different aspect therefore for the three as their past grows almost as problematic as their future.

Of course many of the works that deal with childhood employ a narrative form that allows them to explore a complex double-perspective – so that the reader is simultaneously given the child's and the adult's view of events. In *Great Expectations* incidents from the young Pip's childhood are in fact recalled for us by the mature Pip, who is an altogether different, not to say a thoroughly reformed, character. Emyr Humphreys has deliberately denied us this double vision in *A Toy Epic* by making it unclear when exactly, and how, the words in the text are being 'spoken'. Are they being spoken more or less at the time that the action occurs? They could be, in spite of the frequent use of the past tense. After all, no attempt is ever made in the novel to reproduce the actual thought processes of the characters in a realistic fashion. Instead what is offered is a clearly stylized representation of the states of mind of the different characters, at different ages and on different occasions. Accordingly when the infant Iorwerth 'says' that he 'followed my mother, going to riddle cinders, sheltering behind her skirt' (17), the words are not meant to be those that actually occurred to his mind. They simply stand for, and speak for, the kind of experience he had, and can therefore be regarded as continuous with the experience itself. In other words they are the novel's chosen, artificial way of conveying the experiences of a small boy. They are not the thoughts of a later, much older Iorwerth who is recalling his infancy.

One of the most effective features of the novel is the way it skilfully alternates between the past tense and the historic present tense. Once again it needs to be noted that there is no particular psychological significance attached to this technique – it is for reasons of dramatic effect only that the narrative switches from the one tense to the other. Occasionally this can happen in the very middle of a scene, as when Michael describes how the older boys ganged up on him when he first went to the 'big' school: 'A party of boys came strolling up towards us .. . The leader has reached us . . . "Excuse me", he says laughing' (41–2). Why, though, one might wonder, is the present tense not therefore used throughout, in order to establish a feeling of immediacy? The probable answer is because then the continuous sense of the pastness of the lives being described in *A Toy Epic* would be lost – their pastness, that is, in relation to our, the readers' present. This aspect of the narrative is perhaps clearer in *Y Tri Llais*, the Welsh version of *A Toy Epic*.[27] That novel opens with a narrator who, as he lies on a hilltop in a state between sleep and waking, hears three disembodied voices rising from the valley below, as if issuing out of the great misty gulf of the past.[28] The whole of *A Toy Epic* is therefore as much about a sense of vanished time, and is as full of a sense of belatedness, as is Dylan Thomas's *Return Journey*, which ends with the tolling park bell reminding the narrator that the children his mind's eye has seen at play are all in reality dead and gone. 'Dusk', he realizes, 'was folding the Park around, like another, darker snow.'[29] And *A Toy Epic*, too, ends on a partly elegiac note: 'The earth, bearing continents and seas, shows another hemisphere the sun, and another the outer darkness' (121).

The cycle of the seasons is used throughout the novel as a way of indicating the passage of time. But it is the calendar of the school year that is used as the real index to the boys' growth. *A Toy Epic* is divided into ten chapters, eight of which are of almost equal length while the

remaining two (Chapters Six and Eight) depart only slightly, yet
significantly, from the norm. The first three chapters cover the period
from the boys' infancy right through to the end of their days in primary
school, and this part of the novel concludes with them sitting their
entrance examination to the County School. Their first five years at that
school are then described in Chapters Four to Six and Chapters Seven to
Ten deal with their time in the sixth form, leading up to the fateful
university entrance examination which, in the final chapter, leaves the
boys very differently placed as they prepare to move on and out into
adult life. Indeed their schooling is throughout shown to play a vitally
important part in the formation of the boys' characters, in the
development of their social outlook, and in deciding the eventual course
of their lives. No wonder that large parts of the novel centre on some
aspect or other of the drama of their school careers – the whole of
Chapter Three, for example, is devoted to the experience of sitting the
scholarship exam.

   Other chapters deal not with a single event but with a single phase in
the boys' lives. So Chapter Seven is mainly about their attempts to find a
goal and purpose in life, and Chapter Eight shows them returning to
their separate home backgrounds and exploring them anew, following
both a period of absorption in their new life at County School and a
period of adolescent self-absorption. Moreover the exceptional length
of Chapter Eight marks the fact that it deals with what Albie calls 'a
long, troubled and uneasy summer' (97). Formal symmetry is sometimes used to bind the different sections of a chapter together by
bringing out the thematic correspondences between its different parts.
Chapter Two begins with Albie running from the shade of the house
entry into the May sunshine, before he is hauled reluctantly through
town by his mother and dragged into the nightmare middle of the
striking busmen. The same chapter ends with Michael being called out
of 'the green gloom' of his friend Raymond's tent into the 'harsh
sunlight', before being led home by his father in public disgrace (37).
Both episodes are moments when a boy's mind is opened to a
disturbingly new truth that affects his subsequent psychological
development.

   Structural correspondence is in fact an extremely important device in
A Toy Epic. The opening of the novel, when three voices speak in quick
successsion, is therefore not only a way of immediately establishing that
the work is a triple narrative; it is also a way of establishing the basic
principle on which the whole book is organized. The syntactical

parallelism here at the very beginning is the first example of a pattern of echo and repetition that acts as the infrastructure of the whole work. So for example the beginning of Chapter Three is a very close approximation in structure to the beginning of Chapter One. To notice the similarity is however also to be brought to reflect on the differences between the two passages. In Chapter One the boys successively describe the world that surrounds each of them in early childhood. In Chapter Three, on the other hand, the emphasis is on the different inner worlds that have in each case been created by them in the very image of their different environments.

The brief sections of which each chapter is composed are also frequently interconnected through the repetition of a word, a phrase, or a situation. Section Five of Chapter One consists of Albie's recollections of his father coming home for tea. Section Six opens with Iorwerth's memory of carrying tea out to his father in the fields. The parallelism stimulates the reader, unawares, to compare and contrast the two passages and so to notice the difference between the two milieus, the two worlds of work, the two families. Sometimes a pointed cross-reference is made from one section to another in order to highlight a social contrast. Iorwerth's mother goes to riddle the cinders in the third section of Chapter One, but it is Mary the maid who cleans the grate in Michael's middle-class home in the next section. Dick repeatedly shouts out the name of Nel, the wife around whom the life of Albie's home revolves, whereas the Rector calls for Mary 'in his deep, kind, parsonical voice' (19). At other times the links are of a more abstract or general character, as when the opening sections of Chapter Five prove, on examination, to offer variations on the theme of trust and mistrust. A particularly poignant transition occurs in Chapter Eight when Albie's failed attempt to explain to Frida exactly how it is he loves her is followed by Iorwerth's sad realization 'how ineffective my love for my father is.'

As can then be seen, the structure of *A Toy Epic* is inseparable from the novel's primary concern, which is to explore the interconnections and the divisions between three lives and between three social backgrounds. The structure is profoundly functional, just as the 'poetic' features of the novel are a fully integrated part of its particular style of psychological and social exploration. The early reviews were right when they praised the 'lyricism' of the writing, but were wrong when they treated it as if it were an adornment or a lavish accessory.

Take Iorwerth's description of his first County School assembly, for instance:

> Heads ascend behind us from form to form like the marks on the doorpost which my father has made, makes and will make to register my growth. Exceptions break through the ranks like cocksfoot grass in the hayfield, and Albie is the exception in our row. The hall is filled in the morning by one form after another, as a granary floor is covered by emptying sack after sack of corn. (51)

Beautiful though they are, these similes are first and foremost dramatic in character. In other words they are vividly expressive of the character and state of mind of the perceiver of the scene, as well as being highly evocative of the scene itself. Iorwerth brings his country mind with him to the town school, and domesticates his strange new environment by seeing it in familiar terms. And who but poor Albie, in his state of gloomy mental paralysis, would speak of trudging steadily through the exam syllabus like 'an insurance-man working his weekly way down the terrace'? (101)

It is, then, through its intrinsic qualities as well as through its extrinsic connections with the history of two periods – the thirties and the fifties – that *A Toy Epic* continues to be of worth and of interest. In its Welsh incarnation as *Y Tri Llais*, the novel is still one of the best that is available in the Welsh languge. In its English form, entitled *A Toy Epic*, it remains one of the best novels to have been written about Wales, although it is perhaps surpassed by the same author's magnificent later novel *Outside the House of Baal* (1965). Moreover while it remains, as Emyr Humphreys once put it, 'anchored in historical reality by its landscape', *A Toy Epic* also manages to make daily life in one of the four corners of Wales 'reverberate on that level outside the restrictions of time and place that is an abiding consolation of the human condition.'[30]

6

R. S. Thomas:
The poetry of the sixties [1]

Reading extensively in R. S. Thomas's poetry of the sixties, I found an image was stubbornly forming somewhere at the back of my mind. It kept presenting itself to me as a paradigm of aspects of R. S. Thomas's situation, both during that decade and indeed onward into the following decade of the seventies. Yet all it was, in simple fact, was an episode, or more strictly speaking, a brace of episodes, from R. S. Thomas's childhood as recalled in Y Llwybrau Gynt (1972):

> Another time, going to one of the parks [in Liverpool]: it is the middle of winter and the lake there is frozen over. A crowd of people are sliding on it. Near to the bank, there is a patch which has not frozen. A clergyman comes into view, sailing along like a ship with the wind behind it. Suddenly, to my astonishment, he disappears into the pool. Others come straight away to pull him out, dripping wet. He goes off, crestfallen. Life carries on. It is nice in the park in the summer as well. The breeze is full of the scent of roses. I bend over to sniff one of the flowers – but something nasty is waiting for me there! Quick as a flash it's up my nose, and I start to scream. My mother rushes over to me, scared out of her wits. After I have blown my nose like a dragon into her handkerchief, the enemy is revealed: a harmless little black fly! But I remember the experience to this day, and I still take great care when smelling a flower.[2]

Here we see how life first got up R. S. Thomas's nose – as it has done so notably and so frequently since. In its comically, but calculatedly ingenuous way, the passage is a reflection on the black treachery of life – or rather the black fly treachery of life – and how to guard against it. There are, of course, other elements in the story, such as R. S. Thomas's familiar impatience with his younger self, whom he seems often to want to represent as a cosseted mummy's boy. And in its teasingly modest way, the episode summarizes the tragi-comedy of the encounter of human dreams with reality. But above all, it embryonically suggests the twin fears that seem to me to be the two most important concerns of R. S. Thomas's poetry during the sixties; fears that correspond to the double threat of collapse from within and invasion from without. And bearing in mind those memories from childhood as related above, we could conveniently think of these threats as (a) the disappearing clergyman syndrome, and (b) the black fly syndrome.

Emily Dickinson once spoke of acquiring, in her poetry, 'that uncertain gait some call experience'. R. S. Thomas, watching an old man, sees him 'trying/ Time's treacherous ice with a slow foot. '[3] That 'slow foot' seems sometimes to be the careful measure of his own song. 'Time's treacherous ice' is, in this case, not a metaphysical nicety. It refers to the social, economic and political processes which are putting the skids under everything that makes his Wales culturally distinctive. The question, then, is how to keep one's footing, or how and where to stand one's ground.

In his comprehensive study of the Welsh-language poetry of the sixties, Alan Llwyd refers to the decade as the period when the whole tempo of life seemed to change. He then proceeds to show how a whole host of poets made this acceleration the subject of their poetry, with many deploring its consequences while a few revelled excitedly in the new opportunities – both experiential and linguistic – that the rapidly developing social and cultural situation offered.[4] R. S. Thomas was certainly not among the latter. But neither can he be simply aligned with the former, since although he shared their cultural conservatism he was not as ready as they to express it through unqualified eulogy of the 'peasant', pastoral life of a rural Wales whose time was clearly passing. A poem by perhaps the greatest of contemporary writers of *cynghanedd*, Dic Jones, himself a working farmer, can serve as an example of this genre, although due allowance must be made for the high toll the English language takes on such an irreducibly foreign form of writing:

> Yellow ears' rustle of praise
> Weaves through the valley meadows;
> Grain dances in summer haze;
> They bow to the wind's power
> From ridge to ridge, the patterns
> Of rust and gold interlaced . . .
>
> Once horns would invite our strong
> Elders to the same battle,
> Early scything's fearless men,

Forefathers of his fathers,
Old fellowship, unselfish,
Cheerful reaping's peerless troop.
Oppression had made it strong,
Hardship had made it wealthy.

Mother and children turned out,
And sweetheart, to the cornfield,
In autumn perseverance,
To tie its top-heavy gold,
And an unmatched battalion
Of craft-bound ricks clothed a ridge.

They have not, today's farmers,
One-third of the old crew's craft;
His field will hold tomorrow
Of its long gold drooping ears
Merely the battle's stubble,
And a lustreless clipped mane.[5]

R. S. Thomas himself seemed set to settle in, and to settle for, the country at the beginning of the sixties. Initially, in *Tares*, it seemed that he would stay where, as a poet, he already was; namely in Manafon. As is well known, though, his Manafon, the Manafon of the early poetry, was the product of an educative disillusionment. In the John Ormond film about his life and work, R. S. Thomas spoke of the shock of coming up against 'the harsh realities of rural life', and characterized himself, with characteristic self-deprecation, as coming 'out of a kind of bourgeois environment which, especially in modern times, is protected: it's cushioned from some of the harsher realities.'[6] What he didn't mention there, of course, was the contribution made by Welsh-language literature to the dream of rural beauty he'd brought with him to the Montgomeryshire uplands. 'To him', he wrote in *Neb*, referring to himself in the third person, 'the locality and neighbouring country was beautiful. He wished to continue to write poems of praise to the whole area. But how was he to reconcile this with the farmers' own attitude and way of life?'[7] For more than a century Welsh culture had celebrated the stock figure of cultured shepherd and farmer, who epitomized all that was best in the unique Welsh *gwerin*. And that image was not simply replaced by Iago Prytherch. It survived, in drastically modified form, as one of the several contradictory elements of which the poetic character of Iago is compounded. Furthermore, as late as 1968, the original dream could surface, with its naïvety virtually intact, in a passage from the prose-work *The Mountains*. Ruined buildings remind R. S. Thomas of the men who 'spent long days . . . swapping *englynion* over the peat cutting. They have gone now; the cuttings are deserted, *yr hafotai* in ruins.'[8] An irony worth our notice is the fact that the lonely figure of the farmer in his poetry is the product of the depopulation of the hill country that had been a feature of the preceding half-century. Yet R. S. Thomas freqently treats the figure as an emblem of the eternal condition of rural life, unchanged and unchanging. His farmer is seemingly imbued 'with a tree's patience,/ Rooted in the dark soil.'[9] This is a view of the country very different from that R. S. Thomas offers in *Neb*, when he records 'that more than thirty thousand people had left Montgomeryshire between the two world wars . . . The rector [R. S. Thomas himself] began to sing with longing of the life that had been, and of the life of loneliness and of poverty endured by those who had stayed' (51).

Still, there is no doubt that the Manafon flies did get up R. S. Thomas's nose. Their blue, uncertain, stumbling buzz can be heard throughout his many, perplexed dialogues with the gaunt, remote figure of Iago Prytherch. Yet his poetry evades much more than it admits of the realities of the region. Considered as an approximation to, let alone as an accurate report of, life in an upland rural community, the Prytherch poems are, as we all know, non-starters. As R. S. Thomas himself pointed out, the Manafon district was 'a sociologist's nightmare' – its social structure was so complicated. He himself gives an interesting analysis of that structure, and of the resultant social psychology of the area in *Neb*. The passage includes the following comment:

> The rector's name was expected to head any list of gifts, and they would then adjust their contributions according to the size of the farm: a farmer of two hundred acres would give two pounds, say, a farmer of one hundred acres one pound, and so on – as simple as that. (*Neb*, 57)

But one thing is certain. There were no 'peasants' there, in spite of this Welsh bard and his English reviewers. Indeed, when one reads the social comments passed by Anglo-American critics on these poems, one feels like referring them to Raymond Williams's wise words about the terms appropriate for a mature discussion of Hardy:

> First, we had better drop 'peasant' altogether. Where Hardy lived and worked, as in most other parts of England, there were virtually no

peasants, although 'peasantry' as a generic word for country people was still used by writers. The actual country people were landowners, tenant farmers, dealers, craftsmen, and labourers.[10]

There are, in fact, occasions when R. S. Thomas implicitly makes related points and distinctions in his poetry. For instance, he speaks very deliberately of a hired landless labourer in the poem called 'Hireling' (*Tares*, 28) and of the wealthy farmer with large capital in 'Rhodri'.[11] In other words, he sometimes allows us to glimpse a rural world which does not so much contrast with as reproduce in its own terms the capitalist structure of commercial town and industrial centres. Prosperity, greed, and materialism are not then treated as foreign imports; they are seen as endemic to the rural economy, to rural society, as they are to its urban and suburban counterparts. And this, I take it, is precisely why R. S. Thomas will not, cannot, allow us or himself to contemplate the social structure of the real Manafon for too long in his poetry. If he did, the ground would be cut from under his feet, as surely as the ice disappeared under his Liverpool clergyman's skates. R. S. Thomas's Manafon, as embodied in Iago Prytherch, exists in, and for the sake of, a contrast with the commercial and industrial capitalism which R. S. Thomas regards as the threat of Anglicization:

> He will go on; that much is certain.
> Beneath him tenancies of the fields
> Will change; machinery turn
> All to noise.   (*Pietà*, 41)

Iago Prytherch is also his great, deliberate exercise in mystification. He is the counterpart, in the earlier poetry, of the *Deus Absconditus* who is the dominant dramatis persona of the later poetry. As critics have frequently noted, and as even the poet himself has more or less agreed, the descriptions of Iago's personality border on, if they do not actually cross over into, the self-contradictory. Is he an avid, devoted reader of 'the slow book/ Of the farm'? Or is he as mindless as the soil he tills? And if he is so mindless, is he blissfully, enviably so; or brutishly so? Moroever, to pursue Iago Prytherch is, as Roland Mathias admirably showed in the special, 1972 number of *Poetry Wales*, to become entangled in R. S. Thomas's confusions about the status and character of the natural world itself.[12]

No way seems yet to have been found by commentators to dissolve these contradictions, except perhaps by seeing them as variants of the primitivism which is commonly the bourgeois towny's view of country life. After all, both the pastoral and the anti-pastoral have been popular bourgeois genres. Naturally, though, interpreters are content to talk about the Iago Prytherch poems as consisting of R. S. Thomas's arguments with himself, without enquiring too deeply into the social content, or context, of this arguing. Their explanations tend to gravitate towards these familiar opening lines of 'Servant':

> You served me well, Prytherch.
> From all my questionings and doubts;
> From brief acceptance of the times'
> Deities; from ache of the mind
> Or body's tyranny, I turned,
> Often after a whole year,
> Often twice in the same day,
> To where you read in the slow book
> Of the farm, turning the fields' pages
> So patiently, never tired
> Of the land's story; not just believing,
> But proving in your bone and your blood
> Its accuracy; willing to stand
> Always aside from the main road,
> Where life's flashier illustrations
> Were marginal.[13]

I also find these lines revealing – revealing of the need Prytherch is brought into existence to serve. To identify that need is also to begin to understand why Iago's serviceableness consists of his being an enigma; of his being inscrutable; of his being eminently visible and yet permanently beyond the reach of sight. Iago Prytherch is, for me, a most interesting temporary expedient for dealing with the centuries-old Welsh problem of how to resist the invading, appropriating, eyes of the English.

Behind not only the original construction but also the subsequent eccentric maintenance of the character lies the whole complex matter of the history and the sociology of the picturesque: 'a pose/ For strangers, a watercolour's appeal/ To the mass, instead of the poem's/ Harsher conditions.'[14] In an uncollected 1958 piece for the *Listener*, R. S. Thomas had a fair bit to say about Wales in these terms. 'Because it is a small country', he explains, 'one is always arriving.'[15] For the inhabitant, that rules out the possibility of using physical distance as a trope for the mystery and depth of one's culture – a favourite ploy, of course, of American writers. It also rules out the possibility of using physical distance or vastness as either an actual, or metaphorical, barrier against invasion. All of Wales is exposed as Border Country – a point R. S. Thomas was, however unconsciously, making when he chose to make his stand at Manafon, a mere stone's throw from Offa's Dyke. The 1958 article continues like this: 'Certainly in Wales, the country and the people have, like Mr Eliot's roses, the look of things that are looked at. How tired one is of the South Stack, anchored for ever in its monochrome calm.'

It has been fairly widely remarked that Iago Prytherch was brought into being partly by a counter-cultural, anti-picturesque impulse, but it remains to suggest that it was the same impulse, properly understood as being of national and not merely local or aesthetic origin, that kept Iago in a state of perpetually perplexing existence. It was of the essence, if he was to avoid being appropriated by the very attention the poetry invited. Therefore the more he seemed to abide R. S. Thomas's questioning, the more he remained free. One arrives at Iago very quickly in the early collections, and yet each arrival is only the point of a new departure. One could paraphrase a splendid remark made once by Hugh MacDiarmid and assert that 'the prodigiousness of Iago's character itself becomes a safeguarding excellence.' What it safeguards is the mystery of a way of life which is a synecdoche for Wales.

A useful point may be made here in passing. To the customary talk about R. S. Thomas's indebtedness to the Romantics should perhaps be added a mention of his significant adaptation of at least one important pre-Romantic genre. Some twenty years ago, Geoffrey Hartman wrote a fascinating essay on what seemed to him to be virtually the missing link between eighteenth-century poetry and Romantic poetry.[16] This link was *inscription verse* – verses written as if intended to be carved on a seat, say, or an elm-tree. Verses, too – and this is where R. S. Thomas's poetry comes in – written as if an object, or a feature of the landscape (such as a waterfall) were itself addressing the reader, inviting him to stand and ponder the hitherto unnoticed significance of the scene in front of him. It was, as Hartman pointed out, a genre well suited to the task of conveying the mysterious hidden life of the natural world. 'Invasion on the Farm' can usefully be regarded as just such an inscription poem – verses inscribed on Iago Prytherch, as it were. It is no more an authentic dramatic monologue than lines 'addressed' to the reader by a waterfall are actually, credibly, spoken by it:

> I am Prytherch. Forgive me. I don't know
> What you are talking about; your thoughts flow

Too swiftly for me; I cannot dawdle
Along their banks and fish in their quick stream
With crude fingers. I am alone, exposed
In my own fields with no place to run
From your sharp eyes. I, who a moment back
Paddled in the bright grass, the old farm
Warm as a sack about me, feel the cold
Winds of the world blowing. The patched gate
You left open will never be shut again.[17]

Even as he speaks, Iago's essential existence is left safely wrapped in the impenetrability of muteness. This irreducible distance between him and the inner life of his characters is something that R. S. Thomas seems to value and regret equally, and almost simultaneously, as can be seen in the poem 'The Watcher':

He was looking down on a field;
Not briefly, but for a long time.
A gate opened; it had done so before,
A sluice through which in a flood came
Cattle and sheep, occasionally men,
To fan out in a slow tide,
The stock to graze, the men busy
In ways never to be divulged
To the still watcher beyond the glass
Of their thin breath, the ear's membrane
Stretched in vain, for no words issued
To curse or bless through those teeth clenched
In a long grip on life's dry bone.   (*Tares*, 41)

The ambivalence of this poem is palpable, as Thomas on the one hand wants to participate in the life he is observing and on the other respects the stubborn, impenetrable self-absorption of the workers in their inscrutable tasks. That one long sentence, beginning in the third line and concluding with the poem itself, starts with the promise to the eye of admission to the secret existence of the scene, but ends with the frustration of the ear's attempt to eavesdrop on the meaning of what is going on. The whole passage is rather like a reversal of the famous opening to Wordsworth's 'Michael', where at first the landscape presents a forbidding aspect to the outsider, only to relent once the traveller persists in his willingness to leave the public way, and its public ways, and to learn the customs of this country. Then, says Wordsworth, he may be admitted, or initiated into the discovery that 'the mountains have all opened out themselves,/ And made a hidden valley of their own.'[18]

'The Watcher' is a poem from the collection *Tares* (1962), and that is the last of R. S. Thomas's collections to be devoted to the Manafon experience. Indeed one might venture to suggest that it is the last of his volumes to be imbued with a sense of a particular place – a specific human and natural locality. After that, it could be argued, R. S. Thomas becomes a displaced person. One finds him struggling to realize his dreams, not through a particular place and time, as he was doing, however imperfectly, ambiguously and uncertainly, in the earlier Manafon poems, but *against* the temptation to trust to any human place or time. In retrospect, it can be clearly seen that the poetry after *Tares* was being written somewhere along the road leading from Manafon to Abercuawg, that place which is no place that is extant, but 'somewhere evermore about to be'. It could well be that the social and political events in Wales during the sixties were partly responsible for this change. It is worth noting his bitter comments in 'Movement': 'Move with the times?/ I've done that all right:/ In a few years/ Buried a nation/ . . . None of those farms/ In the high hills/ Have bred children. / My poems were of old men' (*The Bread of Truth*, 35).

Another key poem of this period is 'The Untamed', and it was included in what seems to me to be the key volume of the sixties, *The Bread of Truth*, which is full of the disappearing clergyman syndrome and the black fly syndrome – in other words, fears of inward collapse and of invasion:

> My garden is the wild
>   Sea of the grass. Her garden
> Shelters between walls.
>   The tide could break in;
> I should be sorry for this.
>
> There is peace there of a kind,
>   Though not the deep peace
> Of wild places. Her care
>   For green life has enabled
> The weak things to grow.
>
> Despite my first love,
> ‾ I take sometimes her hand,
> Following strait paths

> Between flowers, the nostril
> Clogged with their thick scent.
>
> The old softness of lawns
>   Persuading the slow foot
> Leads to defection; the silence
>   Holds with its gloved hand
> The wild hawk of the mind.
>
> But not for long, windows,
>   Opening in the trees
> Call the mind back
>   To its true eyrie; I stoop
> Here only in play.   (33)

This poem seems to be constructed out of the tension Thomas feels between his old passion for that realm of independence and freedom which nature had represented for him ever since he was a boy in Holyhead, and a reluctant, wary, yet genuinely affectionate attachment to domestic life. Starting from here, one can see how much of Iago Prytherch there is in R. S. Thomas. The poet is clearly afraid of emotional closeness, or intimacy, because he fears it will render him vulnerable.

The poem ends on a note of heroic, strenuous individualism which reminds me of the writings of Kierkegaard. The similarity is no doubt partly suggested by the fact that two other poems of this period testify directly to Kierkegaard's influence on Thomas's thinking at this time. The one occurs in *Pietà* (1966), the other in *Not That He Brought Flowers* (1968). Critics have nervously noted this but have chosen, perhaps wisely, to make little of it – usually supposing, it seems, that Kierkegaard's influence related only to Thomas's religious convictions. Yet when R. S. Thomas himself mentioned the Dane, during the seventies, he made reference, interestingly enough, to *The Present Age*, which is primarily a work of *social* analysis. In that work Kierkegaard attacks the various devices – of protracted dispassionate reflection – by means of which his age safeguarded its sophisticated inertia, and avoided being brought to the raw moment of decisive, irreversible choice. Yet only in that extremity of personal choice, that moment of self-exposure, does the individual come authentically into being, according to Kierkegaard. Only then does his life acquire the depth – or what Kierkegaard calls the inwardness – which constitutes true character. With that in mind, it is interesting to read the following:

And he dared them;
Dared them to grow old and bitter
As he. He kept his pen clean
By burying it in their fat
Flesh . . .

A recluse, then; himself
His hermitage? Unhabited
He moved among us; would have led
To rebellion. Small as he was
He towered, the trigger of his mind
Cocked, ready to let fly with his scorn.[19]

That, of course, is part of R. S. Thomas's poem about Saunders Lewis, and it is surely a poem which depicts Lewis as a Kierkegaardian hero, a man whose daring commitment to an idea, an ideal, was in itself an indictment of tepid, unresisting modern conformism. What also strikes me, though, is the totally unexpected similarity that lurks within the apparent dissimilarities between the figures of Iago Prytherch and Saunders Lewis, as seen by R. S. Thomas. The words of another poet can help us here, the words of Robert Frost in a poem called 'Reluctance':

Ah, when to the heart of man
    Was it ever less than a treason
To go with the drift of things,
    To yield with a grace to reason,
And bow and accept the end
    Of a love or a season?[20]

What both Iago and Saunders Lewis unexpectedly prove to possess is this distaste for the 'treason' of yielding to 'the drift of things'. It is their blessed unreasonableness in this respect that commands R. S. Thomas's respect. They have an ungracious unyieldingness in common. Yet of course the heroic unreasonableness of the one is fundamentally different in kind from that of the other. This difference is the difference between two periods of R. S. Thomas's writing, and between two reactions by him to the Welsh situation.

Iago Prytherch is invented to represent a communal way of life which possesses the sort of brute integrity that goes with force of habit. He is, to the best of R. S. Thomas's ability, invested with permanence. If he is presented as occupying a non-verbal fastness, then by writing poems about him Thomas constructs a sort of verbal fastness for his own hopes of some principle of endurance in Welsh cultural affairs. 'Not choice for you', as R. S. Thomas puts it in one version, at least, of this myth of permanence, 'But seed sown upon the thin/ Soil of a heart, not rich, nor fertile,/ Yet capable of the one crop,/ Which is the bread of truth that I break' (*The Bread of Truth*, 41). Saunders Lewis, on the other hand, is the contrary individual who chooses quite consciously to devote his accusatory life to the preservation of values which have been jettisoned by the community in its unseemly haste to catch up with what it takes to be progress. The great enemy of such an authentic, committed individual, according to Kierkegaard, is 'the public' – a phenomenon he equates with modern mass society:

> A nation, a generation, a people, an assembly of the people, a meeting or a man, are responsible for what they are and can be made ashamed if they are inconstant and unfaithful; but a public remains a public . . . no single person who belongs to the public makes a real commitment . . . made up of individuals at the moments when they are nothing, a public is a kind of gigantic something, an abstract and deserted void which is everything and nothing.[21]

And then one remembers that Thomas, too, has used that word 'public' and invested it with the same charge of contempt:

> I am invited to enter these gardens
> As one of the public, and to conduct myself
> In accordance with the regulations;
> To keep off the grass and sample flowers
> Without touching them; to admire birds
> That have been seduced from wildness by
> Bread they are pelted with.
>
>   I am not one
> Of the public; I have come a long way
> To realise it.   (*Pietà*, 23)

It may very well be no more than coincidence that the key Kierkegaardian term turns up so prominently in 'A Welshman at St James' Park'. After all, the obvious source for the term is the formal public language of the familiar public notices, the disciplinary courtesies of which the poem begins by mockingly imitating. Nevertheless, the uncompromisingly simple, absolute contrasts – between British 'public' and Welsh man; between seductively trim gardens and wild hills – upon which the poem turns, are the very materials of a Kierkegaardian choice, which brings a genuine individual into existence out of the crowd.

No wonder R. S. Thomas explained, in 'A Grave Unvisited', that he
had deliberately passed by the opportunity to visit Kierkegaard's grave.
He was revolted by the thought that the Danes were now anxious to
profit from the posthumous fame of a figure who had, throughout his
short life, been despised and rejected by his fellow-countrymen:

> What is it drives a people
> To the rejection of a great
> Spirit, and after to think it returns
> Reconciled to the shroud
> Prepared for it?   (*Not That He Brought Flowers*, 9)

For 'people' here read 'the Welsh public'; and for Kierkegaard read
Saunders Lewis – or R. S. Thomas.

'A Welshman at St James' Park' is a poem about the proper use by the
speaker of that little word 'I', which begins with his ungraciously flat
refusal of the official terms of self-description proffered him by the sign.
It is very much a sixties poem, in that it analyses the semiotics of
officialdom, showing how inimical to Welshness is the concealed
ideology inscribed in the ostensibly neutral language of public discourse
in Britain. This was broadly the perception that underlay the
Cymdeithas yr Iaith campaigns during this period against English road
signs and the like. Yet while young Welsh speakers, trained by Saunders
Lewis and others to read the signs of the times, found dramatic methods
of exposing and dismantling the 'homely' instruments of the Anglo-
British state in Wales, it commonly remained the case that the English-
only speakers of Wales had their eyes opened to the incurable
Englishness of a supposedly British state only when they were exiled in
England. In this respect, too, the poem is therefore very much of its time
– and can indeed usefully be described as the classic exile's poem of the
mid-twentieth century, just as Ceiriog's 'Nant y mynydd' ('The hilly
brook') is undoubtedly the classic nineteenth-century Welsh exile's
poem.

Familiar lines from each of these two poems help bring into focus the
difference between two forms of Welsh experience of exile, separated by
a hundred years. Ceiriog presents himself as an innocent child of the
mountains: 'Mab y mynydd ydwyf innau/ Oddi cartref yn gwneud cân.
/ Ond mae 'nghalon yn y mynydd/ Efo'r grug a'r adar mân.'[22] ('I, too,
am a son of the hills, Singing far away from home. But my heart is in the
mountains, with the heather and the small birds.') And R. S. Thomas
turns to similar images:

I think of a Welsh hill
That is without fencing, and the men,
Bosworth blind, who left the heather
And the high pastures of the heart.   (*Pietà*, 23)

Set in the context of the complete poem, Ceiriog's imaginary mountain
seems to be the location, however idealized, however romanticized, of
an actual way of life. He speaks in the person of the 'gwerinwr', or
'amaethwr', who has been uprooted and transplated to barren urban
soil. In other words there is the myth of a particular kind of society
behind 'Nant y mynydd'. Whereas with R. S. Thomas one is constantly
aware of the bareness of that Welsh hill of which he thinks – a hill bare
even, one might say, of Iago Prytherch and his resilient upland life. And
that initial impression is confirmed by the phrase that soon follows: 'the
high pasture of the heart'. Such a genitive construction is extremely
familiar to any reader of Thomas's poetry. And here it seems to
function as a means of creating a deliberate ambiguity of meaning. The
phrase could refer either to actual high pastures that were dear to the
heart, or to high pastures that were a figure of speech for the feelings of
the heart – in other words, for a person's emotional and perhaps
spiritual condition. Either way, the dream is rather a lonely one, centred
not on a society but on an image of lofty self-sufficiency, and a quality of
individual integrity which is proof against all anticipated attempts to
seduce it or to overcome it.

In the early poetry such a dream had been embodied in R. S.
Thomas's highly distinctive vision of the people of an actual, particular
upland community. But during the sixties, judging at least by the
evidence of the poetry, R. S. Thomas began to internalize the dream for
even safer keeping – becoming, in a way, his own Iago Prytherch;
substituting for the upland farms around Manafon his own, internal
'high pastures of the heart'. At the end of 'A Welshman at St James'
Park', therefore, R. S. Thomas heads implicitly back not to a particular
Welsh community, but to the 'high pastures of the heart'. In other
words, he simply exchanges a state of exile for a state of internal exile.
He puts distance between himself and London only in order to come
back and keep his distance from his fellow-Welshmen, most of whom
seem 'Bosworth blind'.

This self-preserving attempt to keep his distance from his supposed
kind is what seems to me to happen repeatedly in his later sixties poetry.
A poem like 'Afforestation', for example, is surely a coded expression of
his distaste for Welsh consumer society, while 'Blondes' is a ferociously

patronizing poem on much the same subject. But above all, it's worth
recalling his experiences 'On the Shore':

> No nearer than this;
> So that I can see their shapes,
> And know them human
> But not who they are;
> So that I can hear them speak,
> The familiar accent,
> But not what they say.
>
> To be nearer than this;
> To look into their eyes
> And know the colour of their thought;
> To paddle in their thin talk –
> What is the beach for?
> I watch them through the wind's pane,
> Nameless and dear.   (*The Bread of Truth*, 29)

What language are these unfortunates speaking, one wonders? It's
doubtful whether they're speaking a Brummy English, although there
are connections between this piece and a poem like 'Eviction', where,
incautiously approaching someone in the Welsh heartlands, R. S.
Thomas finds that 'as in a dream/ A dear face coming up close/ Spits at
us, the reply falls/ In that cold language that is the frost/ On all our
nation' (*The Bread of Truth*, 13). There the black fly syndrome can be
clearly seen. The people on the shore could, though, be speaking
English with a 'familiar' Welsh accent; but what is striking is that one
cannot be sure. It is left deliberately open. They could be speaking
either English or Welsh. It seems to make no difference. R. S. Thomas is
equally estranged from the speakers of both languages. He is thus far
advanced on the road leading from Manafon to Abercuawg.

It is in his essay on Abercuawg (originally a lecture given in Welsh at
the 1976 National Eisteddfod) that we find him saying things like this:

> . . . whatever Abercuawg might be, it is a place of trees and fields and
> flowers and bright unpolluted streams, where the cuckoos continue to
> sing. For such a place I am ready to make sacrifices, maybe even to die.
> But what of a place which is overcrowded with people, that has endless
> streets of modern, characterless houses, each with its garage and
> television aerial, a place from where the trees and the birds and the
> flowers have fled before the yearly extension of concrete and tar-
> macadam; where the people do the same kind of soul-less, monotonous
> work to provide for still more and more of their kind?

> And even if Welsh should be the language of these people; even if they
> should coin a Welsh word for every gadget and tool of the technical and
> plastic age they live in, will this be a place worth bringing into existence,
> worth making sacrifices for? Is it for the sake of such a future that some
> of our young people have to go to prison and ruin such promising
> careers? I have very often put such questions to myself; and I am still
> without a definite answer.[23]

Welsh-speaking Wales is there seen as being itself implicated in the
process of 'afforestation' – to use an image from his own poem which
Gwenallt had made famous before him. In these paragraphs from
'Abercuawg', Welsh-speaking Wales assumes something of the threatening shape of St James's Park in Thomas's imagination, driving him to
take refuge in a name from the Welsh literature of the Middle Ages,
which evokes 'a place of trees and fields and flowers and bright
unpolluted streams, where the cuckoos continue to sing.' It is surely the
lowland equivalent of 'the high pastures of the heart'. In fact,
Abercuawg sounds very like the Afallon (Avalon) to which T. Gwynn
Jones's dying Arthur yearns to go: 'i ynys Afallon i wella fy nghlwy'
('To the island of Avalon to heal me of my wounds').[24] Yet it is actually
presented as an image of dream which is the opposite of Romantic
escapism, and is intended to be the prelude to serious engagement with
present unsatisfactory realities in the name of 'Abercuawg' – that is, in
the name of other, fuller ways of living, memories and hints of which
are preserved in the 'obsolete' terms that haunt the margins of current,
debased speech. Such a potentially constructive argument is indeed
advanced in *Abercuawg*, and seems to be an attractive one. 'In dreams',
as Yeats used to like to quote, 'begin responsibilities'.

Nevertheless, having registered the argument, one is still left in a
situation similar to that described by R. S. Thomas himself in his lecture
'Words and the Poet': 'My own position is usually to allow this as a
legitimate theory, but to ask in practice, "Where are the poems?" '[25]
The answer seems to be that there are no poems, that this positive
interpretation of the dream of Abercuawg has failed to produce an
answering body of work. Instead it is an altogether different and more
disturbing side of the Abercuawg vision of things that seems, from the
sixties onwards, to have issued in poetry. This is the side apparent in the
famous, or notorious, anecdote about Branwen that is included in the
lecture:

> Who has not had the experience of seeing his dreams shattered?
> Branwen was the Helen of Wales, wasn't she? Many of us, I'm sure, hold

an image of her in our hearts, not as she is in her rectangular grave on the banks of the river Alaw in Anglesey, but as she was in her lifetime – the fairest maiden alive. There are still a few Branwens in Wales. Did I not hear the name once and turn, thinking she might steal my heart away? Who did I see but a stupid, mocking slut, her dull eyes made blue by daubings of mascara – a girl for whom Wales was no more than a name, and a name fast becoming *obsolete*?[26]

That is the most recent, and most powerful, example of the black fly of modern Welsh life getting up R. S. Thomas's nose. This Branwen may well have been a Welsh speaker – R. S. Thomas does not stop to find out. It would make no difference. She would be certain to speak only plastic Welsh, in any case. He has no wish to 'paddle in [her] thin talk'. He wishes, no doubt, that he were 'on the shore': 'what is the beach for?' Well, it is clearly for the avoidance of such disenchantment as comes from close encounters of several kinds with his fellow-countrymen and women.

When he writes like this, R. S. Thomas shows an affinity with those conservative intellectuals who were an influential and impressive force in Welsh-language culture during the sixties. Alan Llwyd has summarized their outlook, through extensive quotation, in *Barddoniaeth y Chwedegau*, with particular reference to the observations of Saunders Lewis and Iorwerth Peate. Peate argued that the coming of bilingualism inescapably meant the serious dilution of Welsh-language culture, with the result that no great literature could ever again be produced in Welsh. Lewis likewise concluded that the end of a 'predominantly monoglot community' was 'unmitigated loss, disability, even calamity' for writers. 'English idiom enters unconsciously into Welsh speech today', he sadly noted. 'It is all about us, even in the remotest countryside, in radio set and television screen and daily newspaper. Inevitably there's a landslide of deterioration.' R. S. Thomas, himself a Welsh-learner, took his cultural bearings from prophets like these.[27]

His Abercuawg vision of Welsh-language society – a view that grows parallel to his increasingly jaundiced view of English-language society in Wales – can be seen developing in the poetry of the sixties. The point can most easily be made by a simple, and no doubt simplifying, contrast between two images R. S. Thomas uses for language. One dates from the fifties, the other from the sixties. Writing in the *Listener* (1958), he explained to the English that the Welsh lived not so much on two levels as in two rooms: the kitchen and the front parlour. The former was for family and friends, the latter for visitors. The Welsh, he explained, 'are a homely people; they live in their kitchen. They have their front parlour, of course, and without the language the traveller will never get beyond it.'[28]

This is one of R. S. Thomas's recurrent images of an inviolable inner sanctum. But what one notices is that the inner sanctuary here is not only the Welsh language, but the spoken and the lived language. It is identified with an existent, ongoing, securely hidden kind of social life. It is a view of the Welsh-speaking society which parallels, after an instructive fashion, his view of the Manafon farmers.

Contrast this with the way the language is imaged in the poem 'Welcome', printed in *The Bread of Truth* (1964):

> You can come in.
> You can come a long way;
> We can't stop you.
> You can come up the roads
> Or by railway;
> You can land from the air.
> You can walk this country
> From end to end;
> But you won't be inside;
> You must stop at the bar,
> The old bar of speech.
>
> We have learnt your own
> Language, but don't
> Let it take you in;
> It's not what you mean,
> It's what you pay with
> Everywhere you go,
> Pleased at the price
> In shop windows.
> There is no way there;
> Past town and factory
> You must travel back
> To the cold bud of water
> In the hard rock. (24)

When *The Bread of Truth* was reviewed in the *Listener*, the English reviewer singled out this poem for unfavourable comment, complaining because R. S. Thomas had put such unpleasant sentiments in the mouth of one of his peasant characters. The following week the poet replied, in a letter, that he was speaking for himself in a poem which was about 'the English infiltration of Wales.'[29] But, as any Welshman will realize, the poem is for home consumption, as much as for foreign, English consumption. It is indirectly addressed – addressed, that is, via the English – to the Welsh people whose national anthem, it sometimes seems, is 'We'll keep a welcome'. There-is in any case an element of bravado that lends pathos to the poetry. English is imagined as being spoken only as a Welsh guerilla tactic, used only to fleece the tourists. As if it were possible to use the language without in any way being used, or changed, by it.

There is a great deal to be said about this change of image, from kitchen to 'cold bud of water/ In the hard rock.' And there is something to be said *for* it, as well. The difference between the two images is perhaps in part a measure of the difference between the social experiences of two decades. The 'cold bud of water' is a deeply sympathetic image produced in eloquent defiance of the fact and vile image of Tryweryn – the reservoir that supplied Liverpool with water, and which was created in October, 1965, by drowning the hamlet of Capel Celyn. This remote village had been thoroughly Welsh-speaking, and virtually the whole of Wales had been unanimous in its opposition to the English reservoir scheme which necessitated the disappearance of a whole valley and the dispersal of its Welsh-speaking community.

As a result of such disastrous experiences, the Welsh language had, by the sixties, been partly driven and had partly issued aggressively of its own accord out of the 'kitchen'. The realization that the future of the language was inseparable from social, economic and political affairs revolutionized, as we know, the whole language struggle at this time. And although Thomas speaks pointedly and concentratedly of the cold bud of water in the rock, his metaphor could, at least by extension, be understood as signifying the subtly diffused and therefore infinitely ungraspable nature of a linguistic community.

Yet what strikes me most of all, I must say, is the way that a social phenomenon – language, culture – has here been essentially displaced onto, or into landscape. Maybe in literature topography is always, as Geoffrey Hartman has wittily put it, tropography: a figure of speech. In 'Welcome' we certainly have landscape used as a trope for the Welsh language; and we have it, I would suggest, because R. S. Thomas finds it increasingly difficult to identify with any existing linguistic community. Place replaces people, before itself being displaced later by a purely imaginary place – Abercuawg – 'a place of trees and fields and flowers and bright unpolluted streams, where the cuckoos continue to sing.' Language is de-socialized, de-culturized, de-humanized even, by being elementalized into 'the cold bud of water/ In the hard rock'. It is an image clearly produced under conditions of great social stress, and it creates a picture of pristine linguistic source, forever preserved from corruption by Welsh speakers, as well as from invasion by English speakers. Like Edward Thomas, R. S. Thomas is searching for 'a language not to be betrayed'. His refrigerating use of the adjective 'cold' is incidentally very reminiscent of Yeats: 'the cold/ Companionable streams'; 'cast a cold eye/ On life, on death'; 'cold and passionate as the dawn.' 'Imagination must dance', as Yeats said, 'must be carried beyond feeling into the aboriginal ice.'[30] And he, like R. S. Thomas, used the adjective 'cold' to describe a state of being which would not decay or rot in time. We are, then, back where we began; back with the fears of slippings, of slippage, of erosion and invasion, and all the other treacheries of Time which were suggested by R. S. Thomas's childhood memories of the disappearing clergyman and the black fly.

The pathos of this linguistic crisis, as experienced by Thomas, is very evident in *Pietà* (1966). The collection opens like this: 'Rhodri Theophilus Owen,/ Nothing Welsh but the name' (7). That is a bald example of language completely losing its meaning, because there is no correspondence between the name that is given an object, and the real nature of that object. Under such circumstances, what is the poet to do? Should he abandon this traditional form of nomenclature, since it is now no longer appropriate? Or should he strive to reconnect modern life in Wales with the ancient native language that alone can relate it to its own past? Just two pages later, in *Pietà*, Thomas contrasts the Welshman's alienated relationship to language with the comfortable linguistic situation of the English. He describes a house named 'Rose Cottage, because it had/ Roses. If all things were as/ Simple!' (*Pietà*, 10) Perhaps there is here, in that caustic use of the word 'simple', just a hint that the Englishman's home is altogether too secure a castle, since the English language is so strong as to seem virtually a reality principle in itself. Nevertheless, Thomas's constantly embattled Welshness makes him feel a little envious of the very different cultural condition of the English:

> You chose it out
> For its roses, and were not wrong.
> It was registered in the heart
> Of a nation, and so, sure

Of its being. All summer
It generated the warmth
Of its blooms, red lamps
To guide you. And if you came
Too late in the bleak cold
Of winter, there were the faces
At the window, English faces
With red cheeks, countering the thorns.   (Pietà, 10)

Thomas's own experience has been very different. What he sees in the faces of his fellow-countrymen and women is not a warm welcome but a grim threat. He therefore prefers to keep his distance; to withdraw and keep company with 'the cold bud of water/ In the hard rock.'

Of all the interviews R. S. Thomas has given, one of the most revealing was that shown on the Welsh television arts programme *Arolwg* in the mid-eighties. The interviewer on that occasion was Derec Llwyd Morgan, and thanks not only to his skill but also, perhaps, to the fact that the interview was conducted in Welsh, the poet seemed somewhat less embattled and less combative than usual. One remark he made during the course of that conversation throws interesting light on the relationship between his poetry of the sixties, at least as I understand its character, and the new direction his work seemed to take with the appearance of *H'm* (1972). He explained that during his seventy and more years he had seen extensive and profound changes in Welsh life – changes which had repeatedly undermined his hopes and eroded his ideals. It was, he added, this experience of senseless, or outrightly destructive, change that had prompted him to wonder what view of what kind of God could be compatible with the seemingly pointless events of human history. In other words, the remarkable and frequently anguished religious poetry he has produced since the beginning of the seventies seems to have arisen, at least in part, out of the sorts of acute difficulties in negotiating Time's treacherous ice which he began, on the evidence of the poetry, to have during the sixties.

One particular poem included in his comparatively late volume *Ingrowing Thoughts* seems to capture his uneasy sense of time.[31] It records his reaction to a painting by Ben Shahn, in which a man, muffled in a thick coat, hurries along clutching a shapeless bundle, which is in fact a child, while behind him there are trees like barbed wire, and beyond them a shattered town. The poem open like this: 'Times change:/ no longer the virgin/ ample-lapped; the child fallen/ in it from an adjacent heaven.' He sees Shahn's painting as a drastic modern

reworking of the Madonna and Child painting. Traditionally the
Madonna is always set in the very centre of the picture, with the Christ-
child on her rounded lap, so that she is, in herself, an emblem of a
meaningful, spiritually centred, coherently organized, temporal order.
But times change – and man's idea of Time accordingly changes, in
ways that affect his sense of space. So, in Shahn's painting, there are only
the vertical figures hopelessly, homelessly, slanting across the canvas. In
R. S. Thomas's reading of the picture, the central figure becomes a
refugee, who 'presses, his face set,/ towards a displaced future.'

It would not be true simply to say that R. S. Thomas is that refugee,
that stateless person. But it would, I feel, be true to say that he takes a
particularly well-informed interest in his plight. From the early sixties
onwards a sense of attachment, however grudging and bewildered, to a
particular locality, seems to have been gradually replaced in his own
work by feelings of dislocation and displacement. Conveniently enough
we have a documentary record of the way in which at least one
individual, representative of important sections of Welsh opinion
during the sixties, reacted at the time to this poetry. The provocative
essay by Dafydd Elis Thomas, later Plaid Cymru MP for Merioneth-
shire, appeared in *Poetry Wales*, 1972. It was consciously written from
the point of view of a sympathiser with the young members of
Cymdeithas yr Iaith Gymraeg, the Welsh Language Society, many of
whom were being imprisoned at that time for defacing English-
language road signs in an attempt to gain a place for Welsh in the public
domain. Dafydd Elis Thomas pithily accused the poet of indulging in a
reactionary poetry of despair, at the very time when a young generation
of writers and activists was discovering, and indeed creating, in
contemporary Welsh life the grounds for revolutionary hope.[32]

Now, twenty years on, we can perhaps briefly indulge in the luxury of
regarding the work of both these Thomases as graphic historical
evidence of the crisis psychology of the period. And what is striking is
the way they between them reproduce the ambivalent tone of the
apocalyptic work with which, in 1962, the Welsh experience of the
sixties could be said to have really, if rather belatedly, begun; namely
Saunders Lewis's famous radio broadcast *Tynged yr Iaith* (*The Fate of
the Language*). That 1962 lecture contains the following characteristic
passage:

> The political tradition of the centuries, the whole economic tendency of
> the present age, are against the survival of the Welsh language. Nothing
> can change that except determination, will, struggle, sacrifice, effort.[33]

The first sentence verges on hopelessness. The second confronts it, outfaces it, and so wins through to a well-tempered, steely determination.

Although it was Saunders Lewis's example that inspired the efforts of the young throughout the later sixties, there is a hint of easy, rhetorical optimism in Dafydd Elis Thomas's version of the ensuing struggle. On the other hand, the accusations he levelled against the poetry were fair enough, within limits. R. S. Thomas had not really supported in his poetry the courageous efforts being made at that time to protect and advance the Welsh language. He clearly could not find it in himself as a poet to muster up a coherent, convinced counter-attack against the social, political and economic forces that threatened his Wales. But instead, he made his own lonely way down, through his poetry of the sixties, to the profound and at times tragic misgivings that lie very close to the root of Saunders Lewis's unyielding determination. The result was poetry that speaks with particular power and poignancy to the Welsh-speaking Wales of the nineties.

7

Songs of 'ignorance and praise': R. S. Thomas's poems about the four people in his life

> Existence is
> Not what you say,
> Which does not count
> On Judgment Day;
> It is not even
> What you think,
> Which is but a
> Deceptive link
> Between your God
> And what you are
> – And what that is
> Is far from clear.
> So, Alleluia! loudly raise
> A song of ignorance and praise.[1]

To judge from his poetry, R. S. Thomas shares C. H. Sisson's relieved scepticism about being able to measure the ultimate worth, or indeed to understand the real nature, of his personal being. His poems of unsparing self-assessment seem always to leave a wide margin for eventual correction, even as they insist on facing up to the morally inadequate self-image that 'lies in ambush' for him, regardless of how secretly or obliquely he approaches the mirror: 'And the heart knows/ this is not the portrait/ it posed for.'[2] Similarly, his essays in autobiography – *Neb* and *The Echoes Return Slow* – are constructed to give the impression of a man who does not feel in full possession of his own life: 'A Narcissus tortured/by the whisperers behind/ the mirror.'[3] He writes sometimes like a baffled spectator of his own representatively strange existence – 'ce néant indestructible, qui est moi', as the line from Claudel puts it, which he chose as epigraph for *Neb*. But there are also those others close to him who are the partners in his sorrow's mystery: 'There are four verses to put down/ For the four people in my life,/ Father, mother, wife,// And the one child.'[4] These four have been a significant presence in his writing, yet very little attention has been paid to those poems in which they appear.

In a recent collection, *The Echoes Return Slow*, R. S. Thomas's search for origins has taken him farther back than ever before, although even then it is doubtful whether he himself believes he has got here to the very bottom of what he elsewhere describes as 'time's reasons/ too far back to be known' (*Experimenting with an Amen*, 52). He has, though, gone back as far as the womb, in an astonishing passage invoking pre-natal experience:

> Pain's climate. The weather unstable. Blood rather than rain fell. The woman was opened and sewed up, relieved of the trash that had accumulated nine months in the man's absence. Time would have its work cut out in smoothing the birth-marks in the flesh. The marks in the spirit would not heal. The dream would recur, groping his way up to the light, coming to the crack too narrow to squeeze through.[5]

It would be a crass and impudent piece of reductiveness to insist on explaining the character of Thomas's writing either exclusively or even primarily in terms of what is revealed here. 'Character is built up/' as he has himself reminded us, 'by the application of uncountable/ brush strokes' (*The Echoes Return Slow*, 93). Nevertheless, any reader of his poetry is likely to be struck by the consonances between this memory of birth and R. S. Thomas's reported experiences of living. To put it guardedly thus is to avoid the unanswerable question: is he actually remembering a climate of pain in which his whole being had its genesis?; or is he projecting the pains and frustrations of a lifetime back into the imagined trauma of birth? There is also another possible confusion to which we need to be alert. Even if we hold that a real trauma experienced at birth did (as he himself here seems to suggest) have very far-reaching effects on R. S. Thomas's growth and development, it does not follow that his outlook on life is therefore simply the consequence of that primal trauma; merely the ugly scar of an unfortunate early psychic wound.[6] It would be wiser to speculate that by some such means as those he chooses to mention figuratively at the beginning of *The Echoes Return Slow* he was exposed, and thus sensitized, exceptionally early to those uncomfortable aspects of life his unaccommodating mature poetry has repeatedly explored.

For my purposes it is enough to note that R. S. Thomas was born by Caesarian section, and that when he was in his mid-seventies this fact (recalled as an actual experience) was deliberately chosen by him to serve as an image of the origins of his sensibility. Examined in this light, and read with the corpus of Thomas's mature work in mind, the passage quoted yields up several suggestive meanings. Indeed it would seem to lay bare the deep structure of the poetry's psychology, its fundamental disposition towards life.[7] Here can be seen, for instance, that fear of confinement that is a recurring feature of the poems. Sometimes it is expressed as a passion for freedom (associated with nature); on other occasions it emerges as a nervousness about emotional intimacies, entanglements, commitments, or as a physical distaste for any kind of close encounter with others. Most interestingly of all, it manifests itself in Thomas's identification with a God who is tired of being besieged by men's prayers, or pestered by sentimental petitions, or threatened by the encroachments of the human on his living space: 'My privacy/ Was invaded; then the flaw/ Took over.'[8] In 'The Gap' it is the pressure of human words that God feels: 'God woke, but the nightmare/ did not recede. Word by word/ the tower of speech grew. / . . . One word more and/ it would be on a level/ with him; vocabulary/ would have triumphed.'[9] This kind of perception culminates in that superb exercise in the theology of claustrophobia, 'The White Tiger'. The creature possesses 'a body too huge/ and majestic for the cage in which/ it had been put', and its calm, cold beauty commands awe:

> It
> was the colour of the moonlight
> on snow and as quiet
> as moonlight, but breathing
>
> as you can imagine that
> God breathes within the confines
> of our definition of him, agonising
> over immensities that will not return.   (*Frequencies*, 45)

Arrange the meanings in that prose passage about his birth into a different pattern, and other preoccupations of his poetry seem to emerge. For instance there is a faint intimation of the impenetrable barrier between the divine and the human in that thwarted foetal sensation of 'groping his way up to the light, coming to the crack too narrow to squeeze through.' As for the the brusque, and rather brutal, description of the actual birth, it is disturbingly peculiar. In being referred to as 'the woman', the mother is denied her motherhood: similarly the baby is denied the natural process of birth, and exists in the description only as an inference from the clinically cold fact that 'the woman was opened and sewed up.' Parenthood is the inconvenient production of 'trash', which has then to be disposed of. These aspects of the passage are, perhaps, best left uninvestigated until later, when we consider the ambivalent way in which Thomas has presented his relationship with his parents in his poetry. It is, however, worth noting the undercurrent of savagery in the writing, as if there were in the writer a feeling of resentment at having been 'from his mother's womb untimely ripp'd.' And when R. S. Thomas does use the image of Caesarean birth in his poems, it is as a symbol of the monstrously unnatural – an act of violence done to nature. 'The scientists breach/ themselves with their Caesarian/ births, and we blame them for it', he writes in 'It': 'What shall we do/ with the knowledge growing/ into a tree that to shelter/ under is to be lightning struck?'[10] Again, in 'The Other', he uses the same image to describe the birth of the fearsome Machine:

> They did it to me.
> I preferred dead, lying
> in the mind's mortuary.
> Come out, they shouted;
> with a screech of steel
> I jumped into the world
> smiling my cogged smile,
> breaking with iron hand
> the hands they extended.   (*Later Poems*,180)

Hovering somewhere in the background here are surely Blake's fierce lines from 'Infant Sorrow':

> My mother groan'd! My father wept.
> Into the dangerous world I leapt:
> Helpless, naked, piping loud:
> Like a fiend hid in a cloud.
>
> Struggling in my father's hands,
> Striving against my swaddling bands,
> Bound and weary I thought best
> To sulk upon my mother's breast.[11]

Here baby talk is fighting talk. The infant is precociously aware of being an actor in a tense, emotionally violent family drama: it has to learn early to assume the wiles of disguise, and thus its impulses are, as it were, corrupted at source. Interestingly, there are also shades of the companion piece to 'Infant Sorrow', namely 'Infant Joy', about the poem that partners the prose description of birth in *The Echoes Return Slow*. It will be remembered that Blake's poem begins 'I have no name. / I am but two days old.'[12] This is how the Thomas poem begins:

> I have no name:
> time's changeling.
> Put your hand
> in my side and disbelieve
>
> in my godhead.   (*The Echoes Return Slow*, 3)

Here he names himself the son of Adam, the culpably changeable child of Time. But through the secondary meaning of 'changeling' – 'a child surreptitiously put in exchange for another' (*OED*) – he also declines to consider himself as being, in his essential identity, the child of his parents. Even the surname he inherits from them is given a sardonic twist that turns it from a genealogical fact into a human parable. He is a Thomas who *promotes* doubt – doubt about the divine innocence of infancy. Indeed, the last few lines of his poem read like an ironic commentary on Blake's 'Infant Joy'. Blake's baby is named 'Joy' by its mother in a great surge (or gush) of sentiment which can be read either as mothering or as smothering. In Thomas's poem the baby speaks for itself:

> Her face rises
> over me and sets;
> I am shone on
>
> through tears. Charity
> spares what should be
> lopped off, before
> it is too late.

The power in these lines is in their delicate psychological equivocation. On the one hand, he wants the mother to be kind by being cruel and so grant him an early end to a miserably unworthy existence. On the other hand, he is deeply moved by a tenacious love which seems to involve a redeeming acceptance of him as himself ('I am shone on through tears'). This latter strain of feeling in the poem seems to connect it with the very last prose passage in the collection, where R. S. Thomas brings together, in a single act of religious meditation, his deep passion for the sea and his abiding love for his wife:

Both female. Both luring us on, staring crystal-eyed over their unstable fathoms. After a lifetime's apprenticeships in navigating their surface, nothing to hope for but that for the love of both of them he would be forgiven. (*The Echoes Return Slow*, 120)

In that last phrase, clarity of meaning (with its related determination to hope) is deliberately made to struggle free of a heavy weight of repeated monosyllables and of confusingly repeated prepositions.

The description of Caesarean birth, whether it be remembered or imagined, seems, then, to attract to itself, and to concentrate in itself, a mixture of feelings that is characteristic of R. S. Thomas. There are, for instance, the self-loathing, the dark mistrust of human intimacy, the general sense of alienation and dissociation that permeate his writing. At the same time there is a strong sense of the inviolable integrity of his own separate, independent being. And there is also a shy, almost grudging, doubt-full and dubious tribute to a strength and persistence of love that makes 'a thing endurable which else/ Would break the heart.'[13] These feelings consort together most touchingly, I find, in Thomas's poems about relations within the family. But perhaps because these poems are so few and so far between, secreted away on the odd page of his collections, and only barely existing, it sometimes seems, in the shadow of his towering work on Iago Prytherch and the *Deus Absconditus*, they have so far received very little attention.

R. S. Thomas may have been too painfully close to his mother for him to feel able to write much about her, although he admitted in *Neb* that 'the relationship between mother and son is a strange one, and perhaps crucial.'[14] 'Because my father was often at sea and because my mother was of a domineering nature I was ruled mainly by her', he recently told Ned Thomas.[15] In his interviews and in *Neb* he has repeatedly described her as possessive, neurotic, and infuriatingly false-genteel: 'My mother gave me the breast's milk/ Generously, but grew mean after,/ Envying me my detached laughter' (*Selected Poems*, 52). Yet he has also consciously tried to balance the picture with other qualities, as in the following passage:

But it became time for him to leave Holyhead and go to Bangor as a college student. And his mother came with him! On the excuse that she was anxious to see that he had good lodgings and so on, she came too to share with him his first day away from home. But fortunately, since he was totally unknown to them, the other students didn't stand in rows to make fun of the little baby arriving with its nurse. Those were his feelings at the time. Later he would remember how he returned to his house the previous night and heard the sound of crying from upstairs, and his father's voice trying to silence his wife. Then in bed, after going to sleep, he woke and felt someone kissing him over and over. This was the way a mother came to realise she was on the point of losing the child of whom she had been too possessive. (*Neb*, 19–20)

In all his work there is, as far as I know, only one poem devoted entirely and exclusively to his mother, although one suspects his poetry has, in many intangible and incalculable ways, been 'ruled mainly by her'. Only in his very recent collection, *The Echoes Return Slow*, did he make her approaching end the subject of a poem. Seven years after his father's death it was, he tells us, his mother's turn to go: 'The woman, who all her life had complained, came face to face with a precise ill.'[16] In the opening lines there seems to be a sad, blurred echo of the poem of birth, when the baby had been condemned, by its mother's 'Charity', to live:

> She came to us with her appeal
> to die, and we made her live
> on, not out of our affection
> for her, but from a dislike
> of death. (77)

The double edge of feeling is most sharply sensed in the studied choice of the word 'dislike', where fastidious outward courtesy is drily used to distance inner fear in a manner passingly reminiscent of Emily Dickinson. Moreover the slightly fearful gentility that R. S. Thomas elsewhere associates with his mother now appears, ironically, as an acknowledged feature of his own reserved make-up. Powerful cross-currents of feeling can, then, be sensed under the still surface of the language, and these become even stronger towards the end, as the measured words seem increasingly to act as multipliers of meaning:

> The ambulance came
> to rescue us from the issues
> of her body; she was delivered
> from the incompetence of
> our conscience into the hospital's
> cleanlier care. Yet I took her hand
> there and made a tight-rope
> of our fingers for the mis-shapen
> feelings to keep their balance upon.

Built into the first phrase is a reproachful reminder of the opening line of the poem – 'She came to us . . . The ambulance came/ to rescue us'. Then follows the extraordinary mention of 'the issues of her body', a phrase into which black meanings are so densely compressed that no relieving gleam of comfort is at this point able to escape. Obviously the reference is partly to physical incontinence and to other kinds of bodily effluent. But beyond that is the sense of the mother as having become an insuperable problem, a dilemma; and behind that again lies Thomas's inescapable awareness of his own binding situation as her son, himself literally one of 'the issues of her body.' This last dark shade of meaning in the phrase then colours one's reading of the next sentence so that 'she was delivered/ from the incompetence of/ our conscience' is a kind of grim parody of the process of giving birth, and contains a poignant allusion to the Lord's Prayer, as well as, of course, depending on the modern, humdrum meaning of the word 'deliver'. By the time one has reached the end of the piece, the picture of the son taking his mother's hand and making a tight-rope 'of our fingers for the mis-shapen/ feelings to keep their balance upon' seems applicable to the poem itself. The poet has produced, through words, a precarious miracle of emotional equilibrium, without ever pretending to have straightened out the twisted feelings of a lifetime between his mother and himself.

'Oh, could I lose all father now', wrote Ben Jonson in his great, eloquently restrained elegy 'On my son'. R. S. Thomas's related wish that he could 'lose all son', in his relationship with his mother, is just as restrained, and, yes, just as eloquent too, I would argue. Indeed he is usefully thought of, perhaps, as sometimes being, like Jonson, a superb writer of modern epigrams, in the classical and Elizabethan sense. As a theological student he was, of course, given a grounding in Greek and Latin, and later acquired a knowledge of the great, pungently concise, *cynghanedd* writing of the golden age of Welsh poetry. Particularly interesting is his mention, in *Neb*, of the debt he owed one of his early teachers:

> . . . it is unlikely that the boy would have succeeded in his A level exam . . . but for the Headmaster, Derry Evans, a man who possessed an innate talent for teaching Latin. By him he was provided with an excellent foundation that enabled him not only to succeed academically but also to develop into a poet, because of the emphasis on language. Through having to search for the precise word to translate Latin he learnt the need to do this in poetry too. (18)

But although in his mature poetry Thomas has always been in search of the precise, I do feel that as he has grown older he has become more able to reconcile clarity and complexity, whereas in some of his earlier work there is a tendency to be inflexibly definite and decided. Take, for instance, a poem like the following, entitled 'Sorry':

> Dear parents,
> I forgive you my life,
> Begotten in a drab town,
> The intention was good;
> Passing the street now,
> I see still the remains of sunlight.
>
> It was not the bone buckled;
> You gave me enough food
> To renew myself.
> It was the mind's weight
> Kept me bent, as I grew tall.
>
> It was not your fault.
> What should have gone on,
> Arrow aimed from a tried bow
> At a tried target, has turned back,
> Wounding itself
> With questions you had not asked.
>
> *(Selected Poems, 84)*

The immediate impact of these lines is, surely, powerful, but the piece as a whole does not wear particularly well, I find, perhaps because the images are too insistently definite. The poem is rather like a fine metal bridge that has been built without expansion joints: there is no give in it to allow for changes of temperature in his feelings towards his parents and their relationship to himself. The possible exception to this overall impression is the one sentence that does have an echoing plangency about it: 'Passing the street now,/ I see still the remains of sunlight.' Otherwise the statements border on the dogmatic.

'Sorry', which was first collected in *The Bread of Truth* (1963), seems all the more rigid (as if with suppressed anger) when compared with the opening section of 'Album', a poem included in *Frequencies* (1978):

> My father is dead.
> I who am look at him
> who is not, as once he
> went looking for me
> in the woman who was. (36)

The blank simplicity of the opening statement breaks down into the brooding Faulknerian complexity of the sentence that follows. And as is the case with Faulkner's style, the effect of this spool of syntax is to substitute for the conventional working idea of temporal chronology a sense of time's bewildering circularities: 'What does it mean/ life? I am here I am/ there.' As understood in the opening lines, the relationship between father and son becomes one that reveals a mysterious correspondence between past and present. The parallelism of syntax makes their roles seem interchangeable. Thomas realizes he is now the bringer to life of his dead father, as once his father brought him to life. A particular poignancy seems to attach to that phrase: 'as once he/ went looking for me/ in the woman who was.' Underlying and underpinning these lines there appears to be a pun on the unspoken word 'conceive'. Instead of being merely the by-product of sexual intercourse, the begetting of the child is seen as a great hungering movement of the mind, in the spirit of some deep human need. What the phrase deliberately leaves unclear, however, is whether the 'me' that was actually produced did indeed satisfy that need. In other words it is uncertain whether R. S. Thomas is seeing himself as indeed his father's chosen one, or as the disappointing result of his father's search. And since the syntax makes Thomas's 'search' for his father in the photograph the double of his father's 'search' for him in the act of intercourse, the emotional ambivalence associated with the latter also becomes transferred to the former. Thomas's father is now at his mercy: he exists only in his son's 'conception' of him. And as he acts on the great need to give his father being, the son, by implication, feels both love and resentment.

Judging by the evidence freely offered by R. S. Thomas himself in *Neb*, his impulse to 'go searching' for his dead father came partly from his feeling that he had been impeded – not least by his father's early deafness – from communicating intimately with him when he was alive: 'He had been a man who had seen the world and its customs, and he would have shared his experiences, perhaps, had he been able to have a normal relationship with his son' (*Neb*, 92). R. S. Thomas's painful sense of frustration at being unable to enjoy 'a normal relationship' with his father comes out most poignantly in two sentences he wrote about his death in *The Echoes Return Slow*. 'In the order of things children bid fare-well to their parents. Unable to hear his father bid him fare-well in his stentorian voice' (76). Thomas was, then, prevented from taking leave of his parent, and had to suffer instead his father's

lonely, bellowed goodbye. One wonders how much this has affected the
later Thomas's preoccupation with the silence of God.

   The development of 'Album' is, then, governed by a whole blend of
feelings. Having begun by thinking of himself as specifically desired and
searched for by his father, Thomas goes on to see himself as the addition
to the family that unbalanced the whole picture:

> . . . Look! Suddenly
> the young tool in their hands
> for hurting one another.
>
> And the camera says:
> Smile: there is no wound
> time gives that is not bandaged
> by time. And so they do the
> three of them at me who weep. (36)

The hint of banality, the suggestion of conventional wisdom, in the
words the camera utters, is a sign of the emptiness of the comfort it has
to offer. After all, from the very beginning of the poem, Time is seen as
repeating itself, not as improving on itself. As for the last sentence, it is,
I feel, particularly disarming and deeply affecting because there is
scarcely another one like it in the whole of Thomas's work – hardly
another moment in his poems where he allows himself such an open
display of 'weakness'; of helplessly naked emotion of the kind found in
the work of poets so unlike him in temperament, such as Lawrence's
'Piano', or Whitman's 'Out of the Cradle'.

   A rather different account of the reason for his conception is given in
'The Boy's Tale', a poem where the tension in the speaker (presumably
R. S. Thomas himself) betrays itself in the nervously clipped style of
expression, a kind of psychological telegramese, where the aim seems to
be to expend as little emotion as possible in words: 'Skipper wouldn't
pay him off,/ Never married her' (*Selected Poems*, 87). As the poem
proceeds the abruptness of manner becomes a style of reporting
appropriate to the dry description of a fateful *fait accompli*: 'Caught
him in her thin hair,/ Couldn't hold him'. This sense of the wife–
husband relationship as one, in his parents' case, where the woman
trapped and tamed the man, recurs in R. S. Thomas's writing: 'My
father was a passionate man,/ Wrecked after leaving the sea/ In her
love's shallows. He grieves in me.' (*Selected Poems*, 52) In 'The Boy's
Tale', Thomas sees himself as his mother's chosen instrument for
controlling and dominating her sailor spouse:

> She went fishing in him;
> I was the bait
> That became cargo,
> Shortening his trips,
> Waiting on the bone's wharf.
> Her tongue ruled the tides.　　　　　(*Selected Poems*, 87)

In fact, Thomas's portraits of his father, including the repeated suggestion of marital defeat, with a resulting impression of masculine weakness and inadequacy, are very reminiscent of Robert Lowell's pictures of 'Commander' Lowell, his easy-going, sea-going father. But the comparison between the two writers, once it occurs to one to make it, is somewhat to R. S. Thomas's disadvantage in one respect, at least. Lowell is able to relax in his writing without thereby losing control over it and lapsing into slackness. His consequent achievement, in *Life Studies* particularly, is to invest apparently casual and inconsequential observations with a deeper purpose. His lazily undulating lines work like slow-release tablets, and have to be tucked under the tongue of the mind for a long time in order to allow them gradually to secrete their meanings:

> 'Anchors aweigh,' Daddy boomed in his bathtub.
> 'Anchors aweigh,'
> when Lever Brothers offered to pay
> him double what the Navy paid.
> I nagged for his dress sword with gold braid,
> and cringed because Mother, new
> caps on all her teeth, was born anew
> at forty. With seamanlike celerity,
> Father left the Navy,
> and deeded Mother his property.[17]

Placed next to a passage like that, Thomas's writing can seem cramped, inhibited, even grandiose and portentous. This is partly due to a passion for authoritative, clinching images, the general absence of which in the mature Lowell may help explain why Thomas has a relatively low opinion of the American's work. He told John Barnie in a recent interview that 'Robert Lowell . . . enjoyed an inflated reputation and Heaney came under his influence. It would have been better had he not.'[18] Elsewhere, during the same conversation, he admits his strong preference for the work of Geoffrey Hill, which is, after all, high tension like his own, and tends to be magnificently dense and turgidly pretentious by turns. The irresistible attraction, for Thomas, of the strong image makes it next to impossible for him to write a really successful poem longer than a page or so. For one thing, the series of determinedly arresting images produces a stop/go kind of tempo, and prevents a larger overall structure from forming: for another, the images tend not to collaborate but to clash and compete with each other, rather like a whole chorus made up of prima donnas. A case in point is his extended elegy for his father, 'Salt' (*Later Poems*, 159–63), where he seems intent on exhausting the whole repertoire of nautical tropes in one virtuoso display.[19] Taken in small doses, however, the poetry can have considerable effect, as can be seen in the following passage:

> The voice of my father
> in the night with the hunger
> of the sea in it and the emptiness
> of the sea. While the house founders
> in time, I must listen to him
> complaining, a ship's captain
> with no crew, a navigator
> without a port; rejected
> by the barrenness of his wife's
> coasts, by the wind's bitterness
> off her heart. I take his failure
> for ensign, flying it
> at my bedpost, where my own
> children cry to be born.   (*Later Poems*, 161–2)

His clear signal here that he identifies in some ways, and to some extent, with his father, is worth bearing in mind when he goes on to pity the ageing man's painful ineffectuality, and in particular the world-wide traveller's lack of anything substantial to show for his life's journey: 'What was a sailor/ good for who had sailed/ all seas and learned wisdom/ from none, fetched up there/ in the shallows with his mind's valueless cargo?' How far, one then wonders, was Thomas's invincible determination to be a lifelong mental traveller – a determination so frequently expressed in terms of nautical images, of crossing fathomless depths – shaped by his reaction against that image of his father as left, in old age, bereft of the becoming dignity of 'wisdom'? Certainly his father's example served as salutary warning to R. S. Thomas in several ways, hardening, in particular, his resolve to protect his separate selfhood from being compromised or invaded. Running through his poetry is the constant fear of and contempt for 'weakness', whether it be moral or emotional. He is hardest on himself when he detects such weakness in his own make-up: 'A will of iron, perforated/ by indecision. A charity/ that, beginning at home,/ ended in domestication. / An uxorious valour/ so fond of discretion as/ to defer to it/ as his better half' (*The Echoes Return Slow*, 59). Regardless of whether one takes the reference to marriage here as fact or as metaphor, the relationship of husband to wife is unmistakeably seen, once more, as fraught with danger for the former.

Alongside R. S. Thomas's painful sense of his father's weakness lies his envy of the power he had possessed, when a young sailor, to escape to sea from the nauseating mess human beings had made of modern life. Thomas seems sometimes scarcely able to forgive his father for having finally come ashore – which is tantamount, in Thomas's thinking, to running aground. He imagines his father's corpse as stranded, for ever, on 'this mean shoal of plastic/ and trash' (*Later Poems*, 163). In 'Sailors' Hospital' the town of Holyhead is seen as 'time's waste/ Growing at the edge/ Of the clean sea' (*Selected Poems*, 115). That poem ends, though, in great tenderness, as Thomas finds it impossible to let go of a man whom, on a different level of feeling, he wishes to see released:

> With clenched thoughts,
> That not even the sky's
> Daffodil could persuade
> To open, I turned back
> To the nurses in their tugging
> At him, as he drifted
> Away on the current
> Of his breath, further and further,
> Out of hail of our love.   (*Selected Poems*, 115–16)

These are lines that, rather unusually for R. S. Thomas, enact rhythmically the actual feel of what is being experienced.

As could probably have been anticipated, many of the feelings that Thomas has about his parents recur, but in significantly modified form, in the half-dozen or so poems he has written about his son, Gwydion, beginning with the emphasis that 'It was your mother wanted you;/ you were already half-formed/ when I entered' (*Laboratories of the Spirit*, 16). These, the opening lines of 'The Son', may well remind us of the claim in 'The Boy's Tale', that he had been his mother's idea, but there the resemblance between the two poems rather pointedly ends, because the remainder of 'The Son' is given over to the speaker's progressive admission of his own shyly entranced part in the making and the nurturing of the baby. Even in the act of conception he can now see 'the hunger, the loneliness bringing me in/ from myself.' But what particularly disarms him is that the tiny baby 'is too small to be called/ human.' This is an important discovery for a poet who is otherwise almost indecently quick to detect the smell of mortality in every phase and feature of human life.

Indeed almost all the rest of R. S. Thomas's poems about Gwydion insist on explicitly recognizing, in some way or other, the fact that his son participates in the general human condition, and partakes of the general human frailty. 'Song for Gwydion', a lovely early lyric, approaches this theme via an evocation of the child's 'innocent' natural beauty, to which the father pays enraptured tribute by bringing him a 'trout from the green river'. Its song has been stilled, and its rainbow colours faded by death, but the child selfishly exults in the gift: 'the first sweet sacrifice I tasted,/ A young god, ignorant of the blood's stain' (*Song at the Year's Turning*, 48). Ignorant, may be, but no longer innocent. Father and son are united in a moment of sad communion, partners in sin. Thomas is always ready to see signs of the criminal cupidity of mankind in the gross appetitiveness of young children, even to the extent of describing his begetting of Gwydion, in 'Anniversary', as 'Opening the womb/ Softly to let enter/ The one child/ With his huge hunger' (*Selected Poems*, 67). This seems connected to his attack in *Neb* on man's exploitation and selfish spoliation of the environment: 'the classical term for this was "cupido", the unsatisfiable craving in man that produced machines and planes and missiles and all the technology of the modern world' (*Neb*, 129).

'Is there a leakage/ from his mind into the minds/ of our inventors?' he enquires in a poem from *The Echoes Return Slow* (39). This piece, along with its accompanying prose passage, seems to be an interesting rewriting of Coleridge's great poem 'Frost at Midnight'. There, it will be remembered, Coleridge is gradually reconciled, through listening to his child breathing in the cot at his side, to the natural world which had originally seemed to him so coldly indifferent, or inimical, to human existence. The poem ends with a marvellous verse paragraph celebrating a benign, blessed, organically integrated cosmos, in which Coleridge's son will feel completely at home at all times, and in all seasons: 'Therefore, all seasons shall be sweet to thee . . .' In the prose passage that precedes Thomas's poem, he creates a scene similar to that in 'Frost at Midnight', but very different to it in tone: 'Despite the atmosphere of the nursery, that half-light before the fire, cradling the child, telling it stories, wishing it God's blessing in its small cot, dark thoughts come to the priest in the church porch at night, with the owl calling, or later at his bed-side' (*The Echoes Return Slow*, 38). The process here can be seen to be the reverse of that in 'Frost at Midnight', since Thomas begins with a sense of security, and ends in a state of alienation.

Coleridge was also, of course, disturbed at the beginning of his poem by 'the owlet's cry' that came 'hard and hard again', as if conveying to the human listener all the inhuman hostility of the cosmos. But eventually his disturbed and disordered thoughts are imperceptibly knit together into a new harmony by the rhythm of his son's breathing. In Thomas's case, however, his child's breathing sets the tempo for increasingly disturbed reflections about the unseen presence that haunts the universe:

> What listener
> is this, who is always awake
> and says nothing? His breathing
> is the rising and falling of oceans on remote
> stars. The forbidden tree flourishes
> in his garden and he waters it
> with his own blood.

This leads on to wild fears about a maverick spirit of mischievousness, abroad in the life of the universe, that takes possession of human beings and causes them to tamper with the forbidden: 'The combination/ is yielding. What will come forth/ to wreak its vengeance on us/ for the disturbance?'

Such a vision seems compounded of the stories of both Pandora's Box and the Sorcerer's Apprentice, and the memory of the latter in turn reminds one that the original Gwydion was a wily and resourceful magician whose prodigiously ingenious exploits included, according to the *Mabinogion*, the initially glorious but eventually disastrous act of creating a woman out of flowers. His Blodeuwedd, as she was called, proved to be a veritable Pandora herself, so much so that when Saunders Lewis (R. S. Thomas's great hero) came to reinterpret the story for the twentieth century, he depicted her as a product of human meddlesomeness.[20]

R. S. Thomas's decision to call his son 'Gwydion' is, then, consistent with his determination to see his son as also a son of Adam, instead of fondly and deludedly believing that he is free of original sin.[21] This is very clear in the following passage from *The Echoes Return Slow*:

> The child growing imperceptibly into a boy, the strange plant that has taken root in one's private garden. The apple of the mother's eye. The grudging acknowledgement by the male, so different from the female, that this also is a twig on a branch of the tree of man. The father's share in the promise of fruit and his resentment at canker. (40)

Certain unattractive features of R. S. Thomas's thinking are on view here, such as his tendency to condescend to women and to treat them as the weaker vessels, morally and emotionally.[22] (In this context there are surely shades of Eve in the ironic reference to the boy as 'the apple of the mother's eye'.) There is also a hint of male jealousy and rivalry between father and son in that description of the garden. But permeating the whole passage is a sense of the father having to come to terms with the fact that his child, just like every other, is growing into the fullness of man's fallen condition. The accompanying poem on the facing page, however, deliberately works in an opposite direction. It begins with the father readily admitting that his son 'was sometimes a bad boy', but then follows a lovely compensatory image of a child's open trust and vulnerability: 'Yet I remember his lips/ how they were soft and// wet, when I kissed him/ good-night' (*The Echoes Return Slow*, 41).[23]

More important, though scarcely more numerous, than R. S. Thomas's poems about his son are his poems about his wife. On one reading of his output, these could seem no more than incidental to his primary concerns, those serious subjects that have regularly attracted his consuming interest. At the end of 'Marriage' he seems himself to be ruefully admitting as much, when he regrets that his wife's unassuming qualities have, unlike the brash history of 'kings and queens/ and their battles/ for power', been registered only by 'one man's/ eyes resting on you/ in the interval of his concern' (*Laboratories of the Spirit*, 57). The whole piece is, in fact, a tender, humble reversal of that proud convention whereby a poet simultaneously proclaims and demonstrates his power to immortalize his beloved in verse. Of course, Shakespeare it is who provides the most famous and triumphant examples of this convention, notably in his sonnets: 'And all in war with Time for love of you/ As he takes from you, I ingraft you new' (Sonnet 15). But there is surely reason, in the form of Thomas's passionate admiration of Yeats, to suppose that he has got the Irishman's great poems to Maud Gonne in mind when he apologizes that 'Because there are no kings/ worthy of you; because poets/ better than I are not here/ to describe you . . . you must go by/ now without mention.' In reply to a suggestion made to him recently by Ned Thomas that he is an underrated, but diffident love-poet, R. S. Thomas replied:

> Diffident is the word, is it not? We are all afraid of laughter, at being called soft or sentimental; and certainly such states destroy art. Passion seems to have departed from the poetry I am familiar with in English, Welsh or French. I shy at the word 'darling' which was all too current a while ago. It has something to do with linguistic deflation. Surely most of us would like to write a great love poem to God, to Wales, to our betrothed. It would have to be passionate; but we meander and grow shallow, if subtle.[24]

It seems that he regards Yeats as one of the few modern poets who could grow marvellously impassioned without thereby devaluing his language of love through the use of inflated rhetoric:

> Why should I blame her that she filled my days
> With misery, or that she would of late
> Have taught to ignorant men most violent ways,
> Or hurled the little streets upon the great,
> Had they but courage equal to desire?
> What could have made her peaceful with a mind
> That nobleness made simple as a fire,
> With beauty like a tightened bow, a kind
> That is not natural in an age like this,
> Being high and solitary and most stern?
> Why, what could she have done, being what she is?
> Was there another Troy for her to burn?[25]

It is worth reading this in its entirety, not only because it is so disturbingly magnificent a poem, but also because it brings out for us, so clearly and unmistakeably, the connection Yeats's dazzled, tormented mind is moved to make first between beauty and power, and then between this volatile combination and the artistic imagination. In fact, the whole troubling nexus of experiences in this poem reminds us of the arresting remark Hazlitt made at the beginning of his essay on Shakespeare's *Coriolanus*: 'The language of poetry naturally falls in with the language of power. The imagination is an exaggerating and exclusive faculty . . . a monopolising faculty . . . It presents a dazzling appearance. It shows its head turretted, crowned, and crested . . . Kings, priests, nobles, are its train-bearers . . . Poetry is right-royal.'[26]

In 'Marriage', R. S. Thomas shows an awareness of, and a distaste for, this right-royal aspect of his own imagination as man, and perhaps most particularly as poet: 'You have your battle,/ too. I ask myself: Have/ I been on your side? Lovelier/ a dead queen than a live/ wife?' In this sense, the poem is written to celebrate and protect, as well as to regret, his wife's anonymity. Her non-appearance in his poem is his tribute to her undemonstrative integrity of being, outside that realm of power that frequently proves such an unhealthy attraction for the historian and the poet. (As Hazlitt noted, 'our vanity or some other feeling makes us disposed to place ourselves in the situation of the strongest party . . . The insolence of power is stronger than the plea of necessity.') At the same time Thomas is saddened by his wife's 'passing', both in the sense of her walking by him almost noticed and in the larger, more melancholy sense of her eventual death without proper public or poetic recognition:

> because time
> is always too short, you must go by
> now without mention, as unknown
> to the future as to
> the past, with one man's
> eyes resting on you
> in the interval of his concern.

As usual, Thomas ventures to conclude the poem on a weighty generalization – a considerable risk, in view of his age's dislike of sententiousness. That last phrase has, though, a notable delicacy about it, critically balanced as it is between two meanings. Since Thomas is writing about how he happened to notice his wife as he raised his eyes for a moment from the history book he was reading, he could be using the word 'concern' ironically to refer to his self-important pre-occupation with his studies. On the other hand, the word could mean the very opposite. It could refer to the brief moment when he pays full, conscious, appreciative attention ('concern') to the one person who is *really* important to him, and in the process temporarily (for an 'interval') reorientates his life. What the phrase thus highlights, through its significant ambiguity, is the choice Thomas has to make, between 'concern' (the supposedly important matters of the world) and 'concern' (a care for that which the world at large ignores). He has therefore provided himself with a solution to the dilemma with which his poem opens: 'I have to reconcile your/ existence and the meaning of

it/ with what I read.' No reconciliaton is possible, only the realization
that he is confronted by a test of authenticity, by what Kierkegaard
would call a situation of either/or.

A very different kind of Kierkegaardian situation is brought to mind
by 'Careers', a poem that centres on Thomas's attempt to understand
the relationship between his present 52-year-old self and the boy he
once was: 'How his words/ muddle me; how my deeds/ betray him'
(*Selected Poems*,107–108). At the end he laments that

> where I should
> be one with him, I am one now
> with another. Before I had time
> to complete myself, I let her share
> in the building. This that I am
> now – too many
> labourers. What is mine is
> not mine only: her love, her
> child wait for my slow
> signature.

The attitude here is reminiscent of Kierkegaard's biting comments
about an individual's attempts to avoid, through 'association', the
challenge and responsibility of his own individuality: 'the association of
individuals who are in themselves weak, is just as disgusting and as
harmful as the marriage of children.'[27] One's reaction to the poem is
bound, it seems to me, to be as ambivalent as one's reaction to
Kierkegaard's assertion. While recognizing the possible validity of such
an observation in certain, carefully qualified circumstances, one is also
aware of how it could be used to legitimize selfish individualism and as
a cover for one's fear of intimate, binding relationships. Perhaps the
safest thing one can say about Thomas's adoption of this attitude in
'Careers' is that it seems to be something between a weakness and a
strength. It is only fair to add, however, that he himself seems to regard
it as such. The remark is made in a specific dramatic context, against a
background of mixed feelings. Thomas is being tortured by the
painfully revealing likeness to himself, in all his weakness, that he sees
in his son: 'That likeness/ you are at work upon – it hurts.' Accordingly,
a part of him wishes that he had never married.

The experience of marriage is explored by him in a number of poems
scattered across many of his collections. 'Anniversary' appeared first in
Tares and it celebrates, in its own 'diffident' fashion, nineteen years
spent 'under the same roof/ Eating our bread,/ Using the same air'

(*Selected Poems*, 67). In fact, the present participle dominates the poem, as Thomas tenderly describes a continuous, and continuing, process in which the care of each partner for the other is grounded in mutual carefulness of one another's separateness: 'Sighing, if one sighs,/ Meeting the other's/ Words with a look/ That thaws suspicion.' This sense of marriage constantly involving delicate negotiations and accommodations (both through and about language) is one that recurs in R. S. Thomas's poetry. It can be best seen in the second of the following stanzas from 'He and She' (*Experimenting with an Amen*, 7):

> Seated at table,
> no need for the fracture
> of the room's silence; noiselessly
> they conversed. Thoughts mingling
> were lit up, gold
> particles in the mind's stream.
>
> Were there currents between them?
> Why when he thought darkly
> would the nerves play
> at her lips' brim? What was the heart's depth?
> There were fathoms in her,
> too, and sometimes he crossed
> them and landed and was not repulsed.

Several of the images here partake of the self-consciousness of conceits, thus emphasizing the studied nature of the observations made as if by an authoritatively objective, or judicious third party standing close to but outside of the relationship. An ascetic intimacy of mutual understanding which is expressed only through stressed negatives ('no need . . . noiselessly') is transformed into sensuously physical–mental rapport through that glorious image of 'gold/ particles in the mind's stream'. As for the last stanza, the series of questions there creates an air of mystery, of indeterminacy, with the point of view of the speaker for the first time being appreciably closer to that of the man than that of the woman. The impression of strange, ungraspable correspondences – of mood and of thought – is enhanced by the ghostly presence of rhyme and internal rhyme. 'Darkly . . . play . . . lips' creates an elusive suggestion of consonantal echo, while 'crossed' in conjunction with 'repulsed' offers the rudiments, but no more, of syllabic end-rhyme. The muted effect is, of course, deliberate.

In fact, 'He and She' reminds one, in places, of aspects of Donne's poem 'The Extasie' transposed to a much lower pitch, to allow for the temperate nature of a settled, habitual relationship, as opposed to the extravagant raptures of courtship. R. S. Thomas's poem is a beautiful meditation on the mystery of a mature married love that 'interinanimates two soules' and 'defects of lonelinesse controules.' Indeed the speaker in 'He and She' is the ideal witness imagined by Donne: one 'so by love refin'd,/ That he soules language understood.'[28]

Whereas R. S. Thomas's wife is invoked only as an intensely companionable presence in 'He and She', her character is lovingly detailed in 'The Way of It' (*Later Poems*, 91). Her talents as a professional painter are Thomas's starting point – 'With her fingers she turns paint/into flowers' – and her self-effacing dexterity is gently acknowledged to be the domestic art that has sustained their marriage so resourcefully: 'She is at work/ always, mending the garment/ of our marriage, foraging/ like a bird for something/ for us to eat.' Thomas presents himself as one humbled and chastened by her selflessness, an impression of both partners that is strengthened by the absence of sentimentality in the picture of relationship he paints:

> Her words, when she would scold,
> are too sharp. She is busy
> after for hours rubbing smiles
> into the wounds.

Practical and clear-sighted, his wife is credited, at the end, with having seen through his early strutting courtship display of his qualities and with accepting him, without even the illusion of romantic love, 'as someone/ she could build a home with/ for her imagined child.' At that point, Thomas himself seems like one admirably purged of vanity. Kierkegaard once remarked that most of the time we are subjective towards ourselves and objective in our relationship to others, whereas the great Christian achievement is to be objective in relation to oneself and subjective in one's identification with others. In 'The Way of It' R. S. Thomas succeeds very movingly in achieving this reversal.

But perhaps the most affecting of all the poems he has written about, or to, his wife, are those where she is addressed as his partner in old age, as together they struggle against the clock, 'the continuing/ prose that is the under-current/ of all poetry.' The phrase comes from 'Countering', a poem that ends with a grand flourish of eloquent defiance, all the more powerful for being so uncharacteristic of the late Thomas:

> Then take my hand that is
> of the bone the island

is made of, and looking at
me say what time it is
on love's face, for we have
no business here other than
to disprove certainties the clock knows.

(*Experimenting with an Amen*, 33)

This is a passage of expansive plangency, almost comparable with, say, the end of Hart Crane's *Voyages*,V. But it is permeated by a sad knowingness much more reminiscent of Donne than of Crane. What Donne and Thomas have in common is a sense of 'the continuing/ prose that is the under-current/ of all poetry.' When Donne, in 'The Good-Morrow', produces a whole exuberant array of images to prove that his new love is unique and indestructible, he does so in the certain knowledge that everything mortal is inescapably perishable. The blithe confidence of his last lines is therefore shadowed by secret desperation: 'If our two loves be one, or thou and I/ Love so alike, that none doe slacken, none can die.'[29] If indeed. And the conclusion of Thomas's poem is surely much more 'poetic' than is usual with him precisely because he wants to hint at the empty rhetoric of bravado even while genuinely placing his faith in the triumph of love over time.

R. S. Thomas's celebration of his wife's 'Seventieth Birthday' is a piece as perfect as any he has written about their relationship:

Made of tissue and H_2O,
and activated by cells
firing – Ah, heart, the legend
of your person! Did I invent
it, and is it in being still?

In the competition with other
women your victory is assured.
It is time, as Yeats said, is
the caterpillar in the cheek's rose,
the untiring witherer of your petals.

You are drifting away from
me on the whitening current of your hair.
I lean far out from the bone's bough,
knowing the hand I extend
can save nothing of you but your love.[30]

This is, in its way, a 'language' poem, to use a fashionable term. It offers a contrast between two kinds of discourse, beginning with a pseudoscientific definition of human being, before proceeding to that other mode of speaking, of which poetry is here self-consciously the supreme example. The exclamation that ushers in this other mode draws attention to its own distinctive peculiarity – the peculiarity of a mode of expression where 'heart' can be synonymous with 'person' in a sense that can be covered by the word 'legend'. The touch of the archaic about the expression is defiantly deliberate, as is the suggestion of old-fashioned courtesy, even gallantry, in the paying of the compliment. And as the poem proceeds, metaphor comes ever more proudly into its own, with the paraphrase of Yeats serving to highlight, and to dramatize this process. But the more the writing advertizes itself as 'invention', as artifice, the more sincere and authentic a form it seems to become, and the more perfectly suited it undeniably is to the tracing of the inner truth of a human relationship.

In the last poem of his recent collection, *The Echoes Return Slow*, R. S. Thomas has again attempted a love-poem not only in old age, but also in a sense of old age:

> I look out over the timeless sea
> over the head of one, calendar
> to time's passing, who is now open
> at the last month, her hair wintry.
>
> Am I catalyst of her mettle that,
> at my approach, her grimace of pain
> turns to a smile? What it is saying is:
> 'Over love's depths only the surface is wrinkled'. (121)

Even before this collection had appeared, J. P. Ward had shrewdly noted that Thomas's work was 'suffused with a new sense of the timeless. Poem after poem seems to escape any sense of the present moment, of the pressure of incident, scene or person.'[31] 'I look out' is further confirmation of the move in this direction, and it is surely one of the finest of Thomas's poems in what I have suggested is essentially the genre of epigram. Like many a serious epigram, not only does it conclude with an inscription, it also includes an element of grave wit, which in this case seems to operate as a structural principle. The poem begins with a measured contrast, accentuated by parallelism of phrasing, between 'the timeless sea', and the old lady who is so painfully subject to time. But by the poem's close, the love that the lady continues, in spite of her physical frailty, to embody, is recognized as fundamentally unchanging; and so Thomas ends, through his choice of image, by implicitly associating her with the sea after all.

Since these poems to his wife have been published in random fashion over a long period of time, they have never been supposed by commentators to form a significant part of his achievement, being assumed instead to have been written merely in 'the interval of his concern.' His poem 'The Hearth', which has an unassuming place in *H'm*, should, however, have prompted his devoted readers to reconsider:

> In front of the fire
> With you, the folk song
> Of the wind in the chimney and the sparks'
> Embroidery of the soot – eternity
> Is here in this small room,
> In intervals that our love
> Widens; and outside
> Us is time and the victims
> Of time . . . (18)

Not, then, merely 'an interval of his concern', but rather 'intervals that our love widens . . .' *Those* are the kinds of intervals that R. S. Thomas's poems to his wife occupy in his poetry. As one reads carefully and thoughtfully through his later work, the influence of those poems seems to 'widen', to spread further and further afield, entering for instance into his poems about painting (his late wife was, after all, a painter), and supplying him with the courage to write about 'the victims of time', as he does, say, in 'Beacons' where he dares mention the concentration camps: 'Their wrong is an echo defying/ acoustical law, increasing not fading' (*Between Here and Now*, 100). In short, as he admits in the closing lines of the poem that precedes, and prepares the way for, 'I look out over the timeless sea', he knows himself, and shows himself, to be 'in the debt of love.'

But above all, these poems, like those concerned with the other close members of his family, contribute to and indeed participate in, R. S. Thomas's disinterested exploration of the mystery of being, not least his own. 'Borges suggested that Shakespeare himself did not know who he was', he once said pointedly to Ned Thomas,[32] and R. S. Thomas has given his own essay in autobiography the provocative title 'Nobody'. Speaking of himself recently he has asked: 'But this one, had he ever been anything but solitary?', only to reply with a sentence that should alert us to the other, little-regarded and under-valued aspect of his imagination, the aspect with which this chapter has been primarily concerned: 'And yet in this coastal solitude, far out on a peninsula, the breaking of which by car or aircraft he so much resented, there came to him at odd moments the wisdom of humans' (*The Echoes Return Slow*, 118).

8

Prison, hotel and pub:
three images of contemporary Wales

It is interesting to note the ability shown by some recent authors to register, in the structure quite as much as in the content of their work, significant aspects of what they see as a crisis in Welsh affairs. Two novels in particular between them suggest that a style was evolved capable of conveying something, at least, of the deeply troubled spirit of the undevolved Wales of the eighties. That style could loosely be described as apocalyptic in character, bred as it was in circumstances of social and cultural disorientation.

Wales being its notoriously divided self, the works could not be expected to meet in an agreed vision of disaster. But then, Wales is likely to be one of those countries where even the end of the world will have to come in several different forms before everyone gets the message. The heroine of each of these novels would no doubt find in the aspirations of the other the very nightmare from which she is trying to escape. And yet when a reader exercises the privilege of synchronizing them, they appear as the different victims of a single, poignant historical situation which the two novels jointly succeed in defining. Mutually hostile though they may be on one level, on another they are strangely interdependent, for it is between them that they span contemporary Welsh experience.

As I read these novels consecutively, with a deepening sense of their fateful interrelationship, their unwitting complicity in the work of defining a period, an image came to my mind. It comes from a famous French cartoon from the period of the Algerian war, and it consists of two soldiers standing, facing each other. One has only one leg, and supports himself, slumping slightly, on a crutch. The other stands erect on his two proud feet, but has no arms. And this armless man is blowing a trumpet which is being held, and played, for him by the one-legged soldier. For me, the image suggested aspects of the two hapless linguistic communities in modern Wales, as represented in the two novels I'd read. Both have been differently maimed by a common history, so that neither is now able fully to encompass and express Wales on its own.

It is particularly interesting to note that both novels consciously recognize the long history of the Welsh present. Both choose to deal with life in the eighties at the point when a simple superficial coincidence of dates prompted some Welsh people to rediscover the intimate formative influence of historically distant events on present circumstances. In its highly distinctive way, Mary Jones's novel *Resistance* is an example of the literature, in the broadest sense, marking the seven-hundredth anniversary of Llywelyn's death.[1] Indeed the reaction of Wales in 1982 to the anniversary of the killing of the last native prince of Wales in 1282 is certain to provide wry future historians with evidence of the complex social mentality, the conflicting ideologies, of late twentieth-century Wales. Hywel Teifi Edwards has already taken the opportunity to examine the rhetoric accompanying efforts made for a century (1856–1956) to provide Llywelyn with some kind of national memorial.[2] The attempts at national commemoration described by him are frequently pathetic, sometimes hilarious, consistently ineffectual and never entirely free of farce. They amount to a tragi-comical resumé of recent Welsh history. As he shows, the difficulties the Welsh have had in settling on an agreed image, or estimation, of Llywelyn, derive directly from the longstanding differences and self-contradictions inherent in their views of Wales. And Mary Jones's novel is valuable because she has found contemporary ways of conveying the experiential, visceral feel, as well as the deep structure, of the emotions implicated in this fraught matter of Welshness.

More than a century ago, Gwilym Tawe addressed the National Eisteddfod on the subject of 'Nationalities: their uses and abuses'. It was his opinion 'that we have not been so much conquered as allied to England . . . While we are Welshmen in heart, speech, and behaviour, we need not cease to be Britons in the imperial sense.' To such as he – and by today his kind must be considered to be in a substantial majority in Wales – Llywelyn was at best to be sentimentalized into a simple, inoffensive patriot. At worst, he represented everything that was dangerous about asserting the separateness of Welsh national identity: this could only lead to Wales following the Irish example and resorting to violence in order to break away politically from England.

Since the last century Ireland has been the bogeyman – the bwci-bo – of Welsh politics. The violence of Irish politics down to the present day has become identified in the popular mind with the spectre of nationalism – a fact which certain guileful west British politicians have not been slow to exploit. This is worth mentioning because Mary Jones, although a native of Aberystwyth, has spent the best part of twenty years teaching English in the University of Ulster – an experience that may have made her particularly sensitive to this aspect of the Welsh popular imagination. Reduced to the barest of story outlines, her novel can be shown to follow a pattern characteristic of British public opinion, as that currently exists in Wales. The plot is about Wales, but it is made in Britain. The sub-plot, however, is, as we shall see, a rather different matter.

A woman who has recently discovered she has cancer of the jaw, seeks refuge from her anxieties in a lonely hotel in remote mid-Wales. This is the region which, in this novel, stands in for the Wild West, the Welsh Wales beyond the pale, that used to figure in the symbolic geography of early Anglo-Welsh literature. Everything in this hotel, from the surly clerk to the disjointed, unco-ordinated shape of the building, its mysterious residents and opulently bizarre décor, proves to be emphatically disconcerting and vaguely sinister. A cross between Gothic fiction and twentieth-century expressionist writing, the novel resourcefully exploits this slightly deranged and richly bewildering setting, allowing clarification to materialize only by carefully calculated degrees. Wandering the dank, rankly green countryside behind the hotel, the woman stumbles on the ruins of an old church. Near the altar end stands an oak splashed with what seems like blood: closer inspection proves it to be a wreath of fresh red roses. Add the fact that the date is 1982, and that Llywelyn is supposed to have been buried in Abaty Cwm-hir in Powys, and the picture begins to grow more clear.

Back at the strange hotel, the gauche young man, an isolato with a Mohican haircut that makes him look 'like some moping, brooding cockatoo', turns out to have friends of a kind – Welsh-speaking, uneasy and conspiratorial. The name of this last of the Mohicans is Ceri Griff – short perhaps for Gruffydd, which was of course the family name of Llywelyn – and he is dominated by the authoritative, self-contained and charismatic Aled who is stern guru to the whole group.

In spite of the unspoken connection between them and the burning of holiday homes in the area, the woman Ann is drawn to these men, finding her own personal predicament obscurely mirrored in their cultural plight. However, she awakens one midnight to discover the hotel in flames around her. Having fled with the other guests, she discovers that Aled alone is dead, killed by the explosion of one of his own infernal devices that had ignited the whole building. The morbid fascination which had held her spellbound to the place and its people has been violently ended. She returns to her ordinary life with a renewed appreciation of, and commitment to, the precarious strength of the established order of things: 'infinitely stronger, surely, than one insignificant tumour scraping away at one tiny corner of me! Just as it had been infinitely stronger than what had gnawed at Aled. And yet how frail it all was, too' (149). Returned from her excursion into self-pity and the morbid sympathy that led to such dangerous liaisons, she somewhat guiltily rejoices in her narrow escape: 'It is a base instinct, the will to survive' (149).

Taken as a whole, then, the ending is the best of British responses by English-speaking Wales to the claims made upon it by Welsh-speaking Wales. What we have, says the majority voice speaking through Ann Thomas at the end, we hold: not only out of self-interest but also out of fear of the alternatives, and in the name of what we conceive to be decent, civilized, normal order. In certain respects, this voice continues, Welsh-speaking Wales may be bewilderingly attractive to us, and unnervingly familiar; but it is also foreign and repugnant, representing as it does so radical a threat to what presently exists – economically, socially, politically, culturally – that we can conceive of it only as offering violence to what we are. It is this nexus of feelings and attitudes that the novel *Resistance* brilliantly traces out. This nexus constitutes a vital part of the dominant ideology of modern Wales, the ideology of Britishness; and it was this ideology, surely, that influenced and maybe even decided the vote against devolution in 1979.

So far this chapter has been concerned only with the general outline of the novel – its macrostructure, as one might say. But it is in its microstructure, or infrastructure, that the greatest interest really lies. When Ann passes through the doors of the hotel, 'glinting as they revolved, like the blinding facets of a crystal ball', she is stepping, as she later realizes, like Alice, right through the looking-glass:

The man at the desk looked as if he didn't sleep very much. He also looked as though he might be able to see in the dark.

From the way he stared, you would have thought I was sleep-walking towards him. Clearly, he shared my uncertainty about what I was doing there; about what I was going to do next, he seemed even more apprehensive.

Living in that gloom, I thought, you'd need to be able to see in the dark.

'*Mae'n boeth iawn, ond yw hi?*' he said (instead of whatever he had been on the point of saying).

'Pardon?'

The bulging eyes clouded, but they were still too slippery to hold. He enquired in toneless, formal English whether I could be helped. Close to, his pupils, set in an almost transparent jelly, reminded me of frogspawn.

'A single was it, madam?'

Said like that, it was more suspicious than a double.

He turned his back on me and glanced along the rows of empty pigeon-holes. There were keys dangling beside them, lolling like tongues from vacuous mouths, and I fancied the slots were starting to roll under the little black balls of his eyes, like a roulette wheel speeding up. (1)

Once past the keeper of the door, unconsciously embarked on her strange journey of initiation, she is lost in a blind maze of interminable passages:

Then, in a slight recess, I noticed a hole in the wall, neat, round, six inches or so across, and two or three feet above the ground. The perfect 'o' of a mouth stretched in pain or ecstasy or the panic of death. A little further along there was another. Then none for a while, and then another. They might occur haphazardly, but they were always of the same size and at the same height. The walls were breathing – breathing or spying or listening, and these were the ducts that served as mouth and nose and eyes and ears'. (15)

What the novel is doing is reproducing an experience we have all had: the experience of being in a situation we are aware is highly significant, but we cannot understand how, or what, it signifies. We are trapped in a mysterious system and aware of a secret code of signifiers. It is a shocking lesson in semiotics – a fashionable term that is useful because it illuminates the techniques and procedures this self-consciously sophisticated author is adopting. But it usually comes to us in familiar, even mundane forms – most commonly as quite literally an adventure in a foreign country, when we suddenly feel not geographically but culturally lost, and altogether at a loss for words.

Resistance is a significant novel because it successfully dramatizes the peculiar mixture of fascination and anxiety with which the majority culture and language-group regards the incomprehensible minority culture and language-group in Wales. The latter may be only a sub-culture, in terms of its relationship to power in the society in general, but that only makes it, under certain circumstances, all the more sinister, in ways this novel's underground imagery suggests. A 'foreign' language is a foreign power which can be felt to threaten us in many ways. Those who speak it necessarily constitute a secret society – secret because its workings are by definition impenetrable to the outsider. It has become commonplace to admit to feelings of paranoia, to fears that we are being talked about; but that is only the most accessible feature of a complex of feelings, ultimately grounded perhaps in our disturbed intuition that speakers of another language actually experience, construct, or articulate the world differently from ourselves. This is what Mary Jones has, in the distinctive style and techniques of *Resistance*, found fictional means of exploring. She has mapped out crucial features of what might be described, in rather clumsy terms, as the personal and social psychology of inter-cultural relations in modern Wales.

Lying in bed, and on the very edge of hysteria, Ann listens to the rain dripping off the spaghetti junction of fire-escapes at the back of the hotel, where the windows are 'like crazy-paving all over the wall':

> The mazes of waterlogged wooden decks oozed and dripped, from level to level, in a series of steps, down into the waterlogged yard. And all the noise came from the water gushing along the roof guttering, and gargling and spluttering as it hit the downpipes, and then sloshing down them. Now and again, when the drainpipes choked, they vomited into the pit below. I closed the window and went back to bed. The sounds outside, subdued again now, were astonishingly like language – like garbled rumours spreading about the destruction of the world. (18)

It should be emphasized, however, that these cultural concerns appear really as a second-order of meaning in a novel which primarily examines the state of mind of a woman who knows she has a possibly fatal cancer of the jaw. As a natural, but unconscious consequence, she begins to read terrible new meanings out of her world, since she has become mentally detached from the normal, comfortable 'conventions of reality'. A terror of life's grossly impersonal physical processes; a revulsion against her own body; a humiliating sense of powerlessness; these and many other feelings underly and direct her perceptions. But from the point of view of this chapter, what proves interesting is the social insights that are the by-product of her condition.

Anthropologists and psychologists have long been interested in liminality, and the peculiar experiences that belong to this no-man's-land between clearly established modes of being. In many societies initiation rites mark the transitional period of adolescence, and involve the symbolic departure of the novice from the community, his isolation and eventual return with a different social status. The awe some cultures feel for a confirmed state of adult virginity is partly to be explained by its being an irregular or anomalous state between the two conventional cultural categories of childhood and maturity. It could be defined either as being neither the one nor the other, or as being paradoxically both the one and the other. Legend is full of such peculiar states – the Lady of Llyn-y-Fan is wooed by the lakeside between land and water, and can only be won by bread that is at once baked and unbaked.[3]

The heroine of *Resistance* is in her early middle-age, the period commonly referred to as 'the change of life'. She is still an old maid and virginal. She has recently been made redundant, in a society where work is still one of the chief bestowers of identity. She was a teacher, one of the controlling class, but no longer is. Above all, her illness has set her apart from her ordinary company; the sharp pain in her jaw is the sword come between her present self and what she previously was. Taken all together these are at once the cause and the symbolic expression of her situation: she has ceased to be able to believe in the version of the world by which she was accustomed to live. The hotel is her temporary place of mental residence, between ego and id, and between two cultural ideologies. She is uniquely placed to catch the underlying mood of our period, conveyed in the atmosphere of lethargy instinct with violence that prevails in the novel. The landscape is described in terms deliberately reminiscent both of *The Waste Land* and the *Mabinogion*. 'A hot moist festering where only fungi thrived' is what is produced by 'this summer, rotten to the core, . . . that had grown tired of itself, and sunk into a humid depression.' While the view from the hotel yard from her bedroom window yields only horrors:

> I spent the evenings in my room, like some senseless lover with a host of ladders pitched to the balcony. But all that appeared, in the wake of the frogs, were rats; . . . There was a low scraping sound in the yard one day, an ominously slow sound, and there on the metal blades lay a rat, looking for all the world as though he had lost his footing on ice. The little paws were galvanised into a frenzy, flapping either side of him like the oars of a boat at the brink of a weir. But it was hopeless: the body

they strove to propel was a ton weight, quite beyond his failing strength. For a moment I thought that on top of everything, he was losing the entrails from his abdomen, but all I had seen was his tail. I looked at my watch; I would just be in time for a drink, if I hurried. (75–6)

Sexual tension blends with a fear of physical dissolution in this scene, but it is also a nightmarish social perception. Landscape and yard are partly expressive of her response to the decaying Welsh-language culture in its dual aspects of victim and aggressor, its related modes of hopeless passivity and frustrated violence. But the very same scenes are also partly expressive of her sense of the sinister decay of the other, dominant and hitherto relatively buoyant, culture in modern Wales – the British society to which she normally, 'naturally' belongs. For a brief period she seems to intuit a connection between the state of the two cultures, fused as they are in a single image of the generally derelict state of a neglected and self-neglectful Wales, before the fire in the hotel sends her fleeing back to the dubious safety of her own class, her own society, her own kind.

※   ※   ※

Future historians may well be interested in comparing Mary Jones's scenes of sodden desolation with that other powerful contemporary exercise in the apocalyptic style with which Gwyn A. Williams concludes *When Was Wales?*.[4] But the outstanding work in this eighties genre is the second novel mentioned at the beginning of this chapter, namely *Yma o Hyd*, which is one of the best Welsh books, in either language, to have appeared for quite a time.[5] It is also certainly the bleakest. The author, Angharad Tomos, is probably best known as a militant campaigner with *Cymdeithas yr Iaith Gymraeg* and a former chairperson of that society. She is also a gifted writer, as her popular children's books have shown, and her novel is presumably based on the terms she herself has bravely spent in several prisons. It purports to be a diary illicitly scribbled on prison toilet paper by the aptly named Blodeuwedd – one of the children, as it were, of Saunders Lewis's imagination.

Of this novel's dark cross-hatching of ironies, one of the earliest and best is Blodeuwedd's jaundiced observation that the world's greatest pearls of wisdom have been written on spend-a-penny prison paper. Bonhoeffer, Luther King, Bunyan, the Apostle Paul, it was on snatched scraps of paper they wrote those fierce words that now repose so calmly between gilt covers. For Blodeuwedd such transformations are sinister examples of established society's inexhaustible ability to render serious opposition harmless by assimilating it. And, as she notes, the cult of literature is one of the most effective means by which society currently controls radically dissident opinion.

An example of anti-literature literature, her crabbed entries on disposable paper are written more in anger than in sorrow, and communicate the aggravated ferocity of the caged mind. The prison is here harrowingly well established as being a real, dispiriting place, complete with piss-pots, foul language and human wreckage. But it is also a passionate figure of Welsh speech – a trope for the Wales of today, post-1979, to which Blodeuwedd at times finds it easy to prefer her English prison; and a trope for her cruelly inescapable Welshness – the confines of a state of consciousness determined by the state of the language itself. The novel gives us, unforgettably, the tormented psychology of cultural crisis and of political frustration. 'This is getting from bad to worse. Perhaps I'm gradually going off my head. Think too much, that's what I do. My head's going round and round in circles like a roll of cellotape I can't find a way of starting.'

Yma o Hyd (Still Here) – the title is a reference to Dafydd Iwan's song, the chorus of which became to the eighties what 'I'r Gad' (Into Battle) was to the seventies – the theme song of the Welsh cultural movement. The exchanging of the one for the other signals the change of mood following the referendum of 1979. 'Into Battle', the triumphal political campaign song of militant cultural revivalism, was replaced by 'We're still here', a defiant song of militant cultural survivalism: 'er gwaethaf pawb a phopeth, er gwaethaf pawb a phopeth, er gwaethaf pawb a phopeth, 'rŷn ni yma o hyd.' ('In spite of everything and everyone, in spite of everything and everyone, in spite of everything and everyone, we are still here.') The seven-hundredth anniversary of Llywelyn's death in 1282 came at a singularly inopportune time for the movement. The events of 1979 made it impossible to celebrate the occasion realistically in terms of the reawakening of an independent Welsh consciousness, and all that was then left suitable for the occasion was an elegy for a lost leader, a lost cause, a lost vote, a lost opportunity, and a lost people – a feeling most memorably conveyed in Gerallt Lloyd Owen's bitterly anguished song of betrayal: 'Wylit, wylit, Lywelyn':

> You would weep, you would weep, Llywelyn
> Would weep blood, if you saw this.
> Our heart possessed by a stranger,

> Our crown by a conqueror,
> And a nation of booty-lovers,
> With meek smiles, where there used to be men.[6]

With the help of Dafydd Iwan's prolific song-writing genius, however, an alternative date for celebration was found, the anniversary in 1983 of Macsen Wledig's (Magnus Maximus's) departure from Wales in 383, a semi-mythical event regarded by some as inaugurating Welsh history.[7]

Angharad Tomos's novel is set in the autumn of 1983, and explores the different shades of meaning lurking within that phrase 'Rŷn ni yma o hyd' ('We are still here'). In the process it dissents from, and criticizes, the sentimental glibness with which the words are popularly sung. Survival is in committed practice a matter of grimly persisting even at devastating cost not only to oneself but also to others. It is to be placed by the centuries under an obligation from which one sometimes yearns to be released. In Blodeuwedd's weary experience, to sing 'Rŷn ni yma o hyd' is also to resent the grim Welsh life-sentence that has been handed down.

This interplay between the title and what might loosely be called a popular literary stereotype – between novel and song – is typical of the complex intertextuality of *Yma o Hyd*. The crucial point to remember is that the fight for the Welsh language has been primarily conducted in terms of the survival of the literary culture. Literature is part of the very *raison d'être* of the struggle: the language, the philosophy, the controlling images, in short the whole outlook of those engaged in it has been, and continues to be, fashioned by literature. Angharad Tomos's novel is accordingly a kind of 'inquiry' (to paraphrase Paul Fussell's comment in *The Great War and Modern Memory*) into 'the curious literariness of contemporary Welsh life.'[8] It is in part a sour investigation of what it was like, in the eighties, actually to live out certain lines of literature, until either their lie was exposed or else they took on tortured new meanings unsuspected by those, including sometimes their authors, who were content to take them at their merely sentimental, or rhetorical, word.

T. H. Parry Williams's 'Hon', for instance, became a vogue poem for a generation of Welsh speakers who found in it a flattering image of their frustrating plight:

> Why should I give a hang about Wales? It's by a mere fluke
> of fate
> That I live in its patch. On a map it does not rate

Higher than a scrap of earth in a back corner,
And a bit of bother to those who believe in order.

And who is it lives in this spot, tell me that.
Who but the dregs of society? Please, cut it out,

This endless clatter of oneness and country and race:
You can get plenty of these, without Wales, any place.

I've long since had it with listening to the croon
Of the Cymry, indeed, forever moaning their tune.

I'll take a trip, to be rid of their wordplay with tongue
    and with pen,
Back to where I once lived, aboard my fantasy's train.

And here I am then. Thanks be for the loss,
Far from all the fanatics' talkative fuss.

Here's Snowdon and its crew; here's the land, bleak and
    bare;
Here's the lake and river and crag, and look, over there,

The house where I was born. But see, between the earth and
    the heavens,
All through the place there are voices and apparitions.

I begin to totter somewhat, and I confess
There comes over me, so it seems, a sort of faintness;

And I feel the claws of Wales tear at my heart.
God help me, I can't away from this spot.[9]

Even more popular as an aid to misery was Gwenallt's 'Wales': 'Why
have you given us this misery,/ The pain like leaden weights on flesh and
blood?/ Your language on our shoulders like a sack,/ And your
traditions shackles round our feet?'[10]

Yma o Hyd is a rewriting of such poems in blood – the maddened
blood and distraught mind of the imprisoned young activist Blodeuwedd.
She associates the originals with the masochistic letters sent to her by
well-wishers who the more they squirmed under the lash of their self-
contempt, the more Basildon Bond they used. She may be holed up in
prison, but the fellow-travellers just keep right on travelling, along the
broad M4s of Welsh life. Having been imprisoned many times, she is
used to the elaborate psychological games they play in lieu of decisive
social action. Indeed the novel itself engages mockingly in a related

game with her readers, locking them into a vicious circle of guilt, and guilt at their own guilt, in a way that is positively Dostoevskean, even to the implied despairing message that only a cataclasmic act of grace could possibly rescue the Welsh-language community from this awful sleeping-sickness of the will.

Blodeuwedd's, then, is the voice of experience. She speaks for the second, or even the third generation of activists to whom the straightforward confidence and simple determination of the early days, in the heady sixties and hopeful seventies, seem now as innocent as they are remote. For these hardened young eighties veterans the thumping anti-devolution vote of 1979 was only the most dramatic of a whole series of disillusioning events, which in Blodeuwedd's case led her to commit an act of such apparently wanton violence that it remains inexplicable even to herself. Previously imprisoned for routine offences, like removing English-language road signs, she has this time been convicted of smashing up a shop systematically, in cold-blooded fury. Although she cannot understand why she did this, the causes are surely to be discovered in the state of mind revealed in her diary. What she has sensed is how adept established society, including its Welsh speakers, is at neutralizing any gesture of would-be radical protest simply by treating it as one more move in a game which continues to be played according to the rules of the status quo. Removing road signs may seem to some to be a regrettable, even deplorable form of conduct, and it is certainly illegal; but it is still tolerably reasonable, by prevailing standards. Even the symbolic power of such actions is quickly lost once the ritual has been several times repeated. The offenders are as far as ever they were from effecting a real shift in public consciousness, as the overwhelmingly pro-centralist anti-devolution vote showed. This state of affairs was brought home to Blodeuwedd following her last routine language-society offence, when well-wishers actually joined un-wittingly in the well-established ritual by intervening to pay her fine so as to secure her immediate release. Her subsequent act of 'wanton' vandalism followed directly from this, and was patently her attempt to say No! in thunder, to everything that was the case in Wales. Resorting in desperate circumstances to desperate measures, she did not so much break as smash the very rules according to which both sides were playing these innocuous games of protest.

It is therefore natural for the novel, too, to achieve its effects through partial breaches in decorum. To the anti-literature strain that has already been noted could be added Blodeuwedd's tendency to present herself almost as an anti-heroine, who scorns admiration or sympathy. And instead of the cultivated language of the educated class, we have the sometimes demotic language of the screaming mind, as Blodeuwedd discovers that isolation, even from her own family, is the scarcely bearable price she has to pay for her iconoclastic daring. She stands in a tragically complex relation to her namesake, Saunders Lewis's Blodeuwedd, the woman made of flowers, who told her maid:

> O, you will never understand
> My anguish, never, not you, not anyone.
> You do not know what it is to be alone.
> For you the world is full, you have a home,
> Kinsmen and family, father, mother, brothers,
> And so you are not a stranger in the world.
> The spot where men have walked is familiar,
> And all of Gwynedd, where your forefathers lived,
> Is a hearth to you, a roof constructed
> By generations of your ancestors:
> You are at home in your own land
> As in a bed that was prepared for you
> By loving hands that long awaited you;
> As for me, not a single homestead is mine
> In all the paths of men.[11]

Ironically enough, the Blodeuwedd of *Yma o Hyd* suffers a comparable loneliness precisely because she *does* have a home and a family and a country. Her roots are also the roots of her alienation. She has been rendered homeless by her homeland.

There is in Wales a long tradition of diary-keeping, both as an actual spiritual practice and as a literary convention, and this tradition, in its entirety, is relevant to *Yma o Hyd*. But the main effect, in this instance, of the diary form is to emphasize the difficulties the heroine experiences in establishing a rapport with someone – anyone – sufficient to allow genuine communication to take place. This is not due to a flaw in character, or a peculiarity of temperament, but is the saddest evidence of the cracks produced by contemporary social pressures in the fabric even of the community of committed Welsh speakers to which she belongs. It is symbolically appropriate therefore that she should be marooned in an English prison and that, following a defiant attempt to console herself by making a rag doll, she should eventually be placed in solitary confinement.

Under this most extreme of circumstances she begins to hallucinate extraordinary scenes of visionary intensity. In her disturbed imagination she returns to scenes from her past, only to find that they have been emptied of life, of purpose, of people. Driven to distraction, she wanders the rooms of her family home and the courtrooms Cymdeithas yr Iaith had made ring with their singing, all of which stand deserted and silent now, as if a nuclear explosion had caused language itself to cease to be. (One of the subsidiary themes of the novel, in its latter and latter-day stages, is the military defeat of the Greenham women by that most impeccably, and implacably, British of modern Welshmen, Mr Michael Heseltine.)

All this while, Heledd's great grief-stricken, spine-chilling song of cultural disaster, a ninth-century fragment from a lost saga, is haunting the text: 'Stafell Cynddylan ys tywyll heno,/ Heb dân, heb wely:/ Wylaf wers, tawaf wedy.' ('Cynddylan's room is dark tonight, without fire, without bed: I weep awhile, then am silent.')[12] The choice of a woman as the narrator of 'Canu Heledd' may, so the *Companion to Welsh Literature* informs us, have been determined, if only subconsciously, by the ancient Celtic myth which held the land to be personified by a goddess. By the end of *Yma o Hyd* Blodeuwedd, too, has come to assume a similar role. 'Stafell Cynddylan ys tywyll heno,/ Heb dân, heb gannwyll;/Namyn Duw pwy a'm dyry pwyll?' 'Save for God, who will keep me sane?' In echoing that cry, Blodeuwedd identifies herself not only with Heledd but also with the Myrddin who, following the battle of Arfderydd, was driven beyond all reason, out of his mind and into Celyddon Wood, where he lived as a wild man, communing with the animals. In his madness he received the gift of prophecy and Blodeuwedd, in this novel which is itself an immensely important modern addition to this ancient apocalyptic tradition, moves on to an even stranger plane of vision. Venturing into the cellar of these empty buildings she discovers the place is not, after all, deserted, because there, cowering under tables covered tent-like with tarpaulins in the pathetic manner approved by Civil Defence, is a vast silent crowd. Suddenly a Dafydd Iwan-like figure appears, whose song briefly gives new heart to a cowed people. But then brute reality breaks in, with a sound of breaking glass and rushing feet, and the crowd is forced to move out into the cold:

> We walk together, and through us, between us, around us, there spreads a fear that rises from hidden depths, interconnecting everything. We seem to be walking for ever towards our extinction, and I can think of

nothing. Think of nothing, except that we are still here. Here – still. Yma – o hyd! (128)

There is, then, an apocalyptic style which is common to both *Resistance* and *Yma o Hyd*. And this style is not simply a literary convention, not merely an exercise in hyperbole. It is a perfectly reasonable extrapolation by the imagination from the serious economic, social and cultural situation in Wales during the eighties. The duty of poetry, it was once famously said, is to warn. To which one might add that in this country there is the further duty each of its two literatures owes Wales, which is the duty to heed each other's warning. There is a need for the heroines (as obviously distinct from the authors) of both novels to realize that the road envisaged as leading away from disaster in the one case is a road leading towards disaster in the other. The fear of Welsh-language culture felt by the one needs to affect and modify the fear for Welsh-language culture of the other. In turn, there is Blodeuwedd's awareness of the destructive influence on the Welsh economy of the stubbornly centralized British state, and her sensitivity to the dark encroachments of a purely British ideology on areas vital to the survival of a distinctive Welsh culture, in both languages. This needs to register with Ann, who is so anxious to escape from similar presentiments of her own – the view from the hotel – back to a desperate acceptance of things as they are.

Given that such a mutually, nationally educative interchange of views is indeed possible, then it could be that the awareness of incipient catastrophe – their apocalyptic style – is after all paradoxically the most hopeful thing about these two novels. Otherwise, in the absence of such an extension of sympathy, the linguistic groups in Wales could well be proceeding on two set courses towards one and the same end: the end of a distinctively Welsh identity. The future will then hold a scene rather like the one depicted in a cartoon featured a few years ago in *Private Eye*: where two little men stand by the kerb, watching four skeletal horsemen ride by. 'Typical', says one to the other, 'you wait ages for a horseman of the apocalypse – and then four come along.'

*   *   *

Excellent though they are, these two novels are not the best known fictional studies of Wales to appear during the eighties. That dubious honour undoubtedly belongs to a novel by an outsider, Kingsley Amis, and *The Old Devils*[13] can serve as an useful 'control' for indigenous material like *Resistance* and *Yma o Hyd*.

Such was the hype surrounding the 1986 Booker Prize winner that in the end everyone felt they had read it, even if they had never actually opened the book. Which of course was crap, as Kingsley Amis and his characters are particularly fond of saying. It is in fact crap, or bullshit, that is the rich fertilizer of the whole wide field of social comedy in *The Old Devils* – appropriately enough, since the novel opens with an ageing man's morbid preoccupation with his bowel movements and resultant lavatory humour. But the champion crapper in the novel is undoubtedly Alun Weaver, randy tomcat, multi-media personality, and world-famous professional Welshman, whose return to live in Wales means, he sincerely assures his local-radio interviewer, 'Many things grave and gay and multi-coloured but one above all; I'm coming home. That short rich resounding word means one simple thing to a Welshman such as I, born and bred in this land of river and hill. And that thing, that miraculous thing, is – Wales'(42).

Weaver brings the very best out of Amis, who, like any self-respecting English author, knows an engaging cad when he invents one. Wales, on the other hand, at times brings out the professional Englishman in Amis – who can be roguishly bluff and tetchily blimpish in the best of Brits abroad tradition: 'A sign used to say "Taxi" and now said "Taxi/ Tacsi" for the benefit of Welsh people who had never seen a letter X before'(44). That's crap right enough, but this time from the author himself.

Frequently, though, he is at his funniest, and is most serviceable to Wales, when he plays the part of the Old Devils' advocate. They are a clutch (in more senses than one) of ageing couples, trapped in a vicious circle of friendship. Their Wales for the over-sixties is a land of wine and women, but, alas of all things, no song. Their jaundiced reaction to the contemporary scene is by turns comically querulous and scathingly funny. The grotesquely fat Peter snorts in indignation at an ASH poster he sees in a pub:

> Something between the used glasses and muscular dystrophy collecting box caught his eye and he bent to see better, fumbling for his spectacles. A moment later he gave a kind of snarling bellow, loud enough anyway to cause a nearby head or two to twist in his direction.
> 'Wouldn't you bloody know', he said not much less loudly. 'ASH *yng* sodding *Nghymru. Diolch am . . .* What kind of madhouse . . .'
> 'Never mind, no one understands it', said Charlie soothingly.
> 'Not content with trying to stop me smoking they have the bloody cheek to do it in buggering *Welsh*. It's enough to make you . . .'(111)

To be honest, one would have to admit that this reaction is typical of the attitude of several of the inhabitants of contemporary Wales towards the Welsh language. Perhaps it is only someone from outside Wales, and that someone an Englishman, who would dare ignore the taboo that inhibits so many of Wales's own writers, in both English and Welsh, from treating a subject that creates so much tension in Welsh society. But then, Amis has always been a *connoisseur* of people's prejudices, not least because he realises that they are a far more reliable index to the majority view in society than are the guarded opinions of the intellectuals. The pub frequented by Peter and his cronies is, it emerges, run by English people who litter the place with Welsh-language signs in order to profitably pretend they've gone native. The tendency of Welsh people themselves to pay only fashionably senti-mental lip service to Welsh culture and its past is also the subject of caustic comment. Sign-painters are kept in business by public houses who want to be renamed 'Glyndŵr' instead of 'Glendower'.

Comedy is, then, for Amis the ultimate in national crap-detection, but the comedy in the novel is so consistently good because it is rooted in fears and anxieties – those of the characters and also perhaps those of Amis himself.[14] At a wedding Peter meets Alun's sister-in-law, a woman with 'very red lips and abnormally long teeth thrown in'. She is voracious for company, because she is tethered to a husband who has been overtaken by old age and has inconsiderately gone deaf on her. 'At Rhiannon's front gate they halted again . . . She said, "Take my advice, Mr Thomas, and don't go deaf. Well, it's been nice talking to you." . . . Duncan gave a not quite unsmiling nod of farewell and thanks for not having said anything to him'(279). Irresistible change and decay in all around is what the comic eye sees in *The Old Devils* – from the very beginning when Malcolm steers his morning toast and diabetic honey away from the 'no-go' area in his mouth where there are no longer any teeth worthy of the name, to the very end when, *Western Mail* under his arm, he strolls nonchalantly to the toilet, hoping to catch his temperamental bowel movements offguard, with his trousers down.

Comedy is the dress of various fears of the kind seen grossly naked in Charlie's gibbering terror of the dark. In the end, it is his friend Alun who reduces him to that state deliberately, by way of malicious revenge for Charlie's too-candid critical comments on the book Alun is writing. And that, it seems, is what friends are for in *The Old Devils* – to tolerate each other's weaknesses in order the better to betray each other's confidences. Fear is what bonds them together – fear of terminal boredom, for instance; 'But uglier still is the hump that we get from not having enough to do', as Kipling is quoted as saying (11). And of course fear of death – 'On the way in Malcolm's spirits lifted, as they always did at the prospect of an hour or more spent not thinking about being ill or things to do with being ill' (10).

But there is also fear of life – of modern life, almost every manifestation of which, however trivial, seems to them strange and fathomlessly silly. In other words, 'crap' is their terse understated expression of an apocalyptic view of the world such as is most memorably found in Pope's *Dunciad* – where, incidentally, one of the heroic 'games' played by the idiots involves jumping into an open sewer. Such doom-laden fears, although primarily attributed to his characters and made the butt of comedy, are also in part shared by Amis himself, and this helps explain his attitudes towards Wales.

He summarized these in a recent interview in *The Literary Review*:

> If you're Welsh, according to Amis, 'you want to be for something, and you look around and you can't find anything of which you can say "I'm behind this." It's an awful position to be in. You start saying, isn't it a pity that the Welsh language has declined – and it is, and it's inevitable – but as soon as you start saying let's try and revive it, then you're talking *crap*. . . [Yet] once you've lost your language, you have in a sense lost any past that's worth defending.[15]

In the novel itself the following seems to be a key passsage. The speaker is Malcolm, a Welsh speaker but usually shy of the fact:

> Everything new here is the same as new things in England . . . At last they've found a way of destroying our country, not by poverty but by prosperity . . . It'll be all right with you, when everything's gone and we're left with a language that nobody speaks and Brydan and a few choirs, and Wales is a place on the map and nothing else? . . . You can laugh if you like . . . Specially funny of course to English people. Silly old Welsh bugger. But they'll be laughing on the other side of their faces before long. Because it's going to be their turn next.' (112–13)

Amis has, of course, cunningly arranged it so that we *do* laugh at poor Malcolm. Nevertheless, the fears expressed by him are, one suspects, shared by the author himself, who feels it could easily be England's 'turn next'.

Amis's attitude towards Wales is seen to change, depending on what social or cultural group he's dealing with. First, there's the English-speaking majority, whose cultural disorientation he regards with amused protests of concern. Second, there's the Welsh-speaking minority, whose situation he regards with amused professions of sympathy, provided they do not try to use Welsh as a modern language and do not suppose that anything should or could be done to halt its decline. Together these two groups constitute a 'Wales' that fascinates Amis because its loss of distinctive identity is what he, like Malcolm, believes his England is also (although as yet to an infinitely lesser extent) threatened with. He has therefore created a 'Wales' that allows him to work off, through comedy, his anger and fear and bewilderment at the way things are going in England. Except, of course, that the militant (as opposed to the meekly fading) presence of the Welsh language feeds his paranoid fears of foreign presences and so intermittently provokes his most withering comic attention.

The Wales Kingsley Amis is most attracted to is neither the Wales of cultural nationalism nor the Wales of the comfortable, Anglicized middle class, nor the 'International' Wales of all-purpose concrete and plastic. Rather it is the Wales Rhiannon thinks she sees as she crosses the border, and which she virtually comes to embody by the end of the book: 'There was no obvious giveaway, like road signs in two languages or closed-down factories, but something was there, an extra greenness in the grass, a softness in the light, something that was very like England and yet not England at all, more a matter of feeling than seeing but not just feeling, something run-down and sad but simpler and freer than England all the same' (39). This is an atmospheric evocation of an unpretentiously provincial Wales, decently lower-middle-class, just as (in Amis's conservative imagination) the best of English provinces used to be, but with a little extra local colour to add to its charm. It knows its place and doesn't go in for separatist or socialist politics and all that crap.

Contemporary Wales, on the other hand, is summed up by the hideous decor of the ubiquitous modern pubs which the four friends, zealous drinkers all, literally go out of their way to avoid, because they resemble a 'public lecture-theatre or bit of local government.' But even after they have made every effort to steer clear of such monstrosities they occasionally find they have been caught out:

> Don't you see, I'm saying the place in Harriston was just the same as an *English* pub. That's what they're doing everywhere. Everywhere new here is the same as new things in England, whether it's the university or the restaurants or the supermarkets or what you buy there. What about

this place we're in? Is there anything in here to tell you you're in Wales?
(112)

In fact, the newfangledness of Wales serves Amis as a means of attacking the newfangledness of England.

As Kingsley Amis frankly admitted when he discussed *The Old Devils* on *Desert Island Discs*, his knowledge of Wales is spectacularly limited:

> [As you grow older] you get better at what might be called the tip-of-the-iceberg con. You imply that you know everything about a subject. For example, I try to imply that I know everything about eisteddfods and the Chapel and that sort of life in Wales just by quoting two or three little bits. The implication being, 'I could tell you all about it if I had room, but I'm just letting these little bits out', so that's the tip, but there's a huge iceberg. Of course, there really isn't any iceberg.[16]

At least there is an iceberg, but it is an iceberg the tip of which is Welsh and the submerged mass of which is English. Amis has to a large extent devised a 'Wales' which allows his imagination to create an oblique picture of England – just as sci-fi writers (a genre to which Amis is himself after all addicted) create a picture of life on Mars in 3500 AD in order to give themselves the freedom to explore aspects of human life on earth.

Amis recently published some verse that touches lightly and deftly on the way we view the world from the narrow perspective of the particular culture to which we belong. 'It may seem funny, but my cat/ Is learning English. Think of that/ . . . So when I pick up Sarah's dish/ And ask who's for a spot of fish,/ I have to listen carefully/ But I've no doubt she answers "Me!" '[17] And viewed from the English point of view, has not Wales been over the centuries a creature very like that cat? In other words, the varying treatment of Wales that can be discerned in English literature is less a guide to different aspects and periods of the country's history, than an index to the history of England. This is a vast topic, still relatively little explored, but space allows the mention here of only one or two obvious examples.

For the Honour of Wales is the title of the masque by Ben Jonson performed before the court in London in 1618. It features several naïve, comical characters who between them summarize the characteristic features of the Welsh as seen by the English of that day. Griffith, Jenkin, Evan and the others are fiery, proud patriots who rejoice in their aristocratic pedigree and are forever boasting of the beauty of their ancient land. They insist on paying tribute to James I, because they regard him as the Son of Divination, as prophesied long ago by Merlin. What proof have they of this? Well, by rearranging the letters of the king's full name, Charles James Stuart, they are able to obtain the expression 'Claimes ̄Arthurs Seate, which is as much as to say, your Madestie s'ud be the first King of Gread *Pritan* and sit in *Cadier Arthur*.'[18]

It's not difficult to discern the political implications of the masque. It was clearly an attempt to adapt the Tudor propaganda about Wales to serve the purpose of the new Stuart dispensation. Unlike Henry VII and his descendants, James could not claim that a Welshman descended lineally from Arthur was now occupying the throne of Britain and fulfilling the prophesies of the old bards. Therefore it was necessary for Jonson to invent another flattering, if frankly outrageous, explanation for Wales's special place in the new British state.

But there is also another aspect to the work, because Jonson, rather like Amis three centuries later, creates an imaginary picture of Wales primarily in order to pass oblique comment on the social state of England at that time. The cunning machinations of the hangers-on at court were abhorrent to Jonson and he disliked the greed and ambition of the middle class as well as the pretentions of the *nouveaux riches*. Therefore what he offers in *For the Honour of Wales*, in spite of the patronizing humour that characterizes the writing throughout, is a dramatized description of the substantial virtues which, in his opinion, typified the dependable old families of the minor English gentry: 'stout, valiant, courteous, hospitable, temperate, ingenious, capable of all good Arts, most lovingly constant, charitable.' These are suitably scaled down versions of the values he elsewhere, in poems such as 'To Penshurst', attributed fulsomely to the great houses of traditional England.

More than two centuries later other popular misconceptions about Wales afforded another Englishman an opportunity of challenging aspects of his own cultural background. As Anthony Conran has memorably shown, this is what happened in the case of Gerard Manley Hopkins, after he had spent a period at St Beuno's College in 1877.[19] Partly, perhaps, as a result of the Blue Books Report of 1847 he regarded the 'peasantry' of Wales (as he liked to call them) as a fickle, feckless and sensual people. Indeed he was apparently attracted to Wales originally by rumours of this sensuality, as if, Anthony Conran suggests, he were searching for a way of escaping from the inhibiting influence of his English Victorian middle-class background. And as he began to learn Welsh so, Conran argues, he released the creative energy that had been imprisoned in his unconscious. His imagination was, of course, further excited by the Wales that had been created in Romantic myth – the 'wild Wales' of a semi-pagan people who retained something of an ancient Celtic magic.

One of the last notable English writers to take advantage of this myth was D. H. Lawrence, when he wrote his novella about a majestic Welsh horse called *St Mawr*. An equally important place in the story is reserved for the groom Lewis, who cares for the stallion so lovingly and who has an air about him of quiet strength and aristocratic self-possession. He is a Welshman who comes 'from one of those places where the spirit of aboriginal England [sic] still lingers, the old savage England, whose lost blood flows still in a few Englishmen, Welshmen, Cornishmen.'[20] By contrasting him with the arrogant or subservient, and always inadequate, characters produced by the English class-system, Lawrence is able to suggest that 'the little aboriginal Lewis' (25) is a kind of survivor from nobler times. Indeed he is specifically likened to another character, a Mexican with the 'unforgettable glint of the Indian', because Lawrence regards them both as examples of the survival of primitivism in the effete world of 'advanced' Western civilization.

The Old Devils belongs, then, to a long tradition of using Wales in English literature as a device for highlighting some aspect or other of English society and culture. The novel is a kind of stalking-horse for Amis's Old Fogeyism, the matured version of the Young Fogeyism which he, along with friends like Philip Larkin, first affected and publicized as far back as the fifties. At that time they made a provocative cult of their Little Englandism and their contemptuous xenophobia. Modernism in all its forms became their pet hate, and through the references to Brydan in *The Old Devils* Kingsley Amis mischievously shows that his dislike of Dylan Thomas is still alive and decidedly kicking. In an astute, if acerbic, review in *The Times Literary Supplement*, Tom Paulin recently argued that 'Larkin's real theme' was 'national decline.' His comments on the socio-political dimensions of Larkin's treatment of middle age could easily be adapted to apply to Amis's treatment of old age in *The Old Devils*:

> The autumn leaves [in Larkin's poem 'Afternoons'] fall in ones and twos, rather like colonies dropping out of the empire; the young mothers whose beauty has thickened feel that 'something' is pushing

them to the side of their own lives, and this is a metaphor for a sense of diminished purpose and fading imperial power. Incipient middle age is like a return to the Middle Ages, to the English people's faint, marginal early history.[21]

Paulin further remarked that this England is 'a place of small-towns and allotments where it is for ever 1947 . . . Larkin's snarl, his populism and his calculated philistinism all speak for [Norman] Tebbit's England and for that gnarled and angry puritanism which is so deeply ingrained in the culture.' In *The Old Devils* the very epitome of old-style decency is the long-suffering Rhiannon, a character with whom Amis, like the fictional Malcolm, seems to be in love. Her dependable good nature of the old-fashioned kind shines like a good deed in the naughty modern world, and she becomes the embodiment of everything that 'Wales' should be; straightforwardly sensible, solidly provincial and altogether comfortable. Blake Morrison was surely right when, in his *TLS* review, he unconsciously used English terms to describe Amis's desired country: 'it would be a Wales of pubs and working villages and Orwellian decency.'[22]

*   *   *

Especially when it is taken in conjunction with Mary Jones's *Resistance* and Angharad Tomos's *Yma o Hyd*, Kingsley Amis's *The Old Devils* bears out the important point made by Seamus Heaney some time ago in his essay on 'Englands of the Mind'. He was referring specifically to the poetry of Ted Hughes, Geoffrey Hill and Philip Larkin, but his comments are of more general significance, as he himself suggests:

> I believe they are afflicted with a sense of history that was once the peculiar affliction of the poets of other nations who were not themselves natives of England but who spoke the English language. The poets of the mother culture, I feel, are now possessed of that defensive love of their territory which was once shared only by those poets whom we might call colonial – Yeats, MacDiarmid, Carlos Williams. They are aware of their Englishness as deposits in the descending storeys of the literary and historical past. Their very terrain is becoming consciously precious. A desire to preserve indigenous traditions, to keep open the imagination's supply lines to the past, to receive from the stations of Anglo-Saxon confirmations of ancestry, to perceive in the rituals of show Saturdays and race-meetings and seaside outings, of church-going and marriages at Whitsun, and in the necessities that crave expression after the ritual of church-going has passed away, to perceive in these a continuity of

communal ways, and a confirmation of an identity which is threatened – all this is signified by their language.[23]

Read 'Wales' for 'England' throughout this passage and it will serve as a useful epilogue to both *Resistance* and *Yma o Hyd*. But equally, take the passage simply as it stands, and much of it applies to Kingsley Amis's *The Old Devils*. In other words, his novel is interesting because it shows how the cultural plight of Wales can be seen as certainly anticipating, and perhaps even as closely resembling the cultural predicament of England. The three novels together provide early confirmation of the prescient point made by Emyr Humphreys as recently as 1983:

> ... the Welsh experience prefigures in several essentials what is in effect now the position of most European nations, even the great ones like England, Germany and France. Their position in relation to each other, their inter-national bodies and the guiding power of the United States, bears some resemblance, especially in its cultural and even spiritual aspects to the position of Wales in relation to the greatness of England over four centuries. Under such condition, what is the value of distinct identity? Why should England, for example, resist the massive historic forces that would transform it into an off-shore platform of an American culture vibrating with diverse and exciting forms?[24]

In prison, hotel and pub alike, these and related matters are the central topics under consideration.

Notes

Notes to Preface

1 'Cymru'n un', *Dail Pren* (Gwasg Aberystwyth, 1957), 93.
2 *Talking of Wales* (London: Cassell, 1976), 42.
3 'Of Symbols and Boundaries', in Anthony P. Cohen, ed., *Symbolising Boundaries: Identity and Diversity in British Culture* (Manchester: Manchester University Press, 1989), 19.
4 John Osmond, *The National Question Again* (Llandysul: Gomer Press, 1985), xx.
5 Denis Balsom, 'The Three Wales Model', in *National Question*, Chapter 1 (1–17).
6 Morris Shapira, ed., *Henry James, Selected Literary Criticism* (Harmondsworth: Penguin, 1968), 43.
7 Dai Smith, *Wales! Wales?* (London: Allen and Unwin, 1984), 1.

Notes to Chapter 1

1 *Welsh Outlook* (1914), 178.
2 Olive Ely Hart, *The Drama in Modern Wales: a brief history of Welsh playwriting from 1900 to the present day* (Philadelphia, 1928), 20–21.
3 Cecil Price, 'Towards a National Drama for Wales', *Anglo-Welsh Review* (1962), 12–29. Hywel Teifi Edwards, 'Wythnos yn Hanes y Ddrama yng Nghymru (11–16 Mai, 1914)', in *Codi'r hen wlad yn ei hôl* (Llandysul: Gomer, 1989), 285–315; and *We lead, others follow: Swansea and the Welsh Drama Festival, 1919–1989* (BBC Wales Annual Radio Lecture, 1989).
4 See O. Llew Owain, *Hanes y ddrama yng Nghymru, 1850–1943* (Lerpwl: Gwasg y Brython, 1948). For an example of grudging and very qualified acceptance by a leading Nonconformist of the new drama movement, see the article by Abel Jones, 'Does Wales need the drama?', *Welsh Outlook* (1914), 254–6.
5 'Towards a National Drama', 12ff.
6 Quoted by O. Llew Owain, *Hanes y ddrama*, 32.
7 *Glyndŵr: Investiture Historical Play*, 6.
8 Hart, *Drama in Modern Wales*, 19.
9 D. T. Davies, 'Welsh Folk Drama: its future', *Welsh Outlook* (1920), 65.
10 J. Saunders Lewis, 'Welsh drama and folk drama', *Welsh Outlook* (1920), 167–8. See also Saunders Lewis's article on 'The present state of Welsh drama', *Welsh Outlook* (1919), 302.
11 Note D. T. Davies's own comment on the 'dissatisfaction on the part of a younger generation with the state of affairs produced or perpetuated by their parents. The children are probably giving expression to the

inarticulated but more or less consciously felt needs of the fathers themselves.' ('Welsh Folk Drama', 65) This is brought out in his play through the relationship between Ephraim Harris and the rebellious daughter who dares act out Harris's own repressed desire for freedom.

12 Review of the opening week of the Welsh National Drama Company, May 11–16, 1914 *Welsh Outlook* (1914), 274.

13 *Ephraim Harris* (London/Cardiff: Educational Publishing Company, 1920), 91–4. My translation.

14 'The Literary Outlook in Wales', *Welsh Outlook* (1920), 87–90.

15 *Codi'r Hen Wlad*, 299. The new Welsh drama in English is set interestingly in the context of the English theatre of the day by Gilbert Norwood in the third of his essays on 'The Present Renaissance of English Drama', *Welsh Outlook* (1914), 216–17.

16 'Some recent Welsh plays', *Welsh Outlook* (1914), 29–30.

17 *Welsh Outlook* (1919), 158. Reprinted as Chapter X of J. O. Francis, *The Legend of the Welsh* (London/Cardiff: Educational Publishing Company, 1924).

18 Cf. the remark made by Professor Gilbert Norwood as early as 1914: 'one is beginning to pity the wretched deacon. Just as the writers of morality-plays invariably introduced the "vice", so our Welsh dramatists, it would seem, simply cannot write without a deacon for villain. It is high time some literary deacon took the field of dramatic warfare.' *Welsh Outlook* (1914), 447.

19 'Change', *Welsh Outlook* (Jan., 1914), 30.

20 'The new Welsh drama', *Wales* (Nov., 1913), 6–7.

21 'A vagrant by the Dee', *Welsh Outlook* (1919), 281.

22 See his brief account of his involvement in politics in *The Legend of the Welsh*.

23 *Welsh Outlook* (Jan., 1914), 2.

24 'The crisis of Welsh Nonconformity', *Welsh Outlook* (1920), 57–60.

25 For a succinct account of the growth of the new labour movement, as seen by a leading trade unionist of the day, see 'Labour and Home Rule for Wales', by William Harris, Secretary of the South Wales Labour Federation, *Welsh Outlook* (1919), 145.

26 J. O. Francis, *Change: a Glamorgan play in four acts* (Welsh Drama Series, No. 13; London/Cardiff: Educational Publication Company, 1920), 22.

27 John Davies, *Hanes Cymru* (London: Allen Lane, 1990), 471. For a summary of changing conditions in the south Wales coalfield, see K. O. Morgan, *Rebirth of a Nation* (Oxford: Oxford University Press, 1981), particularly pp. 145–55.

28 Deian Hopkin, 'The Llanelli Riots, 1911', *Welsh History Review* 11 (1982–83), 488–515.

29 *Rebirth of a Nation*, 148.

30 'Evolution or Revolution', *Welsh Outlook* (Jan., 1914), 27–8.

31 *Welsh Outlook* (Feb., 1914), 46.

32 Naunton Davies, *The Human Factor* (Welsh Drama Series, No. 36;

Notes

London/Cardiff: Educational Publishing Company, 1920), 34.

33 *Welsh Outlook* (1914), 132.

34 Raymond Williams, 'The Welsh Industrial Novel', Inaugural Gwyn Jones Lecture (Cardiff: University College, 1979), 11.

35 Gwyn Jones, *Times Like These* (Academi Gymreig reprint; London: Victor Gollancz, 1979), 292.

36 Anonymous review, *Welsh Outlook* (1914), 273. Norwood is identified as the author in the next number of the same periodical.

Notes to Chapter 2

1 John Harris, ed., *My People* (Bridgend: Poetry Wales Press, 1987).

2 An interesting recent essay in *Planet*, however, suggests that Evans's stories reflect very local economic and social conditions in an area of Cardiganshire which remained, during his boyhood, beyond the reviving reach of the railway. See W. J. Rees, 'Inequalities: Caradoc Evans and D. J. Williams', *Planet* 81, 69–80.

3 Octavio Paz, 'In search of the past', *Times Literary Supplement* (Dec. 21–7, 1990), 1374. This is a translation (by Anthony Stanton) of Paz's acceptance speech at the Nobel Literature Prize ceremony, Stockholm, Dec. 8, 1990.

4 Gwyn Thomas, *All Things Betray Thee* (London: Lawrence and Wishart, 1986 reprint), 31–2.

5 An important first step in his re-education is his discovery of a new consciousness of solidarity among the workers throughout the industrial belt (*All Things*, 99–101).

6 *Black Parade* (London: Hamish Hamilton, 1952), 95.

7 Jack Jones, *Unfinished Journey* (London: Hamish Hamilton, 1937). He says of his father: 'In Dowlais works now. Steel – Bessemer. Yes, that's what had finished him and many a-more old iron puddlers. Not wanted now.' (10)

8 Collected in Michael Parnell, ed., *Gwyn Thomas, Selected Short Stories* (Bridgend: Seren Books, 1988), 43–52.

9 Glyn Jones, *The Valley, The City, The Village* (London: Severn Books, 1980 ed.). See particularly 83–91.

10 'Merthyr', in Glyn Jones, *Selected Poems* (Bridgend: Poetry Wales Press, 1988), 34.

11 'Reminiscences of Childhood', in *Quite Early One Morning* (London: Dent, 1974 ed.), 1. For Thomas's picture of Wales see James A. Davies, 'A Picnic in the Orchard: Dylan Thomas' Wales', in Tony Curtis, ed., *Wales: the Imagined Nation* (Bridgend: Poetry Wales Press, 1986), 43–65.

12 Walford Davies and Ralph Maud, eds., *Dylan Thomas: Collected Poems, 1934–1953* (London: Dent, 1988), 13. Note, though, Gwyn Thomas's appreciative comments on Dylan Thomas: 'But it is Dylan as a folk-figure, a piece of twentieth-century Welsh mythology, who remains most fascinating to me. He was a sort of living revenge on all the restrictions and

respectabilities that have come near to choking the life out of the Welsh mind ... At a time when in South Wales alone a whole generation had their lives outraged by a monstrous, State-regimented poverty, he lived with a rebellious abandon that made the rest of us look like sullen convicts.' *A Welsh Eye* (London: Hutchinson, 1984 edition), 94–7.

13 I use the translation by Tony Conran, *Welsh Verse* (Bridgend: Poetry Wales Press, 1986), 280–81. See also the version by Joseph P. Clancy in *Twentieth Century Welsh Poems* (Llandybïe: Christopher Davies, 1982), 97.

14 *Collected Poems*, 73. For a fascinating account of the original version of this poem and the picture it offers, see Roland Mathias, 'Lord Cutglass, Twenty Years After', in *A Ride Through the Wood* (Bridgend: Poetry Wales Press, 1985), 57–78.

15 Vernon Watkins, *Collected Poems* (Ipswich: Golgonooza Press, 1986), 13.

16 Shelley, 'Prometheus Unbound'. In A. S. B. Glover, ed., *Shelley: Selected Poetry and Prose* (London: Nonesuch Press, 1951), 462.

17 Nietzsche, *The Birth of Tragedy*, tr. Francis Golffing (New York: Doubleday Anchor, 1976), 31.

18 'Birches', in Robert Frost, *Selected Poems* (Harmondsworth: Penguin, 1963 ed.), 81–3.

19 *Dylan Thomas: Letters to Vernon Watkins* (London: Dent and Faber, 1957), 29 & 38.

20 See 'Art and Sacrament', in David Jones, *Epoch and Artist* (London: Faber, 1959), 143–79.

21 See John Pikoulis, *Alun Lewis: A Life* (Bridgend: Poetry Wales Press, 1984).

22 *Raiders' Dawn* (London: Allen & Unwin, 1946 ed.), 28.

23 John Pikoulis, ed., *Alun Lewis : A Miscellany of His Writings* (Bridgend: Poetry Wales Press, 1982), 106.

24 *Ha!Ha! among the Trumpets* (London: Allen & Unwin, 1946 ed.), 71.

25 'Nightgown', in *The Best of Rhys Davies* (London: David and Charles, 1979), 100–9.

26 See his preface to *The Collected Stories of Rhys Davies* (London: Heinemann, 1955).

27 'The Chosen One', in *The Best of Rhys Davies*, 5–35.

28 *Unfinished Journey*, 41.

29 *Cwmardy* (London: Lawrence and Wishart, 1978: reprint of 1937 edition), 198.

30 For an interesting account of Gwyn Thomas's life, see Michael Parnell, *Laughter from the Dark* (London: John Murray, 1988).

31 'The Dark Philosophers', in *The Sky of Our Lives* (London: Quartet Books, 1972), 130.

32 'Oscar', in *The Sky of Our Lives*, 13.

33 *The Subsidence Factor* (Cardiff: University College Cardiff Press, 1979), 10.

34 See his autobiographical essay in Meic Stephens, ed., *Artists in Wales*, I (Llandysul: Gomer, 1971), 78.

35 See particularly *The Former Miss Merthyr Tydfil and other stories*

(Harmondsworth: Penguin, 1979), and *Home to an empty House* (Llandysul: Gomer, 1973).

36 *Selected Poems* (Bridgend: Poetry Wales Press, 1986), 81 & 22. For a discussion of Norris's work in its social and biographical context, see James A. Davies, *Leslie Norris* (Writers of Wales Series, Cardiff: University of Wales Press, 1991).

37 *The Sea in the Desert* (Bridgend: Seren Books, 1989), 25.

38 *The Girl from Cardigan* (Bridgend: Seren Books, 1988), 114–115.

39 *Welsh Verse*, 280.

40 *Sliding* (London: Dent, 1971 ed.), 60.

41 John Davies, *The Visitor's Book* (Bridgend: Poetry Wales Press, 1985), 19.

Notes to Chapter 3

1 Emyr Humphreys, *Open Secrets* (London: Dent, 1988), 1, 2 & 3.

2 'Chorus', from W. H. Auden, *Selected Poems* (Harmondsworth: Penguin, 1958), 17.

3 See his autobiographical essay in Meic Stephens, ed. , *Artists in Wales, 2* (Llandysul: Gomer Press, 1973), 165–80; and Elwyn Evans, *Alun Llywelyn-Williams* (Writers of Wales Series, Cardiff: University of Wales Press, 1991).

4 For fuller details see John Pikoulis, *Alun Lewis: A Life* (Bridgend: Poetry Wales Press, 1984).

5 *Cerddi, 1934–1942* (London: Foyle, 1944), 19. The translations are my own, unless otherwise indicated.

6 *Selected Poems*, 27.

7 'Songs for the Night', in *Raiders' Dawn* (London: Allen and Unwin, 1946 reprint), 66.

8 *Artists in Wales, 2*, 173.

9 *Artists in Wales, 2*, 174.

10 'Elegy for the Welsh dead', in Tony Conran, *Blodeuwedd* (Bridgend: Poetry Wales Press, 1988), 14–15.

11 'Spain', in Robin Skelton, ed. , *Poetry of the Thirties* (Harmondsworth: Penguin, 1964), 134.

12 One-volume reprint of *Wales*, numbers one to eleven (London: Frank Cass, 1969), 232–4.

13 Edward Thomas, *Collected Poems* (London: Faber, 1965 impression), 190.

14 *Transactions of the Honourable Society of Cymmrodorion* (1948), 328–9.

15 'The Children', in *Poetry of the Thirties*, 53.

16 'The Conflict', in *Poetry of the Thirties*, 200.

17 'Meeting Point', in *Poetry of the Thirties*, 192–3.

18 *Transactions*, 328.

19 'Ar ymweliad', from *Pont y Caniedydd*. The translation comes from R. Gerallt Jones, ed., *Poetry of Wales, 1930–1970* (Llandysul: Gwasg Gomer, 1974), 272–7. See also the version by Joseph Clancy in *Twentieth Century Welsh Poems* (Llandysul: Gomer Press, 1982), 167–9.

20 *Artists in Wales*, 2, 174.
21 Alun Lewis, *Letters from India* (Cardiff: Penmark Press, n.d.), 39.
22 *Ha! Ha! among the Trumpets* (London: Allen and Unwin, second impression, 1946), 56–7.
23 *Transactions*, 328.
24 'Gwaith ac Adwaith', *Tir Newydd* (Rhif 8, Mai, 1937), 19. My translation.
25 *Artists in Wales*, 2, 174.

Notes to Chapter 4

1 Seamus Heaney, 'The Regional Forecast', in R. P. Draper, ed., *The Literature of Region and Nation* (London: Macmillan, 1989).
2 References throughout are to Emlyn Williams, *The Corn is Green* (London: Heinemann, 1938) and to Emyr Humphreys, *A Toy Epic*, ed. , M. Wynn Thomas (Bridgend: Seren Books, 1989).
3 Emlyn Williams, *George: An early Autobiography* (London: Hamish Hamilton, 1961).
4 Fredric Jameson, *The Political Unconscious* (London: Methuen, 1981).
5 See in particular chapters 23–6 of Emyr Humphreys, *The Taliesin Tradition* (London: Black Raven Press, 1983 and Bridgend: Seren Books, 1989).
6 Lord Raglan, 'I take my stand', *Wales* (October, 1958), 15–18.
7 Emlyn Williams, 'A dyma fi, druan o Gymro, yn sefyll (I take my stand)', *Wales* (November, 1958), 16–20.
8 'Regional Forecast', 13.
9 Emyr Humphreys, *The Little Kingdom* (London: Eyre & Spottiswoode, 1946), 5.
10 'Ynom mae y clawdd', *Deuoliaethau* (Llandysul: Gwasg Gomer 1976), 47.
11 John Gwilym Jones, 'Dawn Emyr Humphreys', *Yr Arloeswr Newydd* I (1959), 17–18.
12 I would like to thank Emyr and Elinor Humphreys for allowing me to see this letter and to quote from it.
13 'There's a certain slant of light', Poem 258 in Thomas H. Johnson, ed., *The Complete Poems of Emily Dickinson* (London: Faber and Faber, 1970).

Notes to Chapter 5

1 All references are to M. Wynn Thomas, ed., *A Toy Epic* (Bridgend: Seren Books, 1989). This essay is reprinted from that edition, with the kind permission of the publishers. For a general survey of Emyr Humphreys's work, see (in English) Ioan Williams, *Emyr Humphreys*, in the Writers of Wales series (Cardiff: University of Wales Press, 1980); and (in Welsh) M. Wynn Thomas, *Emyr Humphreys*, in the Llên y Llenor Series (Caernarfon: Gwasg Pantycelyn, 1989).

2 See Dafydd Jenkins, *Tân yn Llŷn* (Penygroes: Gwasg y Tir, 1975). For an account setting the incident in the context of Saunders Lewis's political philosophy see the essay by Dafydd Glyn Jones in Alun R. Jones and Gwyn Thomas eds., *Presenting Saunders Lewis* (Cardiff: University of Wales Press, 1973), 23–78. The Caernarfon court speech is in the same volume (115–26), as is Emyr Humphreys's important essay 'Outline of a Necessary Figure' (6–13).

3 Saunders Lewis, *A School of Welsh Augustans* (Wrexham: Hughes and Son, 1924).

4 For further information about these figures and other classic Welsh-language authors mentioned in this study, see Meic Stephens, ed., *The Oxford Companion to the Literature of Wales* (Oxford: OUP, 1986). There is a study of Tegla Davies by Pennar Davies in the Writers of Wales Series (Cardiff: University of Wales Press, 1983).

5 See the *Oxford Companion*, and also the study by Derec Llwyd Morgan in the Writers of Wales series (Cardiff: University of Wales Press, 1974).

6 'Ysgrifennu cyfoes-yng Nghymru: I, Y Nofel', *Lleufer* 18 (1962), 4–8.

7 For William Williams see Glyn Tegai Hughes, *Williams Pantycelyn*, in the Writers of Wales series (Cardiff: University of Wales Press, 1983). A fascinating account of the influence of Calvinism on Welsh literature can be found in Dafydd Glyn Jones, 'Some Recent Themes in Welsh Literature', in J. E. Caerwyn Williams, ed., *Literature in Celtic Countries* (Cardiff: University of Wales Press, 1971), 177–92.

8 Emyr Humphreys in conversation with R. S. Thomas, in the programme *Mother's Tongue not Mother Tongue* (BBC Radio Wales and Radio 4UK, August, 1986), presented by M. Wynn Thomas and produced by Lenna Pritchard Jones.

9 Dylan Thomas, *Portrait of the Artist as a Young Dog* (London: Dent, 1956: first published 1940).

10 *Flesh and Blood* (London: Hodder and Stoughton, 1974: London: Sphere Books, 1986). I discuss this motif further in *Emyr Humphreys*, 19.

11 My psychological model here is derived from Madeleine Davis and David Wallbridge, *Boundary Space: an introduction to the work of D. W. Winnicott* (Harmondsworth: Penguin, 1981).

12 This analysis is based on the discussion in Anthony Storr, *The Dynamics of Creation* (Harmondsworth: Pelican Books, 1983 ed.).

13 Horace Gregory, tr., *Ovid: the Metamorphoses* (New York: Mentor Books, 1958), 31.

14 See Sacvan Bercovitch, *The American Jeremiad* (Madison: University of Wisconsin, 1978).

15 *The Taliesin Tradition* (Bridgend: Seren Books, 1989), 195.

16 There is a fine fictional description of this socio-psychological experience in the opening paragraph of 'Lurchers', in Leslie Norris, *The Girl from Cardigan* (Bridgend: Seren Books, 1988), 113.

17 The complicated history of composition of the novella can be found in the Preface to M. Wynn Thomas, ed., *A Toy Epic*.

18 *Lleufer* (1962), 8.
19 Roland Mathias, 'Emyr Humphreys', in James Vinson, ed., *Contemporary Novelists Of the English Language* (London: Macmillan), 327.
20 Chapter 11, 'Perpetual Curates'.
21 From Joseph P. Clancy, tr., *Twentieth Century Welsh Poems* (Llandysul: Gomer Press, 1982), 2.
22 See the *Oxford Companion*.
23 Emyr Humphreys's own interpretation of the Welsh cultural renaissance of the first half of this century can be found in *The Triple Net* (London: Channel Four publications, 1988).
24 The next stage of Michael's education can be found in the Appendix to M. Wynn Thomas, ed., *A Toy Epic*.
25 *Welsh Airs* (Bridgend: Poetry Wales Press, 1987), 44.
26 *New Statesman* (Autumn/Winter, 1958).
27 The two versions are compared in André Morgan, 'Three Voices: Emyr Humphreys's *A Toy Epic* and some comparisons with *Y Tri Llais*', *Planet* (39), 44–9; and in M. Wynn Thomas, 'Hanes dwy chwaer: olrhain hanes *Y Tri Llais*', *Barn* (Ionawr, 1989), 23–5, and *Barn* (Ebrill, 1989), 23–5.
28 *Y Tri Llais* (Penygroes: Cyhoeddiadau Mei, 1985), 3.
29 *Quite Early One Morning* (London: Dent, 1974), 89.
30 *The Taliesin Tradition*, 230.

Notes to Chapter 6

1 A shorter version of this chapter was published in Welsh in M. Wynn Thomas, gol., *R. S. Thomas: Y Cawr Awenydd* (Llandysul: Gwasg Gomer, 1990).
2 The English translation comes from 'The Paths Gone By', in Sandra Anstey, ed., *R. S. Thomas, Selected Prose* (Bridgend: Poetry Wales Press, 1983), 131–45.
3 'An Old Man', *Tares* (London: Hart-Davis, 1961), 27.
4 Alan Llwyd, *Barddoniaeth y Chwedegau: astudiaeth lenyddol-hanesyddol* (Cyhoeddiadau Barddas, 1986), especially Chapter One: 'Mae'r Tempo wedi Newid'.
5 Translation by Joseph P. Clancy, *Twentieth Century Welsh Poems* (Llandysul: Gomer Press, 1982), 216–17.
6 John Ormond, 'R. S. Thomas: Priest and Poet', *Poetry Wales*: R. S. Thomas special number (Spring, 1972), 50.
7 *Neb*, Cyfres y Cewri 6, gol., Gwenno Hywyn (Caernarfon: Gwasg Gwynedd, 1985), 42. My translation.
8 *Selected Prose*, 105.
9 *Poetry for Supper* (London: Hart-Davis, 1958), 37.
10 *The English Novel from Dickens to Lawrence* (St Albans: Paladin, 1974), 82.
11 *Pietà* (London: Hart-Davis, 1966), 7.

12 'Philosophy and Religion in the Poetry of R. S. Thomas', *Poetry Wales* (Spring, 1972), 27–45. Reprinted in Roland Mathias, *A Ride Through the Wood* (Bridgend: Poetry Wales Press, 1985), 186–205.

13 *The Bread of Truth* (London: Hart-Davies, 1963), 41.

14 *Not That He Brought Flowers* (London: Hart-Davis, 1968), 26.

15 'The Welsh Parlour', *The Listener*, 15 Jan., 1958, 119.

16 'Words, Inscription, and Romantic Nature Poetry', in F. W. Hilles and Harold Bloom, eds., *From Sensibility to Romanticism* (New York: O. U. P., 1969), 389–413.

17 *Song at the Year's Turning* (London: Hart-Davis, 1955), 102.

18 'Michael', in Philip Hobsbaum, ed., *William Wordsworth, Selected Poems and Prose* (London: Routledge, 1989), 31.

19 *Welsh Airs* (Bridgend: Poetry Wales Press, 1987), 44.

20 *Robert Frost, Selected Poems* (Harmondsworth: Penguin, 1963), 32.

21 Alexander Dru, tr., *The Present Age* (London: Collins, 1962), 69.

22 T. Gwynn Jones, gol., *Ceiriog: Detholiad o'i weithiau* (Wrecsam: Hughes a'i Fab, 1932), 116.

23 *Selected Prose*, 158.

24 T. Gwynn Jones, *Ymadawiad Arthur a chaniadau eraill* (Caernarfon: Cwmni y cyhoeddwyr Cymreig, 1910), 20.

25 *Selected Prose*, 85.

26 *Selected Prose*, 158–9.

27 *Barddoniaeth y Chwedegau*, 84–5.

28 *Listener*, 15 Jan., 1958, 119.

29 *Listener*, 14 Nov., 1963, 797.

30 'A General Introduction for my work', *Essays and Introductions* (London: Macmillan, 1971), 523.

31 *Ingrowing Thoughts* (Bridgend: Poetry Wales Press, 1985), 13.

32 Dafydd Elis Thomas, 'The Image of Wales in R. S. Thomas's Poetry', *Poetry Wales*, 1972, 59–66.

33 *Tynged yr Iaith* (Cyfansoddiadau BBC, 1962), 26.

Notes to Chapter 7

1 From 'The Spectre', C. H. Sisson, *In the Trojan Ditch* (Manchester: Carcanet, 1979), 78.

2 *Laboratories of the Spirit* (London: Macmillan, 1975), 27.

3 *Experimenting with an Amen* (London: Macmillan, 1986), 52. See also 'Looking Glass' (Op. cit., 40).

4 'Ap Huw's Testament', *Selected Poems, 1946–1968* (London: Granada, 1973), 52.

5 *The Echoes Return Slow* (London: Macmillan, 1988), 2.

6 For a discussion of birth traumas as a possible influence on psychological development in some cases, see D. W. Winnicott, 'Birth Memories, Birth Trauma, and Anxiety', in *Through Paediatrics to Psycho-Analysis*

(London: The Hogarth Press, 1982), 174–93. I am indebted to my friend and colleague, Dr J. F. Turner, for this reference.

7 I deliberately refer to 'the psychology of the poem', in spite of the doubtful validity of such a phrase, in order to avoid imputing directly to R. S. Thomas the characteristics that appear in his work.

8 'Soliloquy', in *H'm* (London: Macmillan, 1972), 30.

9 'The Gap', in *Frequencies* (London: Macmillan, 1978), 7.

10 *Later Poems, 1972-1982* (London: Macmillan, 1983), 182.

11 'Infant Sorrow', *Songs of Experience*, in David Punter, ed., *William Blake: Selected Poetry and Prose* (London: Routledge, 1988), 132.

12 'Infant Joy', *Songs of Innocence*, in *Blake: Selected Poetry*, 58.

13 'Michael', in Philip Hobsbaum, ed., *William Wordsworth: Selected Poetry and Prose* (London: Routledge, 1989), 43.

14 *Neb*, Gwenno Hywyn, gol., *Cyfres y Cewri*, 6 (Caernarfon: Gwasg Gwynedd, 1985), 93. The translations are my own.

15 'Probings: an interview with R. S. Thomas', in *Planet* (80) 28–52.

16 The factual circumstances behind this poem are explained in *Neb*, 91–3. R. S. Thomas concludes the account by saying that 'the whole business left R. S. with a feeling of unease, but he didn't know what the right answer would be, if there was one at all.'

17 'Commander Lowell, 1888-1949', in Robert Lowell, *Selected Poems* (London: Faber, 1965), 40–2.

18 'Probings', 47.

19 It should, however, be noted that the opening sections of 'Salt' are about R. S. Thomas's grandfather, judging by the evidence available in *Neb*, but information about his father's boyhood is at the same time mixed in with this material. See *Neb*, 10.

20 This is a grossly simplified summary of a great and complex play. For an English translation of *Blodeuwedd*, see Joseph P. Clancy, tr., 'The Woman Made of Flowers', in *The Plays of Saunders Lewis*, Volume One (Llandybïe: Christopher Davies, 1985).

21 Information about the legendary figure of Gwydion can conveniently be found in Meic Stephens, ed., *The Oxford Companion to the Literature of Wales* (Oxford: OUP, 1986). R. S. Thomas's friend, the novelist Emyr Humphreys, has created a modern 'Gwydion' in the later novels of his *Land of the Living* series. See particularly *An Absolute Hero* (London: Dent, 1986) and *National Winner* (London: Macdonald, 1971).

22 For an essay that in places throws interesting light on R. S. Thomas's attitude towards women in his poetry, see Anne Price-Owen, 'Provoked by Innocence', *Planet* (73), 62–9.

23 The beguiling attractiveness of the little child's world is also shown in *The Echoes Return Slow*, 36–7.

24 'Probings', 50–1.

25 *The Collected Poems of W. B. Yeats* (London: Macmillan, 1971 ed.), 101.

26 William Hazlitt, 'Coriolanus', in Christopher Salvesen, ed., *Selected Writings of William Hazlitt* (New York: Signet, 1972), 49.

27 Alexander Dru, tr., *The Present Age* (London: Fontana, 1967), 91.
28 'The Extasie', in A. J. Smith, ed., *Donne: Complete English Poems* (Harmondsworth: Penguin, 1971), 53.
29 *Complete Poems*, 60.
30 *Between Here and Now* (London: Macmillan, 1981), 94.
31 J. P. Ward, *The Poetry of R. S. Thomas* (Bridgend: Poetry Wales Press, 1987), 141.
32 'Probings', 36.

Notes to Chapter 8

1 Mary Jones, *Resistance* (Belfast: The Blackstaff Press, 1985).
2 Hywel Teifi Edwards, *Coffáu Llywelyn, 1856–1956* (Llandysul: Gwasg Gomer, 1983). See also 'Coffaú Llywelyn', in Hywel Teifi Edwards, *Codi'r Hen Wlad Yn ei Hôl* (Llandysul: Gwasg Gomer, 1989), 186–237.
3 Victor W. Turner, *The Ritual Process: Structure and Anti-Structure* (London: Routledge and Keagan Paul, 1969). For Llyn-y-Fan, see Alwyn Rees and Brinley Rees, *Celtic Heritage* (London: Thames and Hudson, 1961), 344–5.
4 Gwyn A. Williams, *When Was Wales?* (London: Black Raven Press, 1985).
5 Angharad Tomos, *Yma o Hyd* (Talybont: Y Lolfa, 1985). Other notable recent novels include Christopher Meredith, *Shifts* (Bridgend: Seren Books, 1988) and Wiliam Owen Roberts, *Y Pla* (Caernarfon: Annwn, 1987), English translation, *Pestilence*, by Elizabeth Roberts (London: Hamish Hamilton, 1991). The translations from *Yma o Hyd* are my own.
6 Collected in J. E. Caerwyn Williams, Eurys Rolant, Alan Llwyd, eds. , *Llywelyn y Beirdd* (Cyhoeddiadau Barddas, 1984). 'Wylit, wylit, Lywelyn' was actually written much earlier than 1982 and well before the Referendum of 1979. The comments in it refer primarily to the Investiture of 1969. The translation is my own.
7 See, for instance, Gwynfor Evans, *Aros Mae* (Abertawe: Gwasg John Penry, 1971), 33–6.
8 Paul Fussell, *The Great War and Modern Memory* (Oxford: Oxford University Press, 1977), Preface.
9 Translated by Joseph P. Clancy as 'This Spot', *Twentieth Century Welsh Poems* (Llandysul: Gomer Press, 1982), 71–2. See also Tony Conran's severe treatment of the poem in his introduction to *Welsh Verse* (Bridgend: Poetry Wales Press, 1986), 91–3.
10 *Twentieth Century Welsh Poems*, 95.
11 Joseph P. Clancy, tr. , 'The Woman Made of Flowers', in *The Plays of Saunders Lewis*, Vol. I (Llandybïe: Christopher Davies, 1985), 54–5.
12 For the complete sequence see *Welsh Verse*, 127–8.
13 Kingsley Amis, *The Old Devils* (London: Hutchinson, 1986).
14 My opinion of the novel is considerably higher than that of John Barnie. See his forthright comments in 'The Art of Puffing', *The King of Ashes* (Llandysul: Gomer Press, 1989), 52–7.

InternalDifference

15 *The Literary Review* (1986).
16 Reported in *The Listener* (27 November 1986), 16.
17 'Cat-English', in *The Listener* (11 June 1987), 25.
18 *For the Honour of Wales*, in C. H. Herford and E. Simpson eds. , *Ben Jonson: Complete Works*, vol. VII (Oxford: Clarendon Press, 1963), 509 and 510.
19 Anthony Conran, 'Gerard Hopkins as an Anglo-Welsh Poet', in William Tydeman, ed. , *The Welsh Connection* (Llandysul: Gomer Press, 1986), 110–29.
20 D. H. Lawrence, *St Mawr* (London: Martin Secker, 1930 edition), 76.
21 *Times Literary Supplement* (20–26 July 1990), 779–80.
22 *Times Literary Supplement* (12 September 1986), 994.
23 *Preoccupations: Selected Prose, 1968–1978* (Faber and Faber, 1980), 150–51.
24 *The Taliesin Tradition* (London: Black Raven Press, 1983), 3.

Index